UNDERSTANDING THE SUNDAY SCRIPTURES

A Companion to
The Revised Common Lectionary
Year A

by H. King Oehmig, D. Min.

Contributing Editors:
Isabel Anders, M.A.
Paula Franck, M.T.S.

READ MARK PRESS
Chattanooga, Tennessee

Printed in the United States of America by:

READ MARK PRESS
www.readmarkpress.com
P.O. Box 11428
Chattanooga, TN 37401

Telephone: 800.722.4124
Fax: 423.242.4266
info@readmarkpress.com

$21.95
ISBN Number 978-0-9795581-0-8

INTRODUCTION

Blessed Lord, who caused all holy Scriptures to be written for our learning: Grant us so to hear them, read, mark, learn, and inwardly digest them, that we may embrace and ever hold fast the blessed hope of everlasting life, which you have given us in our Savior Jesus Christ; who lives and reigns with you and the Holy Spirit, One God, forever and ever. Amen.

—The Book of Common Prayer

LECTIONARY BIBLE STUDY

The word "lectionary" means simply "an ordered reading of Holy Scripture." To follow the lectionary is to engage in a disciplined reading of Scripture according to the wisdom of the Church—not necessarily according to one's personal preference. In that way, persons of faith span the entirety of God's Word—the "hard" passages as well as the "consoling" ones—over a three-year period, Sunday by Sunday, as well as day by day. The lectionary keeps us honest—and also from reading the Parable of the Prodigal Son over and over until we turn into mush.

Furthermore, by following this common pattern of Bible study, the individual—at home, in a group study, or at a church on Main Street—becomes a part of that great ocean of Christians participating in the totality of God's self-disclosure from Tulsa to Timbuktu. Drawing from Genesis to Revelation, one becomes part of a worldwide, common rhythm of Bible reflection. Besides keeping us from becoming lopsided in faith, the biblical lectionary also provides us an essential way of staying united—when disagreements over theology and ethics keep us at each other's throats most of the time.

It is perhaps the most basic way that we fulfill Jesus' high priestly prayer: *that the community of believers may be one as he and the Father are one.*

Having briefly touched on the definition of the biblical lectionary—and the overriding reasons for it—let me segue into the origin of UNDERSTANDING THE SUNDAY SCRIPTURES. It all began in an odd place for a Christian minister: at a wedding of a friend at the Mizpah Congregation of Reformed Jews in Chattanooga, Tennessee. In every pew at the temple were copies of a thick, rigorous—and expensive—commentary on the Torah. I knew about its scholarly thoroughness, and its price, since I had bought one in seminary years before and had used it ever since for my own Bible study. It dawned on me that having a commentary on the Torah in the pew enriched the Word for all members of the worshiping Jewish community. Why not do the same for Christians in their parishes? Why not have a resource available in the pew so that if someone came ten to fifteen minutes early to worship, he or she could prepare for the Liturgy of the Word—and make it come alive all the more?

As a parish priest, I also asked: why not have a sound Bible resource designed specifically for the laity—especially for lay leaders—as they prepare for Sunday morning? Good, responsible Bible teaching has never been more in demand than today—particularly for a resource in sync with the Sunday lectionary. For all those involved in worship, not just from the pulpit but also from the pew, there is a hunger to encounter not just what the biblical text *said,* but also what it *says.* We are tired of Bible lite.

And so UNDERSTANDING THE SUNDAY SCRIPTURES came into being—in collaboration with the work of New Testament scholar, Dr. Howard Rhys, retired Professor of Biblical Languages and New Testament from the School of Theology at the University of the South.

Contributing to the background research done by Dr. Rhys are the award-winning skills and insights of Isabel Anders *(www.isabelanders.com),* noted author of *Soul Moments: Times When Heaven Touches Earth* (Cowley, 2006); *Awaiting the Child: An Advent Journal* (Cowley, 2005); and *The Lord's Prayer for a New Millennium* (Magnus, 2001). Anders is also Managing Editor of Synthesis Publications, a resource for preaching and worship that reaches more than 2,100 clergy around the world.

Contributing Editor Paula Franck, Canon to the Ordinary for Education and Christian Formation in the Diocese of Indianapolis, and Exegete for Synthesis Publications, provides research and questions that promote engagement with the texts in "Points to Ponder."

Featured columnist Dr. H. King Oehmig, Vicar of St. Barnabas Church, Trion, Georgia, Editor-in-Chief of Synthesis Publications, and author of *Between the Lines: Reflections on the Gospels Through the Church Year* and *Beyond the Words: Insights on the Gospels Through the Church Year* (Xlibris, 1998, 2004) provides each lesson with its core teaching and challenge to our life in his "On Reflection."

In our Prayer for the Day we have focused on the themes in each day's Lessons and their implications for our lives. A small section on which to write notes accompanies each lesson as well, making *USS* a kind of workbook as well as a devotional study guide.

USS provides a synthesis of varying material centered in the biblical texts that seeks to enlighten and edify the reader in the historic faith—while also being open to the Spirit's newness and wisdom.

USS came into being as a commentary that seeks to incorporate *sound scholarship* without being dry or pedantic. It sets out to engage the reader with the text, without having an axe to grind or a social "agenda" to push. It simply seeks to express a "broad church," theologically sound perspective on Scripture that is faithful to our Lord, and to our sisters and brothers in Christ.

UNDERSTANDING THE SUNDAY SCRIPTURES also has multiple uses apart from preparation for Sunday morning worship. It would be the perfect gift for Christian education teachers, for lay readers, members of a vestry, or a parish council. It can serve as a wonderful resource for older youth groups, or be used in weekly Bible studies to reach out to the homebound, or those in the hospital for an extended period of time. It provides a critical method for young people away from home in college or in military service to stay connected to the Church. And *USS* would also make a perfect gift for newcomers. What better way to welcome them to your community's life, and to stress the value your congregation puts on a study of the Bible that deepens faith?

BACKGROUND ON *THE COMMON LECTIONARY*

That we have a "common lectionary" can be traced to Pope John XXIII, who convened the Second Vatican Council—a seminal event of seismic proportions not only for the Roman Catholic Church, but also for "liturgical" churches everywhere. Pope John summarized his intent on convening the Council when he said: "I want to throw open the windows of the Church so that we can see out and the people can see in." And one of the major ways in which the Second Vatican Council "opened the windows" for the people was in the area of revising liturgy and worship.

The faithful were to be summoned to a "fully conscious and active participation in liturgical celebrations," the Council affirmed, because such participation was the birthright of Christian people as "a chosen race, a royal priesthood, a holy nation, a redeemed people" (1 Peter 2:9; cf 2:4-5). Active participation from the people meant use of the vernacular rather than Latin. It also meant there was to be a revival of the central role of Scripture study in the devotional lives of the faithful—one that was nevertheless open to modern analysis and interpretation.

It was after Vatican II that several North American Churches, beginning with the Episcopal Church, adopted the Roman Catholic three-year lectionary cycle (Years A, B, and C) with some variations. Eventually, in the 1980s, an ecumenical committee was set up to put together—and bring together—a common lectionary from the variations that remained in the Eucharistic readings from week to week. What resulted from the committee's efforts was *The Common Lectionary,* which has evolved into *The Revised Common Lectionary* of today. What began in the 1960s with Vatican II has accomplished a unity that nothing else in ecumenical relations has done: it has brought Christians together—Catholic and Protestant—in reading the same Scripture every week. This much we can celebrate as a common bond among a myriad of Christians around the world.

"THE FEAST OF WISDOM"

And yet, as most of us know, the Good Book—the Book of books, the world's best-known and most widely printed book—is often the least understood. While definitive for faith and as our rule of life, Scripture is not only confusing; the Bible can be one of the world's most dangerous books as well.

The Nazis used it to justify the killing of millions of Jews, calling them "Christ-killers." Slaveholders over the centuries have cited passages to justify owning other human beings, and used passages to justify the subjugation of women and people of color. How many oppressions, inquisitions, and executions have sadly been perpetrated throughout post-biblical history based on a misunderstanding of Holy Writ? One can only guess. As the late Archbishop of Canterbury, William Temple said, "If you have a false understanding of God, the more religious you are, the worse it is for you."

Nevertheless, we believe that the Old and New Testaments contain all that is necessary for salvation. The Book remains the anchor of God's self-disclosure, the gyroscope that guides our lives, and the path through which we most come into contact, and communion, with the Holy One. But, like marriage, the study of the Bible should be entered into soberly, not unadvisedly or lightly, but with dedication, openness, and a willingness to be touched by God through its pages. Lastly, it was old Saint Ambrose, the noted upholder of orthodoxy and Bishop of Milan (339—397) who declared, "Divine Scripture is the feast of wisdom, and the single books are the various dishes." And *USS* sets out to make the enjoyment—and efficacy—of the dishes of Scripture come alive in a new way, for a new time, for a new era of God's people. Through this ministry, we hope you come away refreshed, renewed, and recommitted to the Gospel of Jesus Christ.

H. King Oehmig
Lent, 2007
Sewanee, Tennessee

CONTENTS

Pentecost

Season After Pentecost

A NEW WORLD COMING

Isaiah 2:1-5; Psalm 122; Romans 13:11-14; Matthew 24:36-44

As we begin the season of Advent and a new Church Year, the Lessons focus on Christ's *future* Advent. We are urged to stay awake and be vigilant, for this coming will be unexpected.

The Gospel passage is part of Matthew's fifth and final discourse (24:1—25:46). Jesus is speaking privately to his disciples on the Mount of Olives about the signs of the coming messianic age, which would be preceded by cosmic disturbances, wars, destruction, and persecution.

Just as the leaves on the fig tree indicate when the time for harvest is near, "so also, when you see all these things, you will know that [the Son of Man] is near, at the very gates" (24:33).

Jesus compares the coming of the Son of Man to the days of Noah before the flood. In that time the people went about the events of their daily lives—"eating and drinking, marrying and giving in marriage" (v. 38)—until the rains came and Noah entered the ark.

The people were so absorbed in their day-to-day routines that they failed to notice the actions of God in their midst until it was too late. The same thing will happen when the Son of Man comes. People will be absorbed in their daily concerns and will not recognize the indications of the coming age.

Jesus goes on to give two examples of the unexpected nature of this coming as men and women go about their ordinary occupations of working in the fields or grinding meal, completely unaware that the messianic moment has come (vv. 40-41).

Some will be taken and some will be left. This is not to suggest a judgment on the lives of these individuals, but to emphasize the need to be aware and keep awake so that they do not miss this decisive moment (v. 42).

Similarly, if the owner of a house knew when a thief was coming to break into his home, he would take the necessary precautions and stay awake to prevent it. Thus Jesus urges his followers to be ready, "for the Son of Man is coming at an unexpected hour" (v. 44).

This call for watchfulness and preparation is not to be seen as a threat, but as a reminder not to allow ourselves to become so absorbed in our daily lives that we miss the coming signs. Since no one knows when the Son of Man will come, everyone must watch and be ready.

In Advent, we affirm that God will bring completion to the work begun through Jesus Christ. Although we do not know when or where or how God will come to judge and reign, Paul tells us that "salvation is nearer to us now than when we became believers" (Rom. 13:11b). We have choices of how to live, and these choices are significant as we await the Second Coming.

PRAYER FOR THE DAY

Almighty God, we pray for the grace to forsake darkness, and to put on the armor of light, now in this life, in which your Son Jesus Christ came to us in great humility; and in the last day, when he comes again in glory to bring us life immortal. *Amen.*

Paul's letter to the Romans provides instructions on how Christians are to behave in relation to one another, to their enemies, and to the state. All of the law given at Sinai may be summed up in this one commandment to "love your neighbor as yourself" (13:9b). No person or nation can be excluded, as "love does no wrong to a neighbor" (v. 10a). And in God's intention for humankind, all are neighbors.

Christians find themselves in between two world orders in which the old things are passing away. It is time to wake from sleep (v. 11a), for God's salvation is near, and the followers of Jesus are called to "lay aside the works of darkness" (v. 12b). Just as daylight follows the night, so does the new age of salvation follow the old age of darkness.

Paul says that it is now time to put on new apparel—"the armor of light" (v. 12b)—in order to be ready for the dawning of the new age. This is the time to "live honorably" (v. 13a) and cast aside irresponsible behavior and personal animosity in order to "put on the Lord Jesus Christ" (v. 14).

The words of the Prophet Isaiah, although they were written in a previous era, look forward to a new age when the world will live in peace and unity under the rule of the Lord.

"In days to come" (Is. 2:2), all the nations will come to the height of Mt. Zion. Pilgrims will go to the Lord's house to learn the ways of God. The idea that the God of Israel would be worshiped by all nations was part of the original covenant with Abraham (Gen. 12:3b).

The prophet draws a picture of the reign of an ideal king who shall arbitrate with justice for all. That will in turn lead to a reign of peace, in which "nation shall not lift up sword against nation, neither shall they learn war any more" (v. 4b).

The house of God on Zion's mountain is pictured here as a pinnacle of glory, justice, and peace toward which all the earth can turn. Thus Isaiah calls upon Israel to "walk in the light of the Lord!" (v. 5), just as Paul called the Romans to "put on the armor of light" (13:12b).

ON REFLECTION

We are more than a little unsettled about this last coming of Christ—when he comes to judge "the quick and the dead" at the end of time and history as we know it. Why shouldn't we be? If Michelangelo's depiction of the event in the Sistine Chapel is anything like what is to come, we will see an angry Jesus separating the sheep from the goats with the intensity of a ghostly Conan the Barbarian.

But as theologian Karl Barth says, "In the Bible, the judge is not primarily one who rewards some and punishes others; he is the one who creates order and restores what has been destroyed." So Jesus the Judge, the Jesus of the Second Coming, will arrive as The Restorer of a fallen world in which evil is destroyed, and the reign of Love is ushered in once and for all. It won't be a coming in wrath—a "coming against." It will be, on the other hand, a "coming for." It isn't a message of doomsday, but rather a message of *hope*.

The Light will overcome the darkness once and for all. Suffering and sadness, disease and death, will be no more. The struggle for justice will be over. At long last, every knee will bend and every tongue will confess that Jesus Christ is Lord to the glory of the Father (Phil. 2:10-11). The only thing that life will consist of, after this Coming, will be endless praise and eternal gratitude.

—H. King Oehmig

Therefore the Psalmist rejoiced "when they said to me, 'Let us go to the house of the Lord!'" (Ps. 122:1). As pilgrims travel to Jerusalem, they praise the city itself as a symbol of solidarity—a city "bound firmly together" (v. 3) both in structure and purpose. It is to this place that all the tribes have come, and it is here that they find justice.

As in Isaiah's vision, Jerusalem is a place of peace. Thus the pilgrims pray for the peace, security, and welfare of all, saying, "Peace be within you" (v. 8).

POINTS TO PONDER

1. What is the relationship between the time period preceding the flood of Noah's era and the Second Coming as described by Jesus? How are the "days of Noah" like and unlike our own times?

2. In Matthew 24:38-39, Jesus describes the people of Noah's time as being so occupied with their daily lives that they did not heed God. How do the routines of your daily life influence your ability to hear God—especially at this very busy time of year?

3. What do you think is the point of the illustrations of the men in the field and the women at the mill in verses 40-41, with regard to the coming of the Son of Man? What further warning does the parable of the thief (v. 43) have for us? How are we like these people?

4. The Apostle Paul tells us to put on the "armor of light." How can we prepare for an event when we do not know when or how it will occur? How can we live fully in the present yet anticipate the future?

5. According to these Lessons, what should our conduct and actions be as we prepare for the return of Jesus?

PREPARE THE WAY OF THE LORD

Isaiah 11:1-10; Psalm 72:1-7, 18-19; Romans 15:4-13; Matthew 3:1-12

While the Gospel reading for the First Sunday in Advent always focuses on end times scenarios, Advent 2 and 3 feature John the Baptist, who calls the world to repent in preparation for the coming of the Messiah.

In all four Gospels, the figure of John the Baptist appears at the beginning of the ministry of Jesus, with many of the words and deeds of John foreshadowing those of Jesus.

Although they were both initially well-received as prophets, they came into conflict with the religious authorities and were eventually rejected, arrested, and executed. However, John understood that he was subordinate to Jesus and that his role was to prepare the way for One who was more powerful than he.

Here John is depicted as the archetypal Old Testament prophet dwelling in the Judean wilderness east of Jerusalem. This places him in the Exodus tradition, and implies an expression of religion not centered on the temple and Jerusalem.

John's appearance and life style highlighted his identification with the prophetic tradition of Elijah (2 Ki. 1:8) He wore camel's hair clothing with a leather belt, and he ate locusts and wild honey (v. 4). In fact, some saw him as a new Elijah.

In his prophetic message, "Repent, for the kingdom of heaven has come near" (v. 2), John calls for his listeners to completely turn their lives around and prepare for the coming reign of God. Jesus himself later uses these same words (Mt. 4:17).

The "kingdom of heaven" represents God's coming presence and power, with repentance as the proper response. John goes on to quote from the Prophet Isaiah (40:3) in verse 3, with John himself as the voice in the wilderness calling the people to readiness.

John called the repentant to baptism in the Jordan River, as they confessed their sins. But as Pharisees and Sadducees came forward, John called them evil—a "brood of vipers" (v. 7). The Pharisees and Sadducees were two powerful Jewish religious groups who in Matthew's Gospel represent opposition to the ministry of Jesus.

John goes on to warn them of the impending judgment. The people cannot assume that their ancestry as children of Abraham will protect them from the coming wrath (v. 7). God the Almighty could raise up true heirs to Abraham even from the stones. The only way to avoid destruction is to "bear fruit worthy of repentance" (v. 8). In other words, they must change their lives and do good works or they will be like a barren tree that is cut down and burned.

Thus, while John's baptism is for repentance, the One who is to come is more powerful and "he will baptize you with the Holy Spirit and fire" (v. 11).

PRAYER FOR THE DAY

Thank you, Lord, for your messengers the prophets, who preach repentance and make plain the way of salvation. Give us grace to listen and to forsake our sins, as we await the coming of Jesus Christ our Redeemer. *Amen.*

Jesus is depicted here as judge and not as savior. He is the winnower who will clear the threshing floor by gathering the wheat and burning the chaff. Empowerment and transformation will come through the Holy Spirit, who fuels God's redemption.

In contrast to the "coming wrath" and final judgment of the Gospel passage, the reading from Isaiah describes a time of peace and universal salvation under the rule of an ideal king (Is. 11:1-5). This Messianic king will be a descendant of David, the son of Jesse—thus the image of a green shoot springing to life out of a stump (11:1).

"The spirit of the Lord shall rest upon him" (v. 2), and he shall be endowed with wisdom, understanding, and knowledge. He shall delight in the fear of the Lord (v. 3) and bring equity to the poor. His words shall bring down the wicked as he rules with righteousness.

The coming Messianic age will also be manifested in nature, as wild beasts live in harmony with domestic animals and children. The wolf will lie down with the lamb, and a child will play near the adder's den. This peaceful kingdom on God's "holy mountain" will come about because "the earth will be full of the knowledge of the Lord" (v. 9). Finally, the "root of Jesse shall stand as a signal to the peoples" (v. 10) as the nations turn to the Messianic king.

Paul also refers to Isaiah's image of the "root of Jesse" in his letter to the Romans (15:12), as he proclaims a vision of hope to all believers through Christ Jesus.

The passage for today begins with a reminder of the steadfastness, encouragement, and hope that come to us through the instruction of Scripture. Paul goes on to pray that God's same steadfastness and encouragement will enable the community to live together in harmony.

ON REFLECTION

We don't know how to handle John the Baptist. If only he had come out of Harvard Divinity School—or the College of Preachers. Maybe then he would have legitimacy, or be easier to swallow. But as he is—a fire-breathing prophet who can't be bought off, or kept on the religious reservation—how do we deal with such an ascetic? If only he were on a salary, and had a 401-K plan, and had the security of his children to be concerned about, maybe then we would be more comfortable. Then we know he would give us warmed-over-cream-of-wheat religion.

But this God-drunk, sun-drenched prophet—like the Voice at the burning bush—*will be who he will be,* and remain single-minded in his calling humanity to repent. *Turn around. Awake from your stupor. The fire of God is coming.* Except this fire, John misunderstood, would be the flame of the Holy Spirit that does not char and disfigure, but heals and makes new. Holy fire is a refining fire. A cleansing fire. A fire that loves us too much to let us go to hell in a hand-basket.

George Macdonald, the mentor of C. S. Lewis, put it this way when it comes to Divine fire: the further we move away from God's love the more it burns; the closer we come to it, the more it warms and revives us. At its heart, this is the task of the Baptizer called John: to come close to the fire of God that flames most fully and powerfully in the One to come, Jesus the Anointer. *Come. And come now.*

—H. King Oehmig

Christ, the Messiah, made possible the unity we can experience in harmonious living with one another. When we attain this wholeness in Christ, then we can with one voice praise and glorify God the Father. This unity also calls us to welcome one another into God's family (v. 7).

Paul reminds us that Christ himself became a servant of the circumcised (v. 8a) in order to fulfill the promises given to the earlier patriarchs —and finally even for Gentiles (v. 9a). Verses 9-12 continue with a series of earlier references (Ps. 18:49; Deut. 32:43; Ps. 117:1; and Is. 11:10) that speak of the inclusion of the Gentiles among God's people. "In him the Gentiles shall hope" (v. 12).

Psalm 72, the last Psalm of Book II of the Psalms, offers a prayer that brings to a climax the hope of God's people. There is a desire that, through their king, the nation may grow and thereby extend the Kingdom of God.

In our Lessons today we acknowledge that God *does* endure forever, as the Holy One. Thus we too look forward to the day when God's peace will fill the earth.

POINTS TO PONDER

1. Try to imagine what it would be like to be a witness on the bank of the Jordan River as John preached and baptized those who came. Why do you think Matthew includes the specific details of John's dress and diet? Why do you think people came to hear him?

2. How would you characterize John's message? What do you think might have been the response of those who heard him? What is your own reaction to his words?

3. How do you understand the difference between the baptism John offers and that of the coming Messiah?

4. Why do you think the Pharisees and Sadducees came to John for baptism? Why did John direct his wrath toward these religious leaders? What implications do John's words have for us today?

5. Compare John's vision with that found in the Old Testament reading in Isaiah 11: 1-10. And also consider the final verse in Romans 15:4-13, where Paul speaks eloquently of hope. What gives you hope in the world today?

MORE THAN A PROPHET

Isaiah 35:1-10; Psalm 146:4-9; James 5:7-10; Matthew 11:2-11

The Gospel passage for Advent 3 continues to focus on John the Baptist. It begins with John sending some of his disciples to inquire of Jesus as to whether or not he is "the one who is to come," or another (Mt. 11:3). Earlier, John had identified Jesus as *the one who was to come* (Mt. 3:11-17); but now it would seem that he had doubts.

Soon after the Baptism of Jesus, John had been imprisoned by Herod Antipas and held in the fortress at Machaerus on the heights of Moab near the east central shore of the Dead Sea. John's growing popularity posed a threat to Herod's control over the region; and in addition, Herod's wife wanted revenge against John after he questioned the legitimacy of her marriage to Herod (Mt. 14:1-15).

From his prison, John could no longer proclaim his message of repentance; but he was still eager to know if his heralded judgment was taking place. John had heard about what Jesus was doing, but his ministry of compassion did not conform to the end-times scenario foreseen by the prophet. When John's fiery prophecies did not appear in Jesus' words or actions as John had predicted, he might have wondered about Jesus' authority.

Jesus does not respond directly to the question put to him concerning his identity, but instead points his questioners to what they can observe and hear. His vocation as Messiah is not characterized by judgment or wrath. Nor is he about to establish a Messianic empire over the earth.

Rather his messiahship is one of blessing, healing, and liberation—the blind can see, the lame can walk, lepers are cleansed, the deaf can hear, the dead are raised, and the poor have good news brought to them (11:5). Jesus goes on to bless those who do not take offense (Mt. 11:6) or misunderstand his ministry. For as Matthew repeatedly illustrates, there were many who turned aside and would ultimately reject him.

Jesus then turns to the crowd and begins to speak to them about John, a man resolute and uncompromising, not like a reed that bends and changes direction with the wind. Nor is he like a spoiled prince lounging in his palace—as evidenced by his rough clothing and ascetic life style.

John is clearly a prophet; indeed, he is "more than a prophet" (v. 9); he is the messenger foretold in the Scriptures who was to *prepare the way for the Messiah* (Mal. 3:1; Ex. 23:20). Yet despite his stature as the greatest prophet of his age, "the least in the kingdom of heaven is greater than he" (v. 11). Those in the new era inaugurated by Jesus will be "greater" because they will have an experience of the power and glory of God beyond what John, as a representative of the previous age, imagined.

PRAYER FOR THE DAY

We ask for your power and your mighty presence, O Lord, that your merciful grace may embrace us and deliver us from our sins, through Jesus Christ our Lord. *Amen.*

In essence, the entire Gospel story is an answer to the question posed by John the Baptist; but even Jesus' most intimate disciples did not comprehend his words and actions.

The Prophet Isaiah in 35:1-10 gives us an indication of what we can expect in this new age. The context for the passage is a prophecy on the return of Israel after the exile in Babylon, in which God provides safe passage through the barren wilderness. However, in later times the passage was seen to describe the messianic age.

This will be a time of rejoicing and singing as the desert blooms and God's glory is reflected in nature. Just as the land is restored, so shall the people themselves be renewed (v. 3). There will be no need to fear, for the Lord will save the people from their enemies.

When the Lord comes, the blind shall see, the deaf shall hear, the "lame shall leap like a deer" (v. 6), and the mute shall sing with joy. The earth will be renewed as the streams of water spring forth in the parched desert. A highway shall appear for God's people—the "Holy Way" (v. 8). Even fools will be able to take this route; there will be no danger from wild animals, and the redeemed will travel to Zion in safety and joy (v. 10b).

In this time between the first and second Advents, the writer of the Epistle of James reminds us that we must *be patient until the coming of the Lord* (5:7a).

The people for whom James wrote thought that there would be an immediate return of the Lord, so here James offers them encouragement.

First, he reminds them of the farmer who waits for the precious crop from the earth (v. 7b). The farmers of first-century Palestine had to wait for the early and late rains to come in their time for the results of planting to be revealed.

ON REFLECTION

Of all the people in society who could have impressed Jesus, there was only one who did: John the Baptist. You wonder how Jesus came to regard John so highly? The traditionally learned and wise of the day would have concluded that John's "cheese had slipped off his cracker," or that "he was using a four-digit zip code," what with eating grasshoppers and being clothed in animal hides and living among the jackals and calling the pious a "brood of vipers."

On many issues Jesus and John differed. John maintained a strict diet; Jesus was accused of being a drunkard and glutton (a charge he chose not to refute). John told his disciples to fast; Jesus told his to feast. John said the only way to approach God was through the fruits of repentance; Jesus said the only way was to become as a little child. John distanced himself from sinful society; Jesus hobnobbed with the unclean and irreligious—in full public view—and said that his mission was to be a physician to these sickos and not to the healthy.

Nevertheless, it seems that Jesus had a profound and unique respect for John. It wasn't for his impeccable theology, I suspect, but for his cousin's wholehearted, unabashed commitment to God, and to the mission John understood God to have laid on him. It was John's prophetic authenticity, his complete lack of pretense, which made him the only person in the Gospels Jesus was impressed by—and said so (Mt. 11:11).

—H. King Oehmig

Thus God's people must also be patient and live by the natural cycle of doing God's will as they can understand and perform it. They show their faithfulness by praying for God's Kingdom to come. They are not to be disheartened or weary in waiting.

James goes on to give advice as to how they are to live in the meantime. They are not to judge or to grumble against each other, but are to remain steadfast in their commitments.

Finally James cites the revered prophets of old who endured persecution and suffering while waiting for God to establish justice. James' community of the redeemed must do the same, and wait patiently for the coming Day of the Lord.

Psalm 146 is intended for congregational worship, a corporate praising of God for Divine help. Only God is able to perform good actions dependably with all powerfulness. Happy are those whose help is the God of Jacob.

POINTS TO PONDER

1. Why do you think John the Baptist was concerned about the identity of Jesus?

2. How does Jesus testify to the authenticity of his messiahship? What kind of Messiah does Jesus show himself to be? How do his actions contrast with John's expectations?

3. Read today's Old Testament Lesson in Isaiah 35:1-10 and compare this passage with the response of Jesus to John in Matthew 11:4-6.

4. God's true nature was shown in the world through the actions of Jesus. How are we called to continue Christ's work in the world today?

5. Refer to the Epistle for today in James 5:7-10. What counsel does this passage offer us as we await the second coming of Jesus?

BORN OF A VIRGIN

Isaiah 7:10-16; Psalm 80:1-7, 16-18; Romans 1:1-7; Matthew 1:18-25

The first three weeks of Advent looked toward the future coming of Christ; but this last Sunday of the season focuses on the promises fulfilled in the first coming of our Lord.

Matthew has a primary concern to establish that Jesus is the Messiah who fulfills the historic law and prophecies of Israel. Thus the birth story itself is preceded by a genealogy (1:1-17) that traces Jesus' line of descent from Abraham to David, from David to the Exile, and from the Exile to "Joseph the husband of Mary, of whom Jesus was born, who is called the Messiah" (1: 16).

This genealogy verifies that Jesus' ancestry is rooted in the history of Israel. Furthermore, through Joseph, Jesus is of the royal lineage of David. Matthew begins with a further assertion of the identity of Jesus: "Now the birth of *Jesus the Messiah* took place in this way" (1:18).

In first-century Palestine, it was the custom for parents to arrange the marriages of their children when boys were as young as thirteen and girls as young as twelve. Upon completion of the marriage contract and the establishment of the bride price, the couple were officially and legally bound; however, they often continued to live with their families for one or more years. At the time for the bride to move to the groom's house, the marriage ceremony took place, with a feast afterward at the bride's home.

This period between the espousal and the wedding seems to fit the situation of Mary and Joseph. Any infringement of marital obligations during the engagement period, such as adultery and conception, could be punished by divorce or even death (Deut. 22:13-27).

Thus, when Mary was found to be pregnant, Joseph was justified in divorcing her. However, he was a "righteous man" who did not want to publicly disgrace Mary; so he "planned to dismiss her quietly" (Mt. 1:19).

But before Joseph could take any action, an angel of the Lord came to him in a dream and told him to take Mary as his wife. In the dream, Joseph was addressed as "son of David," reinforcing the messianic ancestry of Jesus. He was assured that it would be no dishonor to take Mary as his wife and accept her baby, as the child had been begotten through the Holy Spirit.

The child would be a son, whom Joseph was to name *Jesus*—or Joshua, which means "God saves." This child would "save his people from their sins" (v. 21) in God's plan for the world.

Matthew provides a Scripture text from Isaiah 7:14 as further proof that the birth of this child would fulfill the ancient prophecies (v. 23). The child would be called *Emmanuel,* "God is with us," as a further indication that Jesus is the Son of God.

Joseph understood his dream as a direct communication from God, and when he awoke he did as the angel directed him and took Mary as his wife (vv. 24-25). Matthew says that Joseph had no marital relations with Mary "until she had borne a son; and he named him Jesus" (v. 24).

PRAYER FOR THE DAY

O God, purify our hearts today, we pray, that your Son Jesus Christ, at his coming, may find prepared within us a fit abode for his presence. *Amen.*

Most of all in this narrative we learn that Jesus is first of all the Son of God, the Messiah—Emmanuel—the *presence of God with us* to set us free from our sins.

The Old Testament reading includes the Isaiah passage that Matthew cites as a proof that the birth of Jesus fulfills the prophets. The historical context of the passage centers around King Ahaz of Judah being threatened with destruction if he did not join an alliance with Syria and Ephraim (Israel) against Assyria (735 B. C.). Ahaz did not want to be caught in a war against the stronger Assyrian forces, and appealed to Assyria for aid. Isaiah came to Ahaz and told him that he should put his trust in God, not the Assyrians, for deliverance (Is. 7:9).

Here Ahaz is told to ask for a sign from God. This sign can be "deep as Sheol or high as heaven" (v. 11). But Ahaz refuses by saying that he "will not put the Lord to the test" (v. 12). To this pious ingenuousness, Isaiah replies that, as far as he is concerned, Ahaz does not regard the Lord as his God at all (v. 13).

But the Lord will give a sign anyway: "The young woman is with child and shall bear a son, and shall name him Immanuel" (v. 14b). The original Hebrew text uses the word *almah* here, which simply means "young woman." However, with the remarkable coming of Jesus, the concept of the virgin birth was reflected in the Septuagint, which used the Greek word for "virgin" as a way to show that the Old Testament foretold the life of Jesus.

The identity of the child in the passage is not clear, but the name Immanuel—God with us—later took on messianic significance.

In his letter to the Romans, Paul also points to the human and Divine origins of Jesus as revealed by Matthew. Paul begins by telling us something about himself: he is servant, Apostle, and one who is "set apart for the Gospel" (1:1). This Gospel comes from God, was foretold by the prophets, and concerns God's Son.

ON REFLECTION

Neither of them asked for the task. Nothing seemed to have prepared them for it either—such as a special aptitude, unusual intelligence, or having an advanced I. Q. Mary and Joseph seem to have been ordinary people, minding their own business, and getting about life.

Bertrand Russell once remarked: "So far as I can remember, there is not one word found in the Gospels in praise of intelligence." If Joseph and Mary had gone about this unplanned pregnancy with intelligence, rather than by faith, the Incarnation would hardly have occurred. Mary's parents would have sent her at once to a counselor—or to Planned Parenthood. Joseph would have called his attorney to annul the betrothal—as well as to put a private investigator on the case to track down Mary's seducer.

W. H. Auden, the noted British poet, wrote: "Dogmatic theological statements [such as the Virgin birth] are to be comprehended neither as logical propositions, nor as poetic utterances. They are to be taken rather as shaggy dog stories: they have a point, but whoever tries hard to get it will miss the point." The point here is that by saying "yes" to God, in a way of being courageous that makes the rest of us look spineless, Mary and Joseph take part in the miracle of miracles: the enfleshment of God as one of us. What happened to them *physically,* must happen with us *spiritually.* Through faith, the Spirit births Jesus into the world through our own flesh and blood. All it takes is for us to say "yes," too.

—H. King Oehmig

Paul then goes on to tell us more about the Son. Jesus was descended in the flesh from the lineage of David and is the Son of God by the power of the Resurrection. Through him we receive the "grace and apostleship" that enables Paul "to bring about the obedience of faith among all the Gentiles" (v. 5), including the beloved in Rome who are called to be saints (v. 7). Faith is the appropriate response to the Gospel, and it is this obedience in faith that enables all people to truly belong to Christ.

As our waiting for the coming of the Christ Child comes to an end, the words of the Psalmist remind us of what this coming means for the world: "Restore us, O God; let your face shine, that we may be saved" (80:3).

POINTS TO PONDER

1. Try to put yourself in Joseph's place, and describe the feelings and inner struggles he and Mary might have experienced as a result of Mary's pregnancy.

2. Discuss the significance of Joseph's dream (Mt. 1:20-21) and his response to what the angel revealed to him. Also look at the other dreams experienced by Joseph (2:13, 19, 22). How do we regard dreams and visions in our world today?

3. We learn here that Joseph was to name the child Jesus, "for he will save his people from their sins" (v. 21). How is the messiahship of Jesus defined by his name?

4. How is the identity of the child further enhanced by being identified with Emmanuel (v. 23)? What does "God with us" mean to you?

5. As you read the other Lessons for today in Isaiah 7:10-17 and Romans 1:1-7, what more do we learn about the life and mission of Jesus as the Messiah?

THE NATIVITY OF JESUS

Isaiah 9:2-7; Psalm 96; Titus 2:11-14; Luke 2:1-14 (15-20)

The waiting of Advent is finally over, and the words of the prophets over the centuries are to be fulfilled: "For a child has been born for us" (Is. 9:6).

Today's Psalm 96 reminds all of us, no matter how many Christmases we have celebrated, that it is always a "new song" that we sing to the Lord. And today we too declare the Divine wonders to all the people.

The passage from Isaiah was written for a coronation celebration and describes the ideal Davidic king. But in time, these words took on messianic overtones, as God's people anticipated the future fulfillment of Isaiah's words.

"The people" here are the Israelites who suffered under Assyrian oppression; but now they will no longer walk in darkness, for "on them light has shined" (9:2) through the promise of the birth of a child. Matthew 4:16 uses these lines from Isaiah as further evidence of the messiahship of Jesus.

The world now rejoices as it is freed from bondage and oppression. Peace and justice shall reign, for the Child who is born has been given authority. His names indicate how he will act (v. 6). As "Wonderful Counselor" he will rule with wisdom. As "Mighty God" he is an expression of God's power and presence. He is called "Everlasting Father" because he will look after the welfare of his people; and as the "Prince of Peace" he brings reconciliation.

His authority will continue to increase, and with his reign will come endless peace. He will establish and uphold his kingdom with justice and righteousness from now until the end of time. This is God's plan—God's "zeal" to save the world.

For us today, the salvation foretold by Isaiah becomes reality through Jesus Christ, whose birth the Gospel of Luke portrays. After setting the stage with the birth of John the Baptist and the Annunciation to Mary that she will bear a child *who will be the Son of God,* Luke intentionally sets the birth itself within the wider Gentile world. He refers to specific geographical details and dates in Roman life.

The census decreed by the Emperor provides the means to place Mary and Joseph in Bethlehem, the messianic city of David. Joseph's lineage connects Jesus to the Davidic line, as foretold in the prophetic tradition. Thus, Jesus is a son of the house of David as well as the Son of God.

Luke tells us that Joseph and Mary traveled from Nazareth to Bethlehem in order to comply with the census decree. While they were in Bethlehem, the time came for Mary to deliver her child (2:6). There was no room for them at the inn, so the baby was born in a stable and placed in a manger.

Thus this Child, who is God's only Son, entered human life in the most humble of circumstances. Born with the barest essentials of hospitality, Jesus in his ministry became host to the dispossessed and displaced of the world.

PRAYER FOR THE DAY

On this festival day, O God, we celebrate the birth of your only Son, Jesus Christ our Redeemer, who now reigns with you and the Holy Spirit in glory everlasting. *Amen.*

How then was the world to know of this miraculous event? The birth of a royal child is normally announced with great fanfare and ceremony. But in keeping with Luke's theology, the birth of the Messiah was told first to the poor and lowly, not the rich and powerful.

In contrast, Matthew's infancy narrative recounts that wise men came from afar bearing expensive gifts to pay homage to the Christ Child (Mt. 2:1-12).

Verses 8-13 of Luke 2 tell of the first proclamation of the birth to a group of shepherds from the fields that surrounded Bethlehem. As "an angel of the Lord stood before them, and the glory of the Lord shone around them" (v. 9), the shepherds were terrified. However, the angel acted quickly to calm their fears by telling them that *in the city of David, a Savior had been born for them—* "the Messiah, the Lord" (v. 11). They could find this Child lying in a manger.

Then an entire heavenly choir appeared, praising God and promising peace to the world that God loved enough to save. *Glory to God in the highest heaven, and on earth peace among those whom God favors!*

Verses 15-20 record the initial responses to this news. First, the shepherds went immediately to Bethlehem to see for themselves what the angel had told them. After finding Mary, Joseph, and the Child, the shepherds told others, who in turn were amazed by this news. In the Gospel of Luke a faithful response to receiving the Good News is to go out and tell others.

We are told that Mary "treasured all these words and pondered them in her heart" (v. 19). Mary continued to reflect on the implications of all the events surrounding this Son whom God had entrusted to her (2:51).

The letter to Titus tells us what we are to do in response to God's gift of salvation in Christ Jesus. We are to renounce all thought and action that is not consistent with the way Jesus lived on earth as we wait for the blessed hope of Christ (2:13).

ON REFLECTION

W. H. Vanstone, a post-World War II theologian in England, expressed the dynamic love so much at the heart of the Christmas event where "God so loved the world. ..." He writes: "The power which love gives to the other is the power to determine the issue of love itself—its completion or frustration, its triumph or tragedy."

It's true. Gathered at Bethlehem's manger, we are poised between love's completion or frustration, between love's triumph or tragedy. The humanization of God in Jesus—the Unlimited becoming limited, the Infinite becoming finite—is God's ultimate risk, the risk of Love. No longer will God be "wholly Other," high in the heavens, but rather here, *as one of us.* It is God's final vulnerability—the Divine risk of love. And the "power of response" is given directly to us. The tragedy or triumph of the Incarnation lies in our willingness to accept or reject the Gift of all gifts.

The writer on the spiritual life, Anais Nin, taught that we do not see things as they are; we see them the way we are. Maybe the whole completion or frustration of Christmas lies in how ready we are to have the Holy Spirit put in our hearts the gift of recognition—to soften us, to empower us, to embrace the blessing of Jesus. Will we recognize in the Incarnation that God is much more than an Uncaused First Cause, or a Ground of Being? God is Love outpouring, going to any length to make the cosmos whole—starting with you and me.

—H. King Oehmig

As he gave himself for us, so we now give ourselves to him in a disciplined life of righteousness. He alone is able to purify our souls from sin and iniquity. And through this marvelous work of salvation, he has united to himself "a people of his own who are zealous for good deeds" (v. 14).

As we seek to perform these deeds to which Jesus inspires us, we find the fullness of Christian believing here and now. Furthermore, we know that one day we will be able joyfully to greet our Redeemer's return in glory. *Praise be to God!*

POINTS TO PONDER

1. How does the light of Christ come to us in our world today? How are we called to bear forth this light to others?

2. What does it mean to "renounce impiety and worldly passions" and to "live lives that are self-controlled, upright, and godly" (Titus 2:12) in our present time? How can we avoid projecting a self-righteous attitude as we seek to live by these high standards?

3. How can our praise to God be an "offering" on this Christmas Day? What are the far-reaching effects of our worship of Christ in a world that may have forgotten the true meaning of this holiday?

4. Why do you think the shepherds were called to the scene of Jesus' birth? How are we like and unlike these first witnesses?

5. What difference does it make to our daily lives that Christ has come among us? How can we share this knowledge and understanding with those around us day to day?

THE WORD MADE FLESH

Isaiah 61:10—62:3; Psalm 147; Galatians 3:23-25; 4:4-7; John 1:1-18

The poetic language of the Prologue to the Fourth Gospel reveals to us the mystery of the Incarnation. Through these words we get a glimpse of God's eternal plan, as well as of the Divine nature and origin of Jesus.

John's Prologue tells us that Jesus existed in the beginning with God the Father and was active in creation. He became incarnate and dwelt among us in human flesh. As the source of light and life in the world, he is the one who makes God the Father known to us.

The opening words of the passage, "In the beginning" (1:1), immediately call to mind the same words in Genesis 1:1 with reference to creation. References to light and darkness throughout the passage further emphasize this connection. And whereas the infancy narratives of Matthew and Luke focus on the earthly origins of Jesus, John is concerned with the heavenly existence of the Word in the beginning—outside the human constraints of time and place.

Here "the Word"—i. e., the Greek *Logos*—conveys the rationality, purpose, and expression of God's creative intent. Jesus as the *Logos* existed in the beginning with God the Father and was active in creation (vv. 2-3). Jesus was with God, and all things came into being through him.

The *Logos* was the agent who gave reality to the Father's design of creation: "In him was life, and the life was the light of all people" (v. 4). This light is such that the darkness of the world—i. e., the world's rejection of Jesus—cannot overcome it.

Verses 6-8 introduce John the Baptist as "a man sent from God" (v. 6). John is the only person in John's Gospel apart from Jesus who is described as being *sent by God*. He was sent to tell the world that Jesus is the true light who enlightens all (v. 9). In verse 15, John acknowledges that, although Jesus comes after him in chronological time, he "ranks ahead of me because he was before me."

The *Logos* brought life to the world, yet those who were his own failed to recognize or receive him (vv. 10-11). However, there were some who did receive the Word and believed in him. To them he gave the privilege of becoming children of God (v. 12).

This was not a matter of human intention, ancestry, individual endeavor, or cultural influence. It was given strictly by God's grace. The adoption by which we are made God's children is the first principle of our lives (1 Jn. 3:1-12).

"And the Word became flesh and lived among us ... full of grace and truth" (Jn. 1:14). This is the true meaning of the Christmas season and the human birth of the *Logos* in Bethlehem. He "lived among us"—he literally "pitched his tent" among us, illustrating the grace and truth that is God's true nature.

PRAYER FOR THE DAY

O God, cause us to shine forth in the world in the light of your incarnate Word: Jesus Christ our Lord, who lives and reigns with you and the Holy Spirit, one God, now and forever. *Amen.*

Law, instruction, and guidance for a way of life were given long ago through Moses (v. 17), but now God's grace and truth come to us through Jesus Christ. No one has ever been able to see God, as the intensity of light and holiness would be overwhelming.

Nevertheless, we who are disciples have seen the only Son, the One who became what we are, and who yet remains forever one with God, "close to the Father's heart" (v. 18).

Thus Paul can write with confidence to the Galatians that the "fullness of time" (4:4) has come with the appearance of God's Son, who was born of a woman and lived as one of us. For centuries the Jewish people had found identity in the Law, a pattern of instruction that Paul refers to as "our disciplinarian until Christ came" (3:24).

The Law was something that the people had obeyed, but Paul knew from his own experience that some relied on their own performance of the Law rather than on the grace of the God who had given the Law.

Paul makes a distinction here between a renewed faith that has been fulfilled through the coming of Jesus Christ, and the former faith under the discipline of the Law. Now the earlier instruction has been turned into the freedom of grace through Jesus. Through his obedience to the will of the Father, Jesus Christ brought reconciliation and new life to believers.

Now, as heirs with Christ, we are no longer slaves to the discipline of the Law, but are adopted as God's children. We can call God "Abba" just as Jesus did, and live with confidence in God's love for us.

While Paul and the Gospel of John could describe the reality of the Incarnation, the prophets could only anticipate the coming of the Messiah. The final chapters of Isaiah (56-66), referred to as Third Isaiah, contain much material that was later seen by Christians as an expression of God's actions through Jesus Christ.

ON REFLECTION

"The primary declaration of Christianity," said Evelyn Underhill, is not, 'This do,' but 'This happened.'"

Frederick Buechner called it the "scandal of the crib." You can see why. Anyone who says that, deep down, all religions are the same, had better look again. With all due respect, no Jew, Hindu, Muslim, or Buddhist would agree with the Christmas message: that at a specific time, at a specific place, a neonate born to peasant Jews from an obscure Judean village was the Son of God.

This happened. God was disclosed, in a unique and unrepeatable way—not in tablets of stone, or in an angel, or in a cloud, a pillar of fire, or a dream. Not in a vision, or in a spiritual feeling—but as a human being. God in skin. God with bones. God in a diaper. God suckling at his mother's breast. God crying himself to sleep. This happened.

A story goes that a mother was putting her young boy to sleep. She told him a story, said prayers, kissed him, and then turned out the light. Right before she left the room, a trembling voice said, "Mommy, don't leave." "Don't worry," the mom replied. "It will be OK … God is here with you." To which the little boy replied, "I know, but I want someone with skin on them."

So there you have what happened: Jesus, God's self-disclosure, in skin, a full human being. Why? Athanasius, Bishop of Alexandria (c. 296—373) perhaps said it best: "He became what we are that he might make us what he is."

—H. King Oehmig

In the reading for today, the prophet rejoices in the expectation of a new era. "My whole being shall exult in my God" (61:10). He conveys a sense of joy and festivity as God's people are compared to a bride and bridegroom clothed with God's salvation and righteousness.

Just as new life sprouts from the earth, so will the Lord God cause "righteousness and praise to spring up before all the nations" (v. 11). All the world will see the glory of the stunning revelation to come.

Zion's glory and salvation will someday become a shining lamp for all the nations to see—"a crown of beauty" and a "royal diadem" (62:3) in the hand of the Lord.

As a further sign, the Lord will give this transformed community a new name. In 62: 4 we learn that Zion will no longer be called Forsaken and Desolate. Instead God will delight in the people as a groom delights in his bride. The people will now be called "My Delight Is in Her" and the land will be called "Married; for the Lord delights in you."

We are called to respond to God's love and delight toward us with praise and thanksgiving. Thus we can proclaim along with the Psalmist: "Hallelujah! How good it is to sing praises to our God!" (147:1).

POINTS TO PONDER

1. The Prologue of the Gospel of John presents John's answer to the question of *Who is Jesus?* What do we learn in this passage about the life and mission of Jesus, as well as about the ministry of John the Baptist?

2. The opening verses of the Gospel passage focus on the creative power of the Word. How do you see the Word's creative activity at work in the world today?

3. What do we learn here about God the Father? What is the relationship between God and Jesus?

4. According to the Epistle reading for today in Galatians 3:23-25, 4:4-7, how do we become adopted as God's children? Compare Paul's words with those of John's Gospel in verses 12-13. What does it mean to you that you are a child of God?

5. Verse 16 states that we have all received "grace upon grace." How would you define "grace"? How have you experienced this gift in your own life?

THE NAME ABOVE ALL NAMES

Numbers 6:22-27; Psalm 8; Galatians 4:4-7; Luke 2:15-21

The lectionary for today focuses on the importance of a name, specifically the *Holy Name of Jesus*. Names carry power, and acts done in the name of Jesus become a revelation of God's presence.

A name also represents the true essence of an individual. The use of the Lord's name invokes the power of God as well as revealing Divine attributes. This can be seen in the Aaronic benediction in the Book of Numbers. It was a priestly function to pronounce a blessing upon the gathered community, and through such a blessing God's presence and protective power were invoked.

Each of the three successive parts of this poetic blessing is longer than the previous one, thus emphasizing God's increasing abundance toward the people. Each verse begins with "the Lord," in recognition that God alone is the source of all blessing.

The first verse (6:24) speaks of God's blessing and protection; while the second (v. 25) recognizes the grace of God. The third verse (26) proclaims the ineffable peace that encompasses the *well-being and salvation* that can come only from God.

This blessing also includes the imagery of God's face shining upon the people. It was a sign of favor when a monarch looked at an individual. Thus the face of the Lord—"the Lord lift up his countenance upon you" (v. 26)—indicates that God's presence is not hidden from the people.

In the final verse, we see that blessing literally means *putting God's name on the people* as an indication of presence, protection, grace, and peace. "So they shall put my name on the Israelites, and I will bless them."

Thus to pronounce a blessing in the name of the Lord is to invoke the Divine presence and give our present action a wider significance that *links us to one another and to God.*

Psalm 8 reflects a similar sense of awe and wonder at the name of the Lord: "O Lord, our Sovereign, how majestic is your name in all the earth!" (vv. 1, 8). The Psalmist goes on to give praise to the power and majesty of the Lord, and to marvel in the trust and love that God has bestowed upon humanity: "What are human beings that you are mindful of them, mortals that you care for them?" (v. 4).

It is for us mortals that Christ came ...

When Christmas falls on a Sunday, the Feast of the Holy Name of Our Lord coincides with the First Sunday after Christmas, and thus supercedes the regular Sunday observance. Falling eight days after Christmas, this feast day was originally called the Feast of the Circumcision, since Luke tells us that on the eighth day after his birth, Jesus was circumcised and given his name.

Except for verse 21, the Gospel text for today in Luke 2 overlaps the optional verses (15-20) of the reading appointed for Christmas Day, in which the shepherds responded to the message of the angels that *a child who is Savior, Messiah, and Lord* had been born.

PRAYER FOR THE DAY

Heavenly Father, you gave your incarnate Son the holy name of Jesus as the sign of our salvation. Now bestow on each of us, we pray, increased understanding and love of him who is the Savior of the world. *Amen.*

They made their way to Bethlehem, where they found the child in the manger. With the angels' words confirmed, the shepherds spread the Good News to others, who responded with amazement.

According to the requirements of Mosaic Law, three ceremonies are to follow the birth of a male child: circumcision (Lev. 12:3); redemption or dedication of the firstborn (Ex. 13:12-13; Num. 18:15); and purification of the mother (Lev. 12:2, 4, 6). Genesis directs that, as a sign of the covenant between God and the nation of Israel: "Throughout your generations every male among you shall be circumcised when he is eight days old" (17:12).

Thus, through circumcision, the Messiah gains solidarity with humanity and becomes subject to the Law—that is, the Messiah is both "born of a woman" and also "born under the law" (Gal. 4:4). However, Luke is more concerned with the naming of Jesus, and this is the only place in the Gospels that describes this event.

In Matthew 1:21, Joseph was told in a dream that he was to name the coming child *Jesus,* "for he will save his people from their sins." In Hebrew the name Jesus means *savior* or *deliverer.* When the angel Gabriel appeared to Mary, Gabriel too declared that the baby was to be called Jesus (Lk. 1:31). Thus, in naming the child Jesus, Mary and Joseph are obedient to God and follow the requirements of their ancestral faith, which include the purification of Mary and a dedication sacrifice for a first-born child (Lk. 2:22-24).

Names in Scripture have great meaning as an indicator of who an individual is and what that person is called to do. Mary and Joseph did not name this child; the naming was part of God's unfolding plan of salvation. Thus this simple obedience on the part of Mary and Joseph was used for the glory of God, as this child grew up to fulfill his vocation as Savior.

ON REFLECTION

Before being referred to as the Divine Physician, the Good Shepherd, the Son of Man, the Bread of Life, the Suffering Servant, Christ, or the Resurrection and the Life, he was known simply as "Jesus."

To the world into which this eight-day-old infant was born, it was one of the most ordinary and common of names—like John, or Joe. Nothing about this name suggested exceptionality or distinction or holiness. The chronicler of the ancient world, Josephus, said in his history, *The Works of Josephus,* that so many men claimed the name "Jesus" that it lacked any individuality at all. But it was the name that the angel told his mother Mary to call him (Lk. 1:31), and she and Joseph did.

You have to wonder what kind of congruence a garden-variety name like "Jesus" would have for one referred to as "Wonderful Counselor, Mighty God, Everlasting Father, Prince of Peace"? Maybe the secret to understanding the naming of Jesus—and the Gospel he would live and die for—is that *the extraordinary is always expressed through the ordinary.* The spiritual is always expressed through the material. The hiddenness of grace most often lies in the place we are least likely to look for it—under our noses. Grace happens in the very place where we live and move and have our being—day in and day out.

—H. King Oehmig

In the letter to the Galatians, Paul writes that "when the fullness of time had come" (4:4), God sent his Son to be our Savior. This son was "born of a woman," and thus could identify with humanity. He was also born "under the law"—indicating his heritage among the Jewish people.

He came to bring redemption so that we might be adopted as God's children. Because Jesus knew God as *Abba Father,* those who accept the reconciliation that Christ brings can also call upon Abba as heirs of *all of which Jesus himself was heir.*

The Feast of the Holy Name reminds us of the salvation Jesus brings to us and to all generations. It is his name that we bless and uphold in all our liturgy and worship. In doing so, we affirm that God the Father also hears us, and that we too are sons and daughters of God through Christ our Lord.

POINTS TO PONDER

1. We read in the Gospel passage that the shepherds left their fields to "see this thing that has taken place" (Lk. 2:15). What might they have been thinking as they approached Bethlehem? What do you think they expected to find?

2. Verse 18 tells us that as the shepherds shared their experience with others, "all who heard it were amazed." As we read the familiar words of the Nativity narrative, how does this story continue to be amazing for us today?

3. In a sense, the shepherds were the first evangelists. During this Christmas season, as well as throughout the year, what can we do to proclaim the birth of the Messiah?

4. In verse 19, we read that "Mary treasured all these words and pondered them in her heart." What do you imagine she might have felt and thought on the night Jesus was born, as well as in the years to follow?

5. What does the name *Jesus* tell us about who he was and the nature of his ministry? What is significant about your own name? What does your name say about who you are as a person?

FLIGHT INTO EGYPT

Jeremiah 31:7-14; Psalm 84; Ephesians 1:3-6, 15-19a; Matthew 2:13-15, 19-23

Only Matthew and Luke include birth narratives in their Gospels; and whereas Luke's focus is on Mary, Matthew tells the events through the perspective of Joseph. Here we see Joseph as a man who cares for his family in accordance to directions from God.

In the first chapter of his Gospel, Matthew establishes evidence that Jesus is the Messiah. Through his genealogy (1:1-17), we see that the humanity of Jesus is derived from his lineage in the messianic house of King David. His Divinity comes through the Virgin Mary's conception by the Holy Spirit (1:18-25). All the Gospel writers sought to show that Jesus was indeed the fulfillment of the ancient prophecies, but none more so than Matthew. Five times in the first two chapters alone, Matthew calls attention to actions he identifies as being in fulfillment of the prophets (1:22; 2:5, 15, 17, 23).

After the Christ Child is born in Bethlehem, Wise Men from the East came to pay him homage (2:1-11). However, the Magi's search for the "child who has been born king of the Jews" (2:2) prompted King Herod to attempt to eliminate a potential rival by ordering the death of all male children in Bethlehem under two years (2:16-18). Already, we see a foreshadowing of the acceptance of Jesus by the Gentiles, as represented by the Magi, and his rejection by the Jewish authorities in the actions of Herod. And in contrast to the peaceful scenes of Luke's nativity, the birth of Jesus in Matthew's account is characterized by threats of danger to the Holy Family.

Soon after the Wise Men depart, Joseph is warned in a dream to take his family and flee to Egypt, where they will be safe from Herod. In verse 15, Matthew recalls the prophecy of Hosea 11:1 to suggest that the sojourn in Egypt recapitulates the history of Israel: "Out of Egypt I have called my son."

When Herod died, Joseph was again told in a dream that it was safe to return to Israel. However, after Herod's death, his kingdom was divided among his three sons. As Archelaus was now ruler in Judea, Joseph was warned once more in a dream to go elsewhere; thus the family went to Nazareth in Galilee. This too was to fulfill the prophecy that "He will be called a Nazorean" (v. 23b).

The stage is now set for Jesus to grow in mind, body, and spirit, according to the will of his heavenly Father, and in obedience to his earthly parents. His life had been spared, and the way was made clear for his ministry. This story also teaches us to listen to God's voice in all circumstances, even in dreams and intuition, as God uses all of these means to prepare us for service.

The birth in Bethlehem, the exile and return from Egypt, the implications of the name Nazarene—all came about in fulfillment of the oracles that were given to God's prophets.

PRAYER FOR THE DAY

O God our Creator, we ask that we may graciously share in the life of your Son, Jesus Christ our Lord, who came to us and humbled himself in order to share our humanity. *Amen.*

Although poetic and imaginative, these prophecies reflected experiences through which the prophets themselves lived. Jeremiah saw his nation conquered and his people marched into exile in Babylon. But in faith, Jeremiah knew that this was not the end; there would be a return. "For thus says the Lord: Sing aloud with gladness for Jacob ... proclaim, give praise, and say, 'Save, O Lord, your people, the remnant of Israel'" (31:7).

The Lord would gather the people from the northland, from the ends of the earth, wherever they had been scattered. Even those too ill-prepared to travel, God would bring home. The prophet recognized that God is a Father to Israel and a shepherd to this flock. On the height of Zion the Lord would cause the people to sing in praise, to rejoice at the nation's bounty. Young and old together would find their mourning turned to joy. When the Lord actually fulfilled this purpose in the Incarnate Son of God, the blessings were not for Israel alone, but for the whole human race, and with hope beyond the present world.

In Ephesians we see another aspect of God's care for all humanity. Every spiritual blessing had been preordained in heaven before the foundation of the world, and was made accessible by the Messiah (1:3). God the Father destined believers for adoption as children through Jesus Christ; therefore we have been and are yet being prepared to participate in this glorious destiny.

Jesus' disciples have been rendered blameless before God, and thus are able to be received into God's family. Because of this fact, we are led to praise this glorious grace that has been freely bestowed on them, and us, through love.

The Apostle Paul goes on to write that he has heard of the faith of the Ephesians and of their spirit of love. He gives thanks for these things (v. 16), and he prays that God, the Father of Jesus, will bestow on them a spirit of "wisdom" and of "revelation" while they continue in their inner life of faith (v. 18).

ON REFLECTION

King Herod did not hate the baby so much as he feared the man the baby would become. And tried to slay him early before the competition for Kingship could begin. Just so would I slay the infant stirring before he shows me the vain emptiness of my reign. O, God, forgive and slay the Herod in me.

—Todd Williams

"The Word became flesh," wrote John, "and dwelt among us, full of grace and truth." That is what incarnation means. It is untheological. It is unsophisticated. It is undignified. But according to Christianity it is the way things are.

All religions and philosophies which deny the reality or the significance of the material, the fleshy, the earth-bound, are themselves denied. Moses at the burning bush was told to take off his shoes because the ground on which he stood was holy ground, and the incarnation means that all ground is holy ground because God not only made it but walked on it, ate and slept and worked and died on it. If we are saved anywhere, we are saved here. And what is saved is not a diaphanous distillation of our bodies and our earth but our bodies and our earth themselves. ... One of the blunders religious people are particularly fond of making is the attempt to be more spiritual than God.

—Frederick Buechner

POINTS TO PONDER

1. As you read the Gospel passage, put yourself in the place of Joseph. How do you think he and his family might have felt throughout this series of dramatic events?

2. Dreams play an important role in this story, as Joseph not only listened to the angel of the Lord in his dreams, but believed and acted accordingly. How do you perceive God directing and guiding your life?

3. Here Joseph is described as a "righteous man" (Mt. 1:19). How is Joseph a model of discipleship for us today?

4. In the Old Testament and Gospel passages, we read of people returning home or to a place of special significance. How does this theme relate to your own life and to your spiritual journey? How do you think someone who has experienced being homeless might relate to these passages?

5. In the letter to the Ephesians, what do you think it means in 1:18 when the writer asks that "the eyes of your heart [be] enlightened"?

LIGHT OF THE WORLD

Isaiah 60:1-6; Psalm 72:1-7, 10-14; Ephesians 3:1-12; Matthew 2:1-12

The Holy Family came to Bethlehem, as Luke records it, and there the Holy Child was born. Thus was fulfilled a prophecy from Micah: "But you, O Bethlehem of Ephrathah, who are one of the little clans of Judah, from you shall come forth for me one who is to rule in Israel, whose origin is from of old, from ancient days" (5:2).

Matthew 2:11 then indicates that the family remained in Bethlehem, that Joseph had found an opportunity to practice his trade and had been able to acquire better accommodations. When the Wise Men came to present their gifts, they did not enter a stable but a house. Theirs had been a lengthy journey. The Holy Child was now one year old.

In the development of God's plan for human salvation, the birth of the Holy Child was the most important event in history. Choirs of angels had been sent to announce it to the ordinary working people of the Covenant nation. Because the salvation was not for that Covenant nation alone, representatives of other nations had to be involved as well. So there is an opening up, a revealing: *an Epiphany*. The chosen representatives of other nations were scholars, scientists who observed phenomena in the skies, especially the motions of the stars. Technically, they were called magi (wise men). They also could be called kings, providing that we do not compare them with European figureheads today. For this most important event in history, there was also a manifestation in the heavens, a conjunction of the planets Jupiter and Saturn in the year 7 B. C.

The astrologers made their calculations. The bright star so created would be visible near the Mediterranean shore. They began their journey in the hope of seeing it, and finally they were rewarded when the star appeared to them in Palestine. Matthew and Luke agree that Jesus was born during the reign of Herod the Great, who died in 4 B. C. So the birth must have been prior to that year, very probably in 8 B. C.

Herod the Great was no more than a vassal of the Roman Emperor; but he was a skilled politician who had secured control of half a dozen provinces. To his court the Wise Men came. They told of their star, which indicated to them that a king had been born; and in Palestine he would be King of the Jews. Herod would have no other king. He had ordered three of his own sons killed to make sure that they could not conspire against him. With the help of Micah's prophecy (5:2), he could direct the Wise Men to Bethlehem with the request that they would report back when they had found their king. God's wisdom circumvented Herod's murderous intent, although not his bloody massacre.

Of the gifts presented to the Child, gold stood for kingship, incense for priesthood, and myrrh, a spice used in burials, for availing sacrifice. Prompted by God, the Wise Men found a different way back to their homes. Herod never saw them again.

PRAYER FOR THE DAY

O God, by a star you revealed your only Son to the inhabitants of the earth. Lead us now, we pray, to shine forth in his presence, that we may continue to reveal him in the world. *Amen.*

The Light has come to dispel the darkness that had covered the earth and all its people. The Isaiah scroll had expressed the hope, even the promise, that the *goyim* (in Is. 60:3 it stands for *nations* rather than *heathen*) would come to God's Light, and kings to the brightness of God's presence. The Wise Men (or kings) not only came and gave their recognition to the Light— they worshiped. These last chapters of the Isaiah scroll anticipate that the Hebrew exiles who have already returned are simply the first installment of a great homecoming. *Your sons and your daughters shall come, and with them shall come treasures of Midian and Ephah and Sheba ...*

The school of Isaiah, and the original prophet himself, taught that God sought for all nations to come to the Light of Divine revelation. Later the commission of Saul of Tarsus received from Christ at his conversion was to bring the *goyim* (nations) to recognize and turn to the Light.

As Paul, the Apostle to the Gentiles, he brought many fellow-workers to take part in that task of conversion. So the letter to the Ephesians (3:6) declares that those nations that have not known the Covenant are to become fellow-heirs with those who have—members of the same Body, sharers in the promises. God, who had created all the nations, was offering to all *access to the Holy One* (v. 12).

A prayer may be offered for the Holy Child who was born to be King. Psalm 72 is such a prayer: "Give the king your justice, O God, and your righteousness to a king's son ..." (v. 1). Actually, the Psalmist was thinking of an ideal earthly king, a messiah. But when the Anointed One did appear, he was much more. As the Wise Men departed to their own country, they could offer such a prayer for the Holy Child whom they had visited, and, indeed, he would more than fulfill it.

ON REFLECTION

Like Noah assembling a triple-decker ferryboat hundreds of miles from any ocean, or Abraham and Sarah leaving the security of Haran for an uncharted land, these Magi set out from Persia following only a star. *A star.* Can't you hear them telling their homefolk the news? To peals of laughter, or to outright cries of anger, maybe they hummed "Twinkle, twinkle, little Star" as they left town headed west to an unknown destination following only an anomaly in the heavens.

Perhaps the two most powerful words in all Scripture are "they went." Hitching their very lives to a star, the Magi "went." Paul Tillich said that faith was a journey without maps, but you were going anyway—trusting your vision, trusting the imagination of your heart, tossing better judgment and common sense to the wind. You go because you trust not only your instincts, but your vision—one that others usually cannot enter—and will certainly question.

The late Urban T. Holmes III, former dean of the School of Theology at the University of the South, wrote in his work *Ministry and Imagination:* "If the Church is to be open to the presence of God in Christ, it has to live a life of imagination." We need to embrace intuition. We need to attend to the "still, small voice" within us—recapture wonder and the ability to be astonished by that which is beyond the rational and the regular.

If that happens, we might find ourselves along with the Magi, lost in adoring the Mystery of the world—a Mystery that, in this instance, is wrapped in nothing but swaddling clothes.

—H. King Oehmig

The compilers of the Isaiah scroll, likewise, could pray in this way for the representative of God's people through whom the Holy One would restore unity and splendor. The letter to the Ephesians could use such words as a thanksgiving for what God had done in Christ. For us today, the Psalm is a *thanksgiving* that by God's grace we are among those enabled to come to the Light.

POINTS TO PONDER

1. Why do you think Herod and "all Jerusalem with him" were troubled when the Wise Men from the East came inquiring about the child "born king of the Jews"? What can still be troubling about Jesus in our midst?

2. When the Wise Men found the Holy Child, they "were overwhelmed with joy" and "knelt down and paid him homage." What do their actions suggest to us about the nature of worship?

3. Why was it significant that people from a foreign country came to pay homage to the Christ Child? What example of faith do the Wise Men set for us today?

4. A star, as the symbol of God's directing guidance, led the Magi to Christ. How does God continue to direct us to Christ in our lives? How do the other Lessons appointed for this day also inform your understanding of the visit of the Wise Men?

5. Today is the Feast of the Epiphany. The word "epiphany" means "to manifest" or "to reveal." During the season of Epiphany, we focus on how the Divine is made known to us through Jesus. What are some "epiphanies" or moments of the Divine that you have experienced in your own life?

THE BAPTISM OF JESUS

Isaiah 42:1-9; Psalm 29; Acts 10:34-43; Matthew 3:13-17

The first public act in the ministry of Jesus was his Baptism in the Jordan River. Thus the Gospel reading for the First Sunday After the Epiphany is always an account of the Baptism.

Following the genealogy and birth narrative in Matthew's Gospel, John the Baptist appears, proclaiming a message of repentance. Now "Jesus came from Galilee to John at the Jordan, to be baptized by him" (Mt. 3:13). Although Jesus is the reason for everything that has happened thus far in Matthew's Gospel, this is the first time that Jesus himself plays an active role in the narrative.

All three of the Synoptic Gospels present an account of the Baptism of Jesus as the first event in his ministry (Mk. 1:9-11; Lk. 3:21-22). The Gospel of John does not include Jesus' Baptism, but John the Baptist does allude to the event (Jn. 1:29-34). Matthew's account closely follows that of Mark, but includes an exchange between John and Jesus (vv. 14-15) not recorded by Mark.

When Jesus presents himself to John for baptism, John's first reaction is to refuse, saying, "I need to be baptized by you, and do you come to me?" The question naturally arises as to why Jesus would submit to John's baptism.

John preached a baptism of repentance for sin and had already stated that Jesus is superior to him. "I baptize you with water for repentance, but one who is more powerful than I is coming after me. ... He will baptize you with the Holy Spirit and fire" (3:11).

Jesus responds to John's objection by answering that "it is proper for us in this way to fulfill all righteousness" (v. 15). These are the first words spoken by Jesus in Matthew's Gospel. Fulfillment and righteousness are important themes for Matthew; and even though Jesus carried no burden of sin, he was nevertheless a part of his nation and people.

By allowing himself to be baptized by John, Jesus claims for himself the sinfulness of Israel, just as he will claim the sinfulness of the world at his crucifixion.

As Jesus came up out of the water, "suddenly the heavens were opened to him and he saw the Spirit of God descending like a dove and alighting on him" (v. 16). The opening of the heavens indicates that there is now a new possibility of communication between God and humans.

The image of the Spirit as a dove has no other scriptural reference, but it does call to mind the image of God's Spirit hovering over the waters at creation (Gen. 1:2).

The vision of the dove is accompanied by a heavenly voice that acknowledges the vocation of Jesus: "This is my Son, the Beloved, with whom I am well pleased" (v. 17).

Thus Matthew makes it clear that these words are not the personal call of a prophet for Jesus alone to hear; this is a public pronouncement of *who Jesus is* as he begins his ministry in the Spirit.

Psalm 29 also proclaims the Lord's glory. The Lord's voice is mighty—it can shatter the cedar trees and shake the Lebanon range. The voice of the Lord is earthquake and fire, but the Lord also gives blessing to the people. In the temple all proclaim "Glory!" as they worship the Lord in the beauty of holiness.

PRAYER FOR THE DAY

Our Father in heaven, who at Jesus' Baptism in the Jordan River called him your Beloved Son and anointed him in the Spirit, give to all of us who are baptized in his name a ministry in the world, as we boldly profess his power. *Amen.*

The opening words from the First Servant Song of Isaiah were echoed by Matthew: "Here is my servant, whom I uphold, my chosen, in whom my soul delights; I have put my spirit upon him ..." (42:1).

Here the nature of the mysterious Servant is described as one chosen by God in the Spirit to bring justice to the world. In God's service, the Servant will be humble and self-effacing, with compassion extended to the weak and needy—"bruised reeds" and "dimly burning wicks" (v. 3).

In verses 5-8, we find the greatness of God the Creator, who calls the people to righteousness, is proclaimed. God has established a covenant with the people who are to be "a light to the nations" (v. 6), to bring freedom to those in bondage and who "sit in darkness" (v. 7). The Lord's incomparable greatness and glory over all others is pronounced.

Thus the "former things have come to pass" (v. 9), as the Lord proclaims a future in which justice will reign and God's covenant will be fulfilled. These "new things" will come to fruition in Christ, whose sacrifice will change the world.

In Acts 10, Isaiah's vision of the extension of God's covenant to all peoples becomes a reality as Peter delivers the first public proclamation of the Gospel to the Gentiles in the home of Cornelius the centurion. Described as "a devout man who feared God" (10:2), Cornelius had a vision in which he was to send for the Apostle Peter to come to speak to him.

Peter had witnessed the Lord's life, death, Resurrection, and Ascension. He had experienced the coming of the Holy Spirit in wind and flames, and had been empowered to perform miracles in Jesus' name. Finally, he also had come to understand in a dream (10: 9-16) that the message of salvation was for Jew and Gentile alike (Acts 10:28).

ON REFLECTION

The Gospel of Philip, a second or third century Gnostic text that never made it into the canon of the New Testament, includes the baptism of Jesus in its narrative—with one interesting, even startling, addition left out of the other Gospel versions. According to Philip's author, when Jesus comes up out of the water, and the Spirit anoints him, and the Voice announces him to be the "beloved" of God—Jesus breaks out laughing.

Can't you just see Jesus now—soaking wet, hair matted down, goosebumps popping up all over, and driplets of water glistening in his beard—all while he is bent over howling. Guffawing. Belly-laughing in the Spirit.

John the Baptist, ever the earnest one, must have thought his cousin had lost his mind. Spiritual people should be serious, by God. Reverent. Do things decently and in order before the Lord—not hugging themselves in side-splitting laughter. Whatever happened to proper piety?

Maybe we need more of this kind of spirituality, the kind that is less self-serious and more self-forgetting and light-hearted. A spirituality that is free and that drips joy and laughter.

The trend in the Church today is to "affirm our baptism," and indeed we should. We need to "return to the river" of adoption by grace alone, to hear over and over the words of *Abba,* "You are my beloved in whom I am well pleased," and then to let this hilarious, fabulously good news take over our entire being. To an ever-serious world, it might be the most effective form of evangelism ever devised.

—H. King Oehmig

Thus Peter went to the home of Cornelius and began by declaring his newfound understanding that "God shows no partiality, but in every nation anyone who fears him and does what is right is acceptable to him" (vv. 34-35). God has sovereignty over all humanity; thus all persons, Jew and Gentile alike, are to be judged with justice and mercy based upon their deeds.

He continued by saying that this message of God's peace was sent to the world through Jesus Christ, who is "Lord of all" (v. 36).

This message began with the Baptism of Jesus, who was anointed with the Holy Spirit and with power. He went about doing good and healing all who were oppressed by the devil.

Jesus was crucified, but God raised him, and he appeared to his chosen disciples. They were commanded by him to testify to the world that *Jesus is the one* who was foretold by the prophets and ordained by God "as judge of the living and the dead" (v. 42), and who will grant forgiveness of sins.

POINTS TO PONDER

1. Imagine that you are a witness to the Baptism of Jesus by John. How would you describe what happened? What do you think John and Jesus might have thought and felt during this momentous encounter?

2. Why do you think Jesus intentionally sought out John in order to be baptized by him at this time? Why do you think John was initially reluctant to baptize Jesus, but finally consented?

3. What is the impact of the appearance of the Dove and the heavenly voice in Matthew 3:16-17? How is the Spirit, as represented here by the Dove, present at every baptism?

4. Refer to today's Old Testament Lesson found in Isaiah 42:1-9. What do these words tell us about the mission of the Messiah? How do you think Jesus might have been influenced and shaped by these words?

5. In the service of Holy Baptism the baptized person is marked with the sign of the cross—"marked as Christ's own for ever." What does it mean to you that you are "Christ's own"?

"COME AND SEE"

Isaiah 49:1-7; Psalm 40:1-12; 1 Corinthians 1:1-9; John 1:29-42

Our readings for today center around the Epiphany theme of *bearing witness to Jesus as the Son of God in the world.*

The Servant Song in Isaiah 49:1-3 tells of the servant's Divine call, and begins with the servant addressing the nations of the world. The servant is aware of being empowered and named by God even before birth. His words are like a sharp sword: "You are my servant, Israel, in whom I will be glorified" (v. 3).

Yet the servant feels that his work has proved fruitless. Those to whom he has been sent by God have totally ignored God's message. Thus he laments and asks why he has been singled out for a task that has achieved so little. However, if there is to be no response in this life, he will at least look for reward from God.

In answer to his complaint, the Lord responds that the servant's mission is no longer just to Israel but to the world: "I will give you as a light to the nations, that my salvation may reach to the end of the earth" (v. 6). Other nations will now see kings and princes prostrate themselves because *Israel is the Lord's chosen one.*

Whereas Psalm 39 ended in despair, Psalm 40, which seems deliberately placed next, begins with hope: *I waited patiently for the Lord and God heard my cry....*

The writer here uses strong, pictorial language in order to make his deliverance seem even more dramatic. God has *set his feet upon a rock* and *put a new song in his mouth* (vv. 2b-3). This is the story of a life of faith, of what it means truly to be a believer.

The Christian community understood Second Isaiah's early inspiration to be fulfilled in the life and the ministry of Jesus Christ.

Also chosen from before birth—indeed, from all eternity—Jesus was more than the light as proclaimed by Isaiah. He was also sacrifice: the *Lamb of God,* as recognized by John the Baptist.

The first chapter of the Gospel of John begins with the Prologue (vv. 1-18), followed by a series of events taking place on four consecutive days (vv. 19, 29, 35, 43). On the first day (vv. 19-28), John the Baptist responds to questions from priests and Levites from Jerusalem. Here we see that the tension with the religious establishment exists from the very beginning.

The Baptist makes it very clear that he is not the Messiah, Elijah, or the prophet (v. 25). He affirms what has already been revealed in the Prologue: John is not the light, but is the one who comes to testify to the light (1:7).

The Fourth Gospel does not have an account of the Baptism of Jesus, but John the Baptist describes the event on the second day (the "next day," in v. 29). When he sees Jesus coming toward him, he hails him as the "Lamb of God who takes away the sin of the world!"

The title "Lamb of God" is used exclusively in John's Gospel, and contains many themes and symbols within it. A connection can be made with the Passover lamb that is slaughtered for the sins of many (Is. 53:7-12). But here the symbol takes on new meaning. Jesus is God's Lamb who brings reconciliation between humanity and God.

PRAYER FOR THE DAY

Almighty God, your Son our Savior Jesus Christ is the Light of the world; so help your people, enlightened by your Word and Sacraments, to shine forth and make Christ known to the ends of the earth. *Amen.*

John further identifies Jesus as the one "who ranks ahead of me because he was before me" (v. 30). John recounts how he saw the Spirit of God as a Dove descend from heaven and remain with Jesus (v. 33). Thus John can testify with certainty that Jesus is the Son of God (v. 34).

On the third day, John is standing with two of his disciples and again watching Jesus pass by. He declares, "Look, here is the Lamb of God" (v. 36); whereupon the two disciples follow Jesus. To "follow" (vv. 37, 38) is more than just going to the same place with another person; the word is used here in the sense of commitment to discipleship.

The focus now shifts from John to Jesus himself. Jesus turns to the two men and asks, "What are you looking for?" (1:38). This is a question that goes to the heart of the impulse to turn to God. The men address Jesus as Rabbi, or Teacher, and ask where he is staying.

Jesus then issues the invitation to "Come and see" (v. 39), and the two men stay with Jesus until late in the afternoon.

The seemingly simple invitation is rich in meaning, and we can only imagine what might have transpired. In the Gospel of John, "coming" to Jesus is a way of describing faith. Seeing, which implies deeper insight, is another level of faith.

A man named Andrew is one of the two who left John to follow Jesus. After meeting Jesus, Andrew goes to his brother Simon and declares: "We have found the Messiah" (v. 41). The actions of Andrew in *immediately bearing witness* illustrate the theme in John's Gospel of *telling others about the truth of Jesus.*

John the Baptist saw Jesus as the Son of God. As the one who first proclaimed him, John illustrates how to make the light of Christ visible in the world.

ON REFLECTION

The season of Epiphany is a two-part season. First, it is about God's self-disclosure in Jesus Christ: the act of *revealing,* along with the content of what is revealed. The Magi story, the Wedding at Cana, the Baptism of Jesus make up the heart of this dynamic.

The second part is what we, as recipients of this revelation, do with it—becoming evangelists of what we have experienced. As someone has said, this mainly amounts to one beggar telling other beggars where to find food.

Andrew, in today's Gospel reading, embodies what it means to be an effective evangelist, and he does so in three ways. He *finds* people. He is not passive, but active about it. He introduces Peter to Jesus (Jn. 1:41); he introduces the lad with five loaves and two fish to Jesus (Jn. 6:8-9); and he brings inquiring Greeks to Jesus (Jn. 12:20-22). He also *tells* his story—what a friend he has found in Jesus. That's about it. Andrew evangelizes not through propositions or convincing theological arguments, but by sharing his own experience, strength, and hope.

The third thing Andrew does is *bring* people to Jesus. He is so stoked by his experience of Jesus, he wants to make sure others show up and find the same "living water" he has tasted. He knows that coming to Jesus is a relational thing. It isn't simply a "coming to" Christ, but a "coming with," too. At some deep level, Andrew knows, when it comes to following Jesus, community begets community. It's a contagious kind of thing.

—H. King Oehmig

Paul's letter to the Corinthians further explains what this service as disciples is to be. The salutations with which Paul begins his letters are important clues not only to the author, but to his view of his audience. When the Apostle wrote to his converts in Corinth, most of them were of Gentile ancestry, and he addressed them as people who belonged to God in union with Jesus the Messiah (1 Cor. 1:1-2).

He was thus affirming not only the legitimacy of his authority over them, but their own identity as a congregation of God's people, sharing belief in Christ and a common life. He proceeds to give thanks for the grace of God they enjoy, and for the fact that the testimony of Jesus has been strengthened among them (vv. 4-6).

When Christ is acknowledged among us, we lack no spiritual gift. As we await further growth, we will receive greater strength to do what is right, through further revelation of Jesus himself (v. 7).

All who call upon the name of the Lord Jesus receive the Divine grace, which makes them rich in expression "in speech and knowledge of every kind" (v. 5). This Christ will also strengthen us to the end, so that we will be "blameless on the day of our Lord Jesus Christ" (v. 8).

POINTS TO PONDER

1. In John 1:34, John the Baptist identifies Jesus as the Son of God. How did he know this to be true?

2. How does John the Baptist define his own mission in relation to Jesus? What do we learn here about the ministry of Jesus as well?

3. In 1:38, Jesus asks the two men who followed him, "What are you looking for?" Why do you think they followed Jesus in the first place—what were they seeking? What are you looking for in your spiritual life?

4. Jesus invites Andrew and the other disciple to "Come and see" (v. 39). What do you imagine might have happened during the time that these two men spent with Jesus?

5. Andrew announces to his brother Simon that he has found the Messiah. What has enabled you to know that Jesus is God's Messiah? What are some of the ways we are called to tell others about Jesus?

FISHERS OF PEOPLE

Isaiah 9:1-4; Psalm 27:1, 5-13; 1 Corinthians 1:10-18; Matthew 4:12-23

Isaiah's prophecy of the coming of the light is a recurring theme in the Epiphany season. The passage today reflects the hope and joy of Israel following liberation from oppression, perhaps from the Assyrians. The entire passage, verses 1-7, describes the ideal Davidic king, and might have been used in a coronation ceremony (cf 2 Cor. 4:6).

The preceding verses paint a grim picture of suffering and despair, as the people cursed their king and God. They saw only "distress and darkness, the gloom of anguish ..." (8:22).

But this darkness was not the final word: the people will be redeemed as darkness is turned into light with the coming of a new peaceful age. Zebulun and Naphtali were among the least of the tribes of Israel, but they too will receive the good news. "The people who walked in darkness have seen a great light ..." (9:2).

The people will exult and their joy will be multiplied, for God has broken the burden of their oppression, as when Gideon was victorious over the Midianites (Jdg. 6-8). Thus the weapons of war will be destroyed, and a child will be born who will rule with justice and righteousness in God's name (Is. 9:5-7).

The Psalm echoes Isaiah's theme of the light and confidence in the salvation of the Lord. "The Lord is my light and my salvation; whom shall I fear?" (27:1). The Psalmist thus sings praises to God, who answers his cries and provides protection from his enemies.

Today's Gospel passage falls into three parts: the beginning of the ministry of Jesus (Mt. 4:12-17); the call of the first disciples (vv. 18-22); and a summary passage on the mission of Jesus (v. 23).

Following his Baptism (Mt. 3:13-17) and a time of testing in the wilderness (4:1-11), Jesus is filled with God's Spirit and ready to begin his public ministry. However, the threat of danger (Mt. 2:13-22) continues to be a factor.

After the wilderness experience, Jesus leaves his home in Nazareth and moves to Capernaum on the northwest shore of the Sea of Galilee, having learned of John the Baptist's arrest by Herod (14:3). In Matthew, Mark, and Luke, all of Jesus' ministry takes place in Galilee until he travels to Jerusalem for his final days. For Matthew, the move of Jesus to the territory of Zebulun and Naphtali fulfills the prophecy of Isaiah 9:1-2.

Jesus' message here: "Repent, for the kingdom of heaven has come near" (v. 17), is the same as that of John (Mt. 3:2). The Kingdom of heaven refers to that time when the truth of God's redeeming power will be fully manifested in the world.

Instead of waiting for followers to come to him, Jesus calls those whom he wants to be his disciples. They will become the nucleus of a new witnessing community.

The first of these followers that we meet are brothers Simon Peter and Andrew, who are fishermen. Jesus comes upon them along the shore of the Sea of Galilee where

PRAYER FOR THE DAY

We pray for grace, O Lord, to respond to the call of our Savior Jesus Christ. May we proclaim the Good News of his salvation to the whole world, that all may know the glory of his redeeming work. *Amen.*

they are casting their nets into the water. Matthew makes no mention of any earlier contact between Jesus and the two men before Jesus says to them, "Follow me, and I will make you fish for people" (v. 19).

The expression to "fish for people" is unusual and may recall Jeremiah 16:16, in which the prophet declares, "I am now sending for many fishermen, says the Lord, and they shall catch them."

The response of the two men is immediate: "They left their nets and followed him" (v. 20). They leave what they are doing so that they may make haste to bring others to God; their new vocation is *discipleship.*

Nearby are other fishermen: James and John with their father Zebedee, mending their nets. When Jesus summons them, they also leave what they are doing at once, just as Simon and Andrew had done. However, the call here does not include Zebedee, who remains in the boat.

The implication is that God calls all to salvation, but often to different vocations. Zebedee and his crew are to go on securing food for others, which is a vital and honorable occupation. But James and John possess other capacities that Jesus will train and refine for God's service.

Thus Jesus continues to travel throughout Galilee "proclaiming the good news of the kingdom" (v. 23) through his teaching, preaching and healing.

Although Jesus was the light who came into the world, there was still strife in the early Christian communities. In the letter to the Corinthians, the Apostle Paul warns his converts of God's judgment on their waywardness and divisiveness. Their loyalty is to the individuals who baptized them. He calls them to forgo their divisions and "be united in the same mind and the same purpose" (1 Cor. 1:10).

Neither Paul nor Apollos nor Cephas had died for anyone's salvation. Baptism simply made those who received it members of Christ no matter who had administered it. No convert came to be a member of Paul or of any other Christian teacher. Paul asks them,

ON REFLECTION

Saint Paul cut to the chase in describing the nature of the followers of Jesus: "Consider your own call, brothers and sisters: not many of you were wise by human standards, not many were powerful, not many were of noble birth. But God chose what is foolish in the world to shame the wise, God chose what is weak in the world to shame the strong; God chose what is low and despised in the world ... so that no one might boast in the presence of God" (1 Cor. 1:26-29).

They had no exceptional college transcripts. No phenomenal I. Qs. No pedigrees. No power in terms of the currency of the world—political influence or exceptional wealth.

In fact, put up before any present committee on ministry, most of them would never have been recommended to seminary, let alone been ordained. What do fisherfolk know about preaching, or what do tax collectors know about doing baptisms or hospital calls?

The First Evangelist makes an interesting point in the call of the first disciples. Jesus never told them to "believe in me," or "worship me," or even "love me." He did tell them to "follow" him. And so, regardless of worldly aptitude or innate talent, those who have climbed to their feet ever since, when Jesus said, "Follow me," have been used in ways beyond what they could ever have asked for or imagined—even being crucified upside down like Peter, or devoured by wild dogs on an X-shaped cross, as happened to Andrew.

—H. King Oehmig

"Has Christ been divided?" (v. 13).

Thus Paul gives thanks that he had baptized only two members of the community at Corinth, for "Christ did not send me to baptize but to proclaim the gospel, and not with eloquent wisdom, so that the cross of Christ might not be emptied of its power" (v. 17). Paul is not diminishing the importance of baptism here, but is affirming the Gospel imperative to spread God's word of salvation in Christ.

To those who have not experienced the saving work of the Cross, Paul's message may appear foolish, as the Cross was seen as a sign of humiliation and weakness. However, there is now a new power in the world—the life-giving message of God's saving entry into our lives through Christ Jesus.

POINTS TO PONDER

1. The first teaching of Jesus as recorded in the Gospel of Matthew is found in 4: 17: "Repent, for the kingdom of heaven has come near." Of what are we called to repent? How would you define the Kingdom of heaven? What is the meaning of this proclamation for us today?

2. In verse 20, and again in verse 22, Matthew tells us that the fishermen "immediately" left to follow Jesus. What do you think their thoughts and feelings might have been as they made this momentous decision?

3. Although James and John were called to follow Jesus, their father, Zebedee, continued as a fisherman. How is *what you are already doing* in your daily life a service to God?

4. Jesus is identified with the *light* in verses 15-16. How would you describe the light that Jesus brings into the world? How have you been touched by this light?

5. In verse 23, we read that Jesus proclaimed the "good news of the kingdom." As disciples of Jesus today, what is our role in proclaiming the good news?

THE GLORY OF ISRAEL

Malachi 3:1-4; Psalm 84; Hebrews 2:14-18; Luke 2:22-40

"When the time came for their purification [forty days after the birth] according to the law of Moses, they brought Jesus up to Jerusalem to present him to the Lord" (cf Ex. 13:2).

Luke carefully pointed out that the Holy Family was strict in observing the *Torah*. Luke 2:21 recorded that Jesus was circumcised on the eighth day. The following verse speaks of a ritual purification.

Israel's *Torah* gave greater emphasis to the Presentation to the Lord of a child than to the purification of the mother. The *Torah* also required that a sacrifice be offered for the child so presented, ideally a lamb; but the offering was proportioned to the resources of the parents.

The offering for Jesus was the two doves proper for a peasant family. But for the Child who was to be God's Messiah it was only right that his Presentation should be embraced by examples of Israel's personal piety.

One example was Simeon, whose devotion had opened him to the presence and guidance of God's Holy Spirit. He had also received the promise, "You will indeed see the consolation of Israel." Simeon had total trust in that promise. Therefore he was able to recognize the consolation as present in the Child who was being presented.

Simeon enjoyed universal respect. Mary and Joseph counted it a privilege for him to embrace the Child.

We may paraphrase the Song of Simeon:
I bless and I thank you, O Lord.
I need ask no more of life now that I have seen your salvation.
The salvation you have prepared is not for us alone, but for all peoples.
In being a light to the Gentiles, your salvation is the glory of your people Israel.

To Simeon God's Spirit manifested the future when the Holy Child would bring down the powers that were now misleading God's people. The Spirit would raise up others to perform God's will. Simeon foresaw the controversy and opposition, and the cost in grief to Mary herself—yet he saw it all as blessing.

There was more to take place at the Presentation. There was the voice of prophecy resident in Anna. Through these many years as a devout widow she had lived in the temple. She also would praise the Lord for all that was to be accomplished through this Child. Those who would look for redemption needed to look no further.

When all that tradition required was done, the Holy Family could return to Galilee. Luke's Gospel does not note the interval in Egypt recorded by Matthew (2:13f). This account concludes by telling how God's wisdom and favor remained with the Holy Child as he grew.

PRAYER FOR THE DAY

O God, on this day when your only-begotten Son was presented in the temple, may we bring to you pure and clean hearts, through Jesus Christ our Lord. *Amen.*

So *the Lord came to his temple.* Malachi 3:1 predicts that the Lord will indeed come suddenly. The prophet was predicting a coming in judgment that the members of a sinful nation would be unable to endure.

In so coming, the Lord would be experienced as a fire to melt away the apostate sinfulness that rendered God's people unable to present acceptable offerings in their worship. The prophet also uses the figure of a solvent to purify sinful lives (v. 3). Formerly offerings had represented the commitment of those who presented them. The aim of all the Hebrew prophets was that it might be so again.

Psalm 84, which serves also for the Second Sunday After Christmas, celebrates the coming of pilgrims to meet with the Lord in the temple. As the abode of the Lord of hosts, the temple has a loveliness all its own. It is a place of security where even sparrow and swallow may nest (v. 3).

Those who are privileged to make their home in its precincts may offer ceaseless praise. The joy of those who make the pilgrimage is scarcely less. Even the desolate country through which they travel will provide refreshment.

Under the Lord's protection pilgrims will find such days as they can spend in the Divine presence worth more than a thousand days of absence from this place of blessing.

The Christian Apostles and their interpreters could look at the fulfillment of the hopes expressed by prophets and psalmists. The letter to the Hebrews describes the Person and the work of Christ.

In the words we read today, Christ's sharing of our humanity, our flesh and blood, enabled him to be our representative, our champion in setting us free from death.

It is the likeness that Christ shares with us that makes him merciful and compassionate.

ON REFLECTION

He had been duly circumcised and named and therefore had formally been taken into the Covenant community. And so now Jesus is ready to be presented to the Lord. The practice was taken from Exodus 13:1-2, where the firstborn male is to be dedicated to the Lord. Just as the "first fruits" of the harvest were set aside to the Lord as the tithe, so also were the "first fruits" of an Israelite family set aside for God, the Provider, the Giver of life.

It was common practice for a price of five shekels to be offered to God to "redeem" the child from this servitude. However, Luke never mentions that any offering was made in the case of Jesus. At no time would he ever be "undedicated" to the Father, Luke wants us to know. With every breath, Jesus would be in the service of the Holy One—up to the last breath he would take on Golgotha.

This "presentation" ceremony might seem odd to us moderns, but think about it: all parents sacrifice their children to their gods. Money. Success. Addictions. Love interests. That is why in the sacrament of Holy Baptism, we do the most important "dedicating" that can be done in human life. It is none other than the presenting, the giving over—the dedicating—of a child to the One who is our final dependability, the One who has come to give us life and the abundant life. And only in the dedicated service of this Jesus is there perfect freedom.

—H. King Oehmig

In his faithful actions as our High Priest he presents himself as a sacrifice of Atonement to God our Father for the sins of his people (2: 17). It is his suffering that brings assurance that he *understands* and *can help us* in whatever we must suffer.

And so on this Holy Day we remember not only the actual events, the blessings, and the promises. We experience also our own identification with the Son of God, and give thanks for all that he means to us: *Jesus,* the hope of the world.

POINTS TO PONDER

1. What do we learn about Jesus, his family, and the practices of first-century Judaism from today's Gospel on the Presentation?

2. Describe Simeon and his actions in Luke 2:25-32, as the infant Jesus is brought to the temple. What is the vision of the Messiah that Simeon proclaims here?

3. Read the words that Simeon addresses to Mary in verses 34-35. What impact do you think these words might have had on Mary at the time? What meaning do they have for us today?

4. Anna and Simeon are among the faithful who watch and pray. How do you think they must have felt on this occasion? What contribution do their testimonies make to our faith communities, and what can we learn from them?

5. Imagine that you are Mary or Joseph. What thoughts and feelings do you think they might have shared with each other after they left the temple?

THE WAY OF BLESSEDNESS

Micah 6:1-8; Psalm 15; 1 Corinthians 1:18-31; Matthew 5:1-12

The nature of *discipleship* is a major theme of the Epiphany season.

The Prophet Micah, along with Amos, Hosea, and Isaiah, was one of the 8th-century B. C. prophets. He came from a small village in Judah, and was chiefly concerned with social justice and ethical issues.

Our Micah text for today is in the form of a "covenant lawsuit" brought by God against the people for their infidelity and ingratitude. The mountains, hills, and foundations of the earth serve as jury and cosmic witnesses to the covenant between God and Israel.

In Micah 6:4-5, God presents the case against Israel by recalling God's saving acts in liberating Israel from slavery in Egypt through Moses, Aaron, and Miriam. The Lord protected the people in their wilderness wandering by sending Balaam, when King Balak of Moab plotted against them (Num. 22–24). They were insured a safe crossing of the Jordan into Canaan when the waters parted for them (Josh. 3-5). *Why then, the Lord asks, has Israel abandoned their God?*

In verses 6-7, the defendant, Israel, responds by asking what offerings are acceptable to the Lord. God answers in verse 8 by declaring that *the Lord does not require any of these things,* but will show them a better way than material sacrifice. The Lord has told them, "O mortal, what is good; and what does the Lord require of you but to do justice, and to love kindness, and to walk humbly with your God?"

The heart of the prophetic ethical tradition is summarized in these words. This is also the spirit of the Beatitudes of Jesus—a radical devotion to doing God's will that is often the exact opposite of what the world requires or expects.

The Beatitudes comprise the opening verses of the Sermon on the Mount (Mt. 5:1—7:27). As the first and longest of five discourses in Matthew, the sermon is a collection of sayings that define *what it means to be a disciple of Jesus.*

The word "blessed" itself is used in the sense of being *in favor with God.* The Gospel of Luke also includes Beatitudes (6:20-26) with four blessings and contrasting woes.

At this point in the Gospel, Matthew has named his first four disciples and has been traveling throughout Galilee teaching, preaching, and healing. Like other pivotal events in Matthew's Gospel, this first major sermon takes place on a mountain.

First Jesus calls for blessings on the "poor in spirit" (v. 3). This phrase refers not so much to economic deprivation, as in Luke's Beatitudes (6:20), but to a deeper acknowledgment of spiritual dependency before God.

The next blessing is for those who mourn (v. 4). This does not necessarily mean consolation for the loss of a loved one, but in the broader sense, *grief* over the wrongs and sufferings of the world (cf Is. 61:2-3).

The third blessing is for the meek, who "will inherit the earth" (v. 5). This reflects the sentiment of Psalm 37:11: "The meek shall inherit the land, and delight themselves in abundant prosperity."

PRAYER FOR THE DAY

Almighty God, all things both in heaven and on earth are in your hands. We your people ask today for your peace and blessing, through Jesus Christ our Lord, who lives and reigns with you and the Holy Spirit. *Amen.*

The word *meek* here means essentially the same as the poor in spirit of verse 3, and inheritance of the earth can refer to their acceptance into God's Kingdom.

While Luke claims a blessing on those who are hungry now (6:21), Matthew speaks of those who hunger and thirst *for righteousness* (v. 6). This refers to a desire to see God's will and justice on earth, along with vindication for those who suffer.

The fifth blessing is for the merciful, who will receive mercy (v. 7). God's *mercy* is freely extended to all, used here in the sense of *forgiveness*. Those who are recipients of this mercy and forgiveness are called to do likewise. Only those who practice mercy will have the understanding to receive it themselves.

Next comes the "pure in heart" (v. 8), which recalls Psalm 24:3-4 and refers to those who have risen above temptation and seek God's will in all aspects of life. Thus they will see God not only in the age to come, but now.

A seventh blessing is pronounced for the peacemakers (v. 9) who seek to bring about reconciliation, especially in the sense of loving one's neighbor. Those who work to heal the brokenness around them will be called "children of God," since peace is the nature of God's work in the world (Jn. 16:33).

The final words pronounce God's favor upon those who suffer persecution for their loyalty to God (vv. 10-12). They can be compared to the former prophets who were persecuted as well. Thus they can "rejoice and be glad" (v. 12a), for there is eternal reward for them in heaven.

Just as the Beatitudes illustrate a reversal of the expectations of the world, Paul proclaims another reversal as he calls the Corinthians to set aside their understanding of human wisdom, for "God's foolishness is wiser than human wisdom, and God's weakness is stronger than human strength" (1 Cor. 1:25).

ON REFLECTION

A spiritual "law" seems to be that you cannot—or should not—ask people to change unless you offer them something better than what they are presently experiencing.

So when Jesus begins the most evangelistic teaching ever given—the Sermon on the Mount—he begins by offering the *blessings* of the Kingdom of heaven. *Fortunate* are the "poor in spirit," those who "mourn," those who are "meek," as well as those "who are persecuted for his sake." The promise of reward is offered. *"Blessings abound where'er he reigns,"* as the old hymn says. And these blessings surpass all worldly possibilities and promises as we the followers move from allegiance to the "lords" of this world and surrender to the one true Lord, Jesus.

Psychiatrist James T. Fisher, in his work *A Few Buttons Missing: The Casebook of a Psychiatrist* (J. B. Lippincott, 1951), offered medical wisdom about these promises of Jesus when he wrote: "If you were to take the sum of the total of authoritative articles ever written by the most qualified of psychologists and psychiatrists on the subject of mental hygiene—if you were to combine them and refine them and cleave out the excess verbiage—if you were to … have these unadulterated bits of pure knowledge concisely expressed by the most capable of living poets, you would have an awkward and incomplete summation of the Sermon on the Mount."

—H. King Oehmig

As Paul attacks the spiritual pride of the Corinthians, he declares that God has made foolish the wisdom of the world through the paradox of the Cross, which has been seen as "a stumbling block to Jews and foolishness to Gentiles" (v. 23).

God did not choose those of high birth, intellect, or influence among them. Instead, God called the foolish, the weak, the low, and the despised "so that no one might boast in the presence of God" (v. 29). Therefore: "Let the one who boasts, boast in the Lord" (v. 31).

Thus we return to the question posed by Micah concerning *what the Lord requires*. As disciples, we are called to put aside human assumptions and trust in Jesus Christ as the source of our life.

Furthermore, the Psalmist reminds us that those who would dwell with the Lord will "walk blamelessly, and do what is right, and speak the truth from their heart" (15:2).

POINTS TO PONDER

1. The Beatitudes describe a way of life that Jesus expected from his followers. List the qualities of blessedness as found in the Gospel passage, and draw from them a profile of what it means to be a disciple.

2. How can those who are poor in spirit, those who mourn, the meek, and the persecuted be considered *blessed*? How would you define the word "blessed" as used here? How have you been blessed in your own life?

3. How does the understanding of blessedness as described by Jesus compare with that of our contemporary world? In verses 10-12 Jesus speaks to those who suffer persecution. When have you or others you know faced adversity in some way because of commitment to Christian principles?

4. Also refer to the other Lessons for today, and discuss the way of life that these passages, as well as the Beatitudes, call us to follow as disciples of Jesus. In particular, what is the challenge of Micah 6:8? Contrast the wisdom of God with the wisdom of the world, as presented by Paul in his letter to the Corinthians.

5. What are the challenges presented by these readings—to you personally and to the Church as a whole?

SALT AND LIGHT

Isaiah 58:1-9a (9b-12); Psalm 112:1-9 (10); 1 Corinthians 2:1-12 (13-16); Matthew 5:13-20

"Such fasting as you do today will not make your voice heard on high" (Is. 58:4b).

In this chapter the prophet addresses a grave spiritual crisis in the people's actions before the Lord. The text highlights the lack in the people's ethical response to maintaining or keeping justice. Today we may think of "justice" as largely a legal term. But the Old Testament prophets were more concerned with the everyday needs and practical working out of life in community. It is such basic rights that seem to be at risk here.

There is also the hopeful note of a coming action of God "soon." It appears that discouragement had settled deeply in the people's hearts. In contrast to the high expectations and sweeping promises of the second section of the Book of Isaiah (chs. 40-55), where the prophet had heralded a day of new things and of God's glorious future—here we perceive fear and downheartedness. The earlier promises were in the context of the return from exile and the beginning of a new life for Israel.

But it had not all come to fruition. After 70 or so years, the Israelites had been allowed to return home. But they expected more: for God to come and to establish dominion on the earth. That this has not happened as they anticipated adds to their discouragement.

Yet God will give the people strength for whatever is ahead. "Then you shall call, and the Lord will answer; you shall cry for help, and he will say, Here I am" (v. 9a).

Psalm 112 declares that *happy are those who follow the commandments of the Lord.* They are "gracious, merciful, and righteous" (v. 4), and will be blessed with prosperity and numerous descendants.

The blessed will be remembered for their righteousness, their sense of honor, and their steadfastness in adversity. They will be exalted—in contrast to the wicked who "gnash their teeth" in frustration and anger. "The desire of the wicked comes to nothing" (v. 10).

Unless your righteousness is greater than that of the scribes and Pharisees you are not going to enter the Kingdom of heaven at all.

It's hard to imagine the shock value of that statement. The scribes were the people who defined what was right and wrong. The Pharisees were the people whose lives came closest to fulfilling what the scribes defined. How could anyone do better than they? And what could it mean to tell ordinary folk that they were *the salt that preserves the world* or the *light by which people see?*

Offhand, the people who were listening might suppose that what was being put forward was a whole new ethical system. But Jesus put all such revisions out of consideration when he declared that he had come not to destroy the Law or the Prophets, but to fulfill them. No single phrase or letter should be canceled; and the person who performed the Commandments and taught others to do likewise would be counted great in the Kingdom.

PRAYER FOR THE DAY

We pray that you may set us free, O God, from the burden of our sins, and grant to us the freedom of abundant life, through your Son, Jesus Christ our Savior. *Amen.*

So how can anyone attain to a greater righteousness than the scribes and Pharisees? By making the Commandments internal. External observance can be hypocritical; but internal character determines who we are.

We can preserve the world or be its light when good works come to be what we do naturally without having to think first. The sort of righteousness Jesus was talking about wasn't totally a new idea. Something like it had been evident in some of the Psalms, such as: "The Lord is my light and my salvation. One thing I asked of the Lord ... to behold the beauty of the Lord" (Ps. 27: 1, 4).

It is fitting that these words in today's Gospel constitute an introduction to the remainder of the "Sermon on the Mount" in which things of old will be held up against the new way of Jesus, and thereby opened to fresh, expanded understanding.

Just as only the human spirit can discern the inmost intentions of an individual, so the intention of God can be revealed to us only by the action of God's Spirit. "We speak God's wisdom, secret and hidden, which God decreed before the ages for our glory" (1 Cor. 2:7).

The Apostle Paul, who had lived out the righteousness of a Pharisee, and had found no ease of conscience in doing so, knew firsthand the need for a different sort of righteousness. And he knew how he had found it. It was God's gift and he had been able to receive it only by putting total trust in what God had done for him.

So he could feel no confidence in human attainments. In his telling of the good news of salvation, whether in Corinth or anyplace else, Paul would not rely on persuasive argument or intellectual demonstration of God's power.

ON REFLECTION

The reality of discipleship is that every act we do is an act of ministry. Wherever we are, whatever we do, we are Jesus-bearers—an expression of the Body of Christ, for better or worse. It is a glorious truth to fathom, and a mighty responsibility to acknowledge. As Norman Cousins said about the human body: "If we could contemplate our own composite wonder, we would lose ourselves in celebration and have time for nothing else."

But the "salt and light" teaching of Jesus wasn't flattery—it was a warning to his disciples that they could go bland and tasteless, dim and dark—like flat salt or a lamp that has run out of oil. Staying connected with the Source of "salt and light" is the key to effective discipleship. You cannot have the Kingdom of God without God.

Agnes Sanford, a true spiritual master, wrote in her book *The Healing Light:* "If we try turning on an electric iron and it does not work, we look to the wiring of the iron, the cord, or the house. We do not stand in dismay before the iron and cry, 'Oh electricity please come into my iron and make it work.' We realize that while the whole world is full of that mysterious power called electricity, only the amount that flows through the wiring will make the iron work." Sanford said that the same principle is true concerning the power of God. The whole universe is full of it, but only the amount of it that flows into us will work for us—and through us.

—H. King Oehmig

What God does and why God does it is beyond human comprehension. Paul describes it as a *mystery* that has been concealed from human thought and knowledge. He supports this claim with a citation of Isaiah 64:3 (64:4 in some English versions): "From ages past no one has heard, no ear has perceived, no eye has seen any God besides you, who works for those who wait for him."

The Spirit searches everything—even the depths of God. Here is the promise in Paul's rendering: "What no eye has seen, nor ear heard, nor the human heart conceived, what God has prepared for those who love him— these things God has revealed to us through the Spirit" (vv. 9-10).

Even the way we speak of these things is not of human understanding, but is spiritually discerned (v. 14). Although no one can know the mind of God, we do have the mind of Christ to instruct us (v. 16).

POINTS TO PONDER

1. In Matthew 5:13, Jesus tells his disciples that they are to be like salt. Think about the particular qualities of salt. How are the followers of Jesus similar to salt? What do you think Jesus means when he speaks of salt losing its taste? What happens when we lose our saltiness, and how can it be restored?

2. In verses 14-16, Jesus says that his disciples are to be a light to the world. What special responsibilities are inherent in carrying the light?

3. Beginning with verse 17, how does Jesus define his relation to the Law and the Prophets? Why is this point important for us to remember today? In particular, discuss the difference between external and internal observance of the Commandments.

4. According to this passage, what is necessary for citizenship in the Kingdom of heaven? What warnings for us today are contained here in the words of Jesus?

5. How are the promises of the Old Testament passage in Isaiah also a call to us to practice justice and trust in God for our future? Consider also the words in today's Epistle. What insights have you gained about faithful discipleship from today's passages?

KINGDOM RIGHTEOUSNESS

Deuteronomy 30:15-20; Psalm 119:1-8; 1 Corinthians 3:1-9; Matthew 5:21-37

In Deuteronomy 30, Moses speaks to the people of Israel as they are poised to cross the Jordan River and take possession of the promised land. God has been with them in the wilderness after their escape from Egyptian slavery. But now there are choices to be made.

If they decide to obey the commands of the Lord, loving the Lord their God obediently (v. 20a), they will be blessed with prosperity, long life, and many descendants. But if they are led astray and bow down to other gods, they shall perish.

They are being given the long-awaited land in which to enact God's purposes for them by *loving God, obeying God, and "holding fast" to God's will.*

Psalm 119, sometimes called "The Great Psalm," is a lengthy and stylized meditation on God's Torah, or "teaching."

The entire Psalm 119 consists of twenty-two eight-line strophes, or stanzas, in which every line of a given stanza begins with the same letter of the Hebrew alphabet. This would have enabled the worshiper to learn it more readily by heart.

In the first stanza, which begins with the letter *aleph,* we read that God's commandments have been established, and "Happy are those who keep his decrees ... " (v. 2). Further, these statutes should be the subject of unceasing study so that people may grasp their full meaning and follow them.

"I will praise you with an upright heart ... I will observe your statutes; do not utterly forsake me" (vv. 7-8).

The church at Corinth was situated near the center of the Roman province of Achaia. Corinth was one of the most important cities of Greece. Paul himself had first brought the message of Christ to these people and helped establish them.

In his first letter to the Corinthians, he writes to his "brothers and sisters," but calls them, not true grown-ups, but "infants in Christ" (v. 1). Thus he must feed them with spiritual "milk," rather than the stronger food he would love to give them.

Much of what Paul stresses here is an answer to pastoral problems in that congregation; and no problem is taken more seriously than that of divisiveness. As long as the people were following "human inclinations" (v. 3), they fell into jealousy and quarreling.

Paul would not accept the suggestion that he was father of the Christian faith. Nobody got baptized in the name of Paul (1:13). The other leader mentioned, Apollos (vv. 4b, 5), the philosopher of Alexandria, had come to Corinth later. He was ready to appeal to the arts and arguments of human wisdom. But it was unacceptable to Paul to allow the Christian faith to become elitist.

PRAYER FOR THE DAY

O Lord our God, accept our sincere prayers; and because we are helpless without you, enable us by your grace to keep your commandments, and to please you in will and deed. *Amen.*

Whether it was presented by Paul or Apollos, the Gospel centered in Jesus. Paul's answer to the cults of personality was to affirm that all share a common faith.

Paul's work may have been to plant, and that of Apollos to water, but it is always God who makes the faith grow (v. 6).

In today's Gospel, Jesus begins by defining the "righteousness" that "exceeds that of the scribes and Pharisees" (v. 20). From early times, interpreters of Matthew 5:21-48 have identified in Jesus' teaching here a series of six statements of "opposition" to the Law of Moses and the rabbinic tradition. But Matthew's Jesus plainly intends another interpretation of Jesus' message and his motives for bringing up these points of the Law.

No commandment of the Law is here "abolished" (v. 17) or broken (v. 19) in these sayings. One who practices the teachings of Jesus will violate no commandment of the Law. In every case, Jesus instructs his disciples to serve not only the "letter" of the Law (v. 18), but also its spirit and intention.

Wherever Matthew's Jesus quotes Scripture: "It was said to those of ancient times"—he refers to several Old Testament passages. "You shall not murder" is found in Exodus 20:13 and Deuteronomy 5:17, and points to the teaching of God through Moses. Jesus' words, "But I say to you..." serve to establish Jesus alongside Moses. Therefore, Jesus cannot be seen to contradict what God spoke through Moses. Rather, he seeks to amplify it.

It is the "urge to kill" that troubles Jesus. "If you are angry with a brother or sister, you will be liable to judgment" (v. 22a). Jesus truly knows the weaknesses of all humans. It is their nature that he seeks to change.

ON REFLECTION

The followers of Jesus will get angry—didn't Jesus himself? Or do we think Jesus hurled the moneychangers out of the temple with a smile on his face? To get angry as Jesus did is not the problem. To *hold on to* anger is. The New Testament scholar, C. H. Dodd, properly translates the passage on murder-anger as meaning: anyone who *nurses* anger against his brother or sister. This comes closest to the true meaning of Jesus' teaching.

As human beings, we will get angry. As Christians, we are to be aware of it, feel it, express it in a responsible way—and then let it go. Don't nurse it. Give it to God before it turns from hot anger to cold anger. Nursed, it seeps down into the very marrow of the soul—with murderous consequences.

Perhaps the truest sign of conversion is the presence of an "enlarged heart" in the believer. A spirit of love takes hold—one that "bears all things, believes all things, hopes all things, endures all things" (1 Cor. 13:7).

At the execution of Stephen, Saul witnessed a mystery that made perhaps as much of an impact on him as did the Damascus Road vision. He saw a man being stoned to death who actually forgave his executioners—*forgave them and him.* What he saw in the eyes of the first martyr, Stephen, would disclose the supernatural power of Jesus-love, and then lead Paul to say that this love was the only thing that would have survival value in this world (1 Cor. 13:8).

—H. King Oehmig

Jesus' view is not simply idealistic, but practical and appropriate. "So when you are offering your gift at the altar, if you remember that your brother or sister has something against you, leave your gift there before the altar and go; first be reconciled to your brother or sister, and then come and offer your gift" (vv. 23-24).

Jesus' standards for sexual relationships are introduced by the appropriate words from the Decalogue, and their scope is extended to include the inner attitude as well as the external act. It must be recognized that, in Israel at this time, adultery was a less inclusive term. Adultery could occur only if the *woman* involved had a living husband.

This standard derives from the oppressive belief that a wife was her husband's "property." This falls appallingly short of the Christian view of marriage. Jesus supported marriage, and sexual desire within marriage; he blessed a wedding by his presence (Jn. 2:1-12).

But he was against lust without love. The warnings added to this teaching must be seen as exaggeration (vv. 29-30).

Since lust is primarily a matter of the mind or heart, the destruction of eye or hand, or of any other body part, will not cure it. But nothing, no matter how valuable to a person, can be cherished when it leads to sin.

Oaths refer to something that was a fact of life in the Hebrew Bible. The particular problem here is with a person who intended deceit. Whoever supports the truth of a statement with impressive sounding phrases but leaves a loophole to claim later that God was not involved, does not adhere to the righteousness of the Kingdom.

The simple statement of promise, "yes" or "no," must be as dependable as the most solemn oaths of others (v. 37).

POINTS TO PONDER

1. What does it mean to us today to follow God's call to "Choose life"?

2. What does the Psalmist pray for as he attempts faithfully to observe the Law? What are the joys and rewards of keeping the Lord's statutes?

3. What insights does Paul provide in his letter to the Corinthians about the growth of faith in the Christian community?

4. In the Gospel passage, how do the teachings of Jesus bring the old Law to completion? How does Jesus continue to challenge us to go beyond the letter of the Law?

5. In light of all these Lessons, what does our relationship with our neighbor have to do with our worship of God?

GOSPEL LOVE

Leviticus 19:1-2, 9-18; Psalm 119:33-40; 1 Corinthians 3:10-11, 16-23; Matthew 5:38-48

The holiness of any place dedicated to God, whether a movable tent of meeting, or a permanent structure of stone and timber—or a community of worshipers—is derived from *the holiness of God who is to inhabit it.* So in Leviticus 19:2 the people of God are called upon to be holy as their God is holy.

Then verses 9-18 tell what it will mean for the people of God to be holy. Holiness is compassion.

At harvest, landowners will not totally strip their fields or their vineyards. They must leave something to be gathered by the poor and the strangers who possess no land. Verse 11 adds that God's people must not steal nor deceive.

And no one may take an oath by God's name to mislead others regarding what is intended. In verse 13 this could end in robbing the neighbor, failing to give the laborer the wage earned for the day.

Holiness also requires honest impartiality in the just administration of law. Justice for Leviticus is a matter of facts. There is neither a preferential option for the poor, nor any deference to the rich and powerful.

Verses 16-18 sum this up, prohibiting slander or even the circulation of damaging information about another—even if that information is true.

God's people must abstain from malice and hatred against one another, and must never take vengeance into their own hands. Holiness is summed up in the word of the Lord that *you must love your neighbor as yourself.*

"Teach me, O Lord, the way of your statutes, and I will observe it to the end." Verses 33-40 of this Psalm honoring the wisdom of God's word and its power in the believer's life are *a prayer to understand the Law.*

With understanding, one will be able to keep God's word and live within the parameters of the commandments with a *wholeness of heart* and an integrity that extends to every area of daily life.

A number of images have been used to designate the people of God. One found in several New Testament writings, and still popular in the following century, is that of a *living temple.* It is a structure composed of the members of the community themselves as "living stones."

The foundation—the only possible foundation of the living temple—is Christ. Christ's Cross has dealt with the totality of human sin, and his Resurrection has opened the way to eternal life.

The Apostle Paul, acting under God's inspiration as a skilled architect, has shown his converts where that foundation is. Now they can build on it.

So in 1 Corinthians 3:16 we read that the members of the community constitute God's temple. The temple is a dwelling-place for God, who operates in the world through the Holy Spirit. So Paul can tell his converts that the Spirit of God dwells in them.

It is an awesome responsibility. God's temple must be kept holy as God is holy. Therefore the disciples must renounce the worldly wisdom that is foolishness with God.

PRAYER FOR THE DAY

O God, we pray, send your Holy Spirit into our hearts in love, that we may experience the true bond of peace that unites us forever in you, through Jesus Christ our Lord. *Amen.*

As verse 21 declares, we can have no reason to boast of our own achievements, for God has already given to us everything we have: the Apostles who have brought us God's revelation, the world in which we live, and life present and to come. We belong to God, united as we are with Christ the Son—who is one with Abba, the Father.

Life in the Christian community, according to Jesus' Sermon on the Mount, calls for a much higher standard of righteousness than an external code of "dos" and "don'ts." Jesus knew that people would never solve the problem of moral behavior by changing outward rules; the heart must change.

Behavior, according to Jesus, begins in the heart; and behavior that is evil begins in impurity of heart (Mt. 15:18-20). Our behavior *should* be based on God's love for us, and on God's own character.

The Law permitted and even encouraged retribution for injury to person or property. Jesus quotes the catchwords "eye for eye" and "tooth for tooth" (Ex. 21:24; Lev. 24:20; Deut. 19:21).

Followers of Jesus are not to seek justice for themselves. They are to abandon even the desire for revenge or restitution. Jesus also says, "Do not resist an evildoer" (v. 39). And certainly the life of Jesus offers the best illustration of the teaching. He was falsely accused, abused, and finally put to death.

Yet he says that physical violence must not be met with violence. It must be suffered. A blow to the "right cheek" would indicate a back-handed, demeaning slap across the face. *Yet those who have been called into God's Kingdom are not to reciprocate evil as a way of conquering it.* They are to give more than is required.

Jewish men wore two garments: a tunic of linen wool worn next to the skin, and a heavier cloak worn over it. The outer garment was specifically protected by the Law. It was not to be required as security for a loan (Ex. 22:25-27).

Matthew's Jesus envisions a lawsuit in which the plaintiff is awarded a person's tunic. The loser is to hand over his cloak as well, essentially giving up his legal rights.

ON REFLECTION

A breathtaking moment occurs in the movie *Gandhi,* one that shows us the nature of Christian love through the lives of a Hindu and a Muslim—a message sorely needed in our world of religious violence. The time is 1947 after Gandhi's famous walk to the sea, the final act that led India to independence from the British. Fighting had broken out between Hindus and Muslims over who would rule the country. Calcutta, Delhi, and Bombay were in a state of emergency.

Gandhi had gone into a near-fatal fast to stop the violence. In Calcutta, some Muslim fighters visited him at his bedside, and laid down their swords to show that they wanted peace. At that point, a wild-eyed Hindu man burst through the gathering and threw a piece of bread at Gandhi and exclaimed, "Here, eat! Eat! I am going to hell, but not with your debt on my soul."

Gandhi quietly answered the man, "Only God knows who goes to hell." The tormented man replied, "I killed a child. I smashed his head against a wall." "Why?" Gandhi asked the man.

"They killed my son, my boy; the Muslims killed my son."

Gandhi looked at the man and said, "I know a way out of hell. Go, and find a child whose mother and father have been killed, and raise him as your own—only be sure he is a Muslim and that you raise him as one."

—H. King Oehmig

Likewise, the followers of Jesus must comply when compelled to perform some service, much as Simon of Cyrene was compelled by Roman soldiers to carry the cross of Jesus (Mt. 27:32).

What should a disciple of Jesus do when faced with a beggar or borrower? The answer is: Give what is asked.

The point Jesus makes is that his followers must consider the other person's need as more important than one's own.

The final saying in the list of personal duties deals with the question of the limits to be set upon one's love of neighbor. The precept is quoted from Leviticus 19:18. Disciples of Jesus are not to limit their love to those who love them, or they would be just like everyone else.

Just as God the Father shows loving partiality in giving sunshine and the rain—so needed in arid Palestine—to the righteous *and* the unrighteous (v. 45), so also should the disciple show unqualified love for brothers, sisters, and enemies.

What is the motive for such a radical response? "Be perfect, therefore, as your heavenly Father is perfect" (v. 48).

POINTS TO PONDER

1. In the Leviticus passage we read that the people of Israel are holy because the Lord their God is holy. What then is required of Israel truly to be God's people?

2. The Psalmist prays for understanding in order to keep God's commandments and live. How is keeping God's precepts connected to the good life?

3. As you read Paul's letter to the Corinthians, what does it mean that we are each a part of God's holy temple?

4. In Matthew 5:48, Jesus calls us to be perfect as God is perfect. Here the word "perfect" is used in the sense of wholeness. What do you need to do in your own spiritual life to move toward this goal?

5. As you reflect on all of today's readings, how are *we* called to live *if we truly are the people of God?*

ON UNDIVIDED COMMITMENT

Isaiah 49:8-16a; Psalm 131; 1 Corinthians 4:1-5; Matthew 6:24-34

Jesus and his disciples were nurtured by the Hebrew Bible. If any portion of the Scriptures was more frequently on the lips of Jesus and his followers than the Psalter, it was the Isaiah scroll. In particular, we find throughout the New Testament references to the chapters of that prophet of the first days of return from the Exile, the Second Isaiah.

As the caravans were being assembled in the land beyond the Euphrates, the few who remembered Jerusalem saw God's Covenant as being renewed. So did their much more numerous grandchildren, who planned not only to make the journey, but to undertake the rebuilding of imagined glories. All of them celebrated how their God had helped them in a day of salvation.

It may have been an overstatement to speak of the exiles as prisoners (Is. 49:9), since they had been able to engage in trade while in captivity. Yet their situation might have seemed little better than a dungeon.

It was no easy journey that the exiles were undertaking. So in verses 9-10 the prophet assured them that God would provide them with food and would lead them to flowing springs. Second Isaiah promised that the sun would not strike them down. Verse 11 presents the hope that God will level out a highway through the mountains.

Return has been made possible, not only for those who have been forcibly deported to return to Judah from the north. Those who fled the advance of their conquerors shall have a highway prepared for them from the west, from Egypt and other places of refuge. So when the Lord has brought comfort to the people, the prophet calls on heaven and earth to break forth in songs of celebration (v. 13).

Then comes a change of tone, a reference to the lament of Zion for the loss of God's protection. This leads to the assertion of verse 15 that God's steadfast love is even less subject to change than the love of a woman for her child. Even though a mother might forget, God will remember. "See, I have inscribed you on the palms of my hands" (v. 16a).

The Psalmist's own prayer of humble submission in Psalm 131 is also a petition for personal guidance through life's difficult passages. The petitioner likens his soul to a quieted child that is being calmed upon its mother's breast. This is a song of trust in the One who knows us intimately, better than we know ourselves.

In writing to the Corinthians, Paul takes the lessons of Old Testament and Gospel and applies them to his own task. He and his colleagues draw from this tradition in presenting the good news that *God in Christ has already freed the world.*

The lessons apply also to the manner of human response to God's act. Founding Apostles, missionaries—even pastors and teachers—are administrators of that Divine work. "Think of us in this way, as servants of Christ and stewards of God's mysteries" (v. 1).

PRAYER FOR THE DAY

Loving Father, we pray that you will deliver us from a lack of faith, so that nothing in this mortal life may overshadow the light of your immortal love, which you have manifested to us in your Son, Jesus Christ our Lord. *Amen.*

' spoke as one who was seeking absolute
~~ ~n dealings, and he was not
~ilure. Yet he would
not pres~ ate of his own
faithfulness. He ~ not even judge
myself. ... It is the Lor~) judges me" (vv.
3-4b).

No need to worry! You will always have everything that you need. Lucky Numbers 12, 13, 14, 19, 20, 39.

As verse 5 has it, we cannot know the value
of our own stewardship until the Lord comes
in final judgment. Therefore none of us has the
right to pass judgment on anyone else.

The Lord will "bring to light the things
now hidden in darkness and will disclose the
purposes of the heart" (v. 5). Then each will
receive the correct commendation from God.

The thought of the *power and love of God*
reached a new expression in the teaching of
Jesus. Today's Gospel declares that "no one can
serve two masters; for a slave will either hate
the one and love the other, or be devoted to the
one and despise the other" (Mt. 6:24a).

"You cannot serve God and wealth" (v.
24b). It is not that possessing wealth and
serving God are in themselves incompatible
occupations. But rather, it is impossible to
serve one's possessions ("mammon," from
an Aramaic word that means "property" or
"riches" and is sometimes used without any
negative connotation) and simultaneously be
about serving the One God.

Jesus teaches that to *love the Lord above
all things* is crucial. When our priorities are
straightened out, there should then be no room
for anxiety concerning food or drink, clothing
or shelter (though shelter was not a great worry
in Palestine).

In this familiar verse, Jesus reminds
believers, "Do not worry about your life, what
you will eat or what you will drink, or about
your body, what you will wear. Is not life more
than food, and the body more than clothing?"
(v. 25).

ON REFLECTION

Unless the eye catch fire, The God
Will not be seen.
Unless the ear catch fire, The God
Will not be heard.
Unless the tongue catch fire, The God
Will not be named.
Unless the heart catch fire, The God
Will not be loved.
Unless the mind catch fire, The God
Will not be known.
   —William Blake (1757—1827)

The fruit of silence is PRAYER.
The fruit of prayer is FAITH.
The fruit of faith is LOVE.
The fruit of love is SERVICE.
The fruit of service is PEACE.
   —*The Simple Path*, Mother Teresa

Yet if one has such anxiety it would certainly demonstrate that there is in that person a divided loyalty of trying to serve God and mammon. However, Jesus is not here being insensitive to persons in real need of the core components of survival. Rather, the teaching reaches out to those who are seeking true meaning in life—what lies as treasure beyond human fulfillment.

Verse 26 shows that nature itself reveals the futility of great worry over bodily needs. Birds live from day to day, for they have no barns. Worry does not enlarge life; it renders life miserable.

Similarly, in the following verses, the beauty of the lilies simply happens because God designed it, and even the most costly human adornment cannot equal it.

The Father, who cares about the transient beauty of the fields, can surely be trusted to provide for the needs of human beings. Therefore, the only way to live is in total dependence on God.

Worry about material needs is heathenish. For believers, saving faith includes the reliance that God's grace shall supply everything we need, whether actual resources or the capacity to do without them.

This belief includes the understanding that the human order is good. It is good since God created it; and we experience it as good day to day in *the blessings of this life*. We are to "strive first for the kingdom of God" and God's righteousness, and "all these things will be given to you as well," Jesus promises (v. 33).

POINTS TO PONDER

1. What are the promises to God's people as expressed in today's passage from Isaiah? How are these promises relevant to us today?

2. The Psalmist speaks of trust in God as our central concern and confidence. How does dependence on God underlie our understanding of discipleship? What is God's part and what is ours?

3. What does the Apostle Paul in his letter to the Corinthians suggest our response should be to God's saving of the world through Jesus Christ?

4. In the Gospel passage, Jesus tells us not to worry about tomorrow. As you read this passage, think about how your life would be different if you truly followed Jesus' advice. List some concrete ways in which you would make changes.

5. The theme of God's care is interwoven throughout all of today's readings. In what different ways is this care expressed in the various passages? How have you experienced this care in your own life?

_____

_____

_____

_____

_____

_____

TRANSFIGURED IN LIGHT

Exodus 24:12-18; Psalm 2 or 99; 2 Peter 1:16-21; Matthew 17:1-9

The Transfiguration of Jesus, one of the most dramatic stories in the Gospels (Mk. 9:2-8; Mt. 17:1-8; Lk. 9:28-36), is always read at the close of the Epiphany season. Here the glory of Jesus as God's Chosen is stunningly manifested in the shining radiance of Jesus on the mountain.

The Old Testament reading for today of Moses on Mt. Sinai is an earlier occasion of Divine theophany. Israel has been liberated from bondage in Egypt. As God leads the people through the wilderness, they receive the Law, which ultimately defines their identity as a nation.

Israel has accepted God's covenant (Ex. 24:7-8), and now Moses is commanded to go up to the mountain with God to receive the stone tablets containing the Law and the commandments (v. 12).

Previously Moses had been accompanied by seventy elders as well as Joshua (24:9), but they are now to remain behind as Moses continues his ascent alone. In his absence, Aaron and Hur are authorized to assume leadership roles among the people.

As Moses was summoned into the Divine presence, "the glory of the Lord settled on Mount Sinai, and the cloud covered it for six days" (v. 16). To the people below, the glory appeared as a "devouring fire" (v. 17), but Moses was embraced in the cloud as God's chosen spokesman.

The Ten Commandments form the basis of God's Law, but they are not the total rule of life for the people of Israel in their relationship with God. Thus Moses remained in God's presence for forty days and nights to receive the wider implications of this revelation.

Like Moses, Jesus also ascends a mountain where his human appearance is transfigured into *the glory that belonged to God the Son* from all eternity. But whereas Moses left his assistant Joshua down below, Peter, James, and John, the first disciples called by Jesus (Mt. 4: 18-22), were witnesses to this glory.

As Jesus and his disciples traveled throughout Galilee, his teaching, preaching, and healing drew ever larger crowds. At Caesarea Philippi, Peter's confession of Jesus as none other than "the Messiah, the Son of the Living God" (16:16) was followed by Jesus' prediction of his Passion (v. 21). Peter was not able to accept this reality, and this brought a strong rebuke from Jesus (vv. 22-23) and further teachings on the true cost of discipleship (vv. 24-28).

Thus six days later, Jesus would take Peter, James, and John to witness a vision that would sustain them through the dark days to come in Jerusalem. Jesus "was transfigured before them, and his face shone like the sun, and his clothes became dazzling white" (Mt. 17:2).

Matthew alone adds the detail of the face of Jesus shining like the sun, which recalls the face of Moses as he came down from Mt. Sinai (Ex. 34:29-35), as well as the vision of the Risen Jesus in Revelation (1:16).

PRAYER FOR THE DAY

Almighty God, who revealed the glory of your only-begotten Son on the holy mountain, give us strength to bear our own cross, as we are being changed into his likeness from glory to glory. *Amen.*

This "transfiguration" is not a metamorphosis in the Hellenistic sense, but is an epiphany or revelation of Jesus in his undimmed, heavenly glory—a glimpse of the future.

Two figures also appeared with Jesus: Moses the lawgiver and Elijah the prophet. Both Moses and Elijah had their own mountain experiences (Ex. 24:13-18; 1 Ki. 19:8-13) and were "taken" by God (Deut. 34:6; 2 Ki. 2:11).

In response to this vision, Peter wanted to build three dwellings—perhaps similar to the booths erected at the Feast of Tabernacles (Lev. 23:39-43) that had taken on eschatological connotations—to memorialize and prolong this experience.

As Peter was speaking, a bright cloud overshadowed the scene, just as Mary was "overshadowed" by the power of the Most High at the Annunciation (Lk. 1:35).

A voice from the cloud then proclaimed the words spoken at Jesus' Baptism: "This is my Son, the Beloved; with him I am well pleased" (cf 3:17).

But here the voice also added, "Listen to him!" (v. 5b). Jesus is more than a lawgiver (Moses) or a prophet (Elijah); he is God's Son. Thus they are to give heed and to obey his words.

At this point, the disciples became overwhelmed by this manifestation of the Divine, and fell to the ground in fear. When they came to themselves, the vision was gone, and Jesus was alone once again. Jesus told them not to be afraid, and as they began to descend the mountain, he ordered them to "Tell no one about the vision until after the Son of Man has been raised from the dead" (v. 9).

Second Peter assumes that the readers are familiar with one of the Gospel accounts of the Transfiguration and refers to this event as evidence of the truth that *Christ will come again in glory.*

The letter was written late in the first century in response to the false teachings of those who said that *since Jesus had not already returned, the Christian hope of the Second Coming was clearly mistaken.*

ON REFLECTION

Giovanni Bellini (c. 1430—1516), who brought Venetian painting into the High Renaissance, in his work *The Transfiguration,* depicts three different poses of the disciples that convey responses we can identify with.

Get away quickly as possible. In the face of *The Mystery,* we feel overcome with fright—or stark fear. As Emily Dickinson wrote, "The truth must dazzle gradually, or every man be blind." We run, too, because we don't want our reality changed too drastically, our world turned too much upside down by a Divine presence we cannot deny.

Kneel in adoration. No doubt this disciple in the painting would be Peter, who implores Jesus to build three booths on the spot, perhaps to preserve the "Kodak moment." This expression tells us that there is another part of *The Mystery* that fascinates and enthralls us. As the hymn says, we become lost in "wonder, love, and praise." But it can be a dangerous pietism, too.

Closeness to the Gospel brings recognition of the Incarnation. The third response centers less on the three disciples than it does on the other figures in the painting, who go about their work in the fields, or chat with friends on the roadside—unaware of what is happening. That the extraordinary happens in and among the ordinary could well be the point here—or another one. That is, the individuals who come closest to Jesus, who truly follow him, are the ones who experience the deepest mysteries God has to share: the greater the intimacy, the greater the blessings.

—H. King Oehmig

Thus Christian ideals of morality and right living were also unnecessary.

Peter emphasizes that the teachings of the power and coming of Christ are true and not merely "cleverly devised myths" (1:16). The promises of Christ are supported by the experience of the Apostles who were eye-witnesses to this glory at the Transfiguration. They heard God the Father speak and declare that "This is my Son, my Beloved, with whom I am well pleased" (v. 17), recalling the heavenly voice at the baptism of Jesus (Mt. 3:17).

As one of the Apostles present on the holy mountain, Peter saw for himself the majesty of Jesus, and proclaimed the vision to be a confirmation of the power of the Risen Christ that would be fulfilled at the Second Coming.

Therefore, believers should pay attention to the prophetic word just as they would to a "lamp shining in a dark place, until the day dawns and the morning star rises in your hearts"—at the Second Coming (v. 19b).

The morning star in their hearts indicates the indwelling of the Holy Spirit, which brings transformation. Thus believers will be guided by the word of prophecy until the Lord returns again. But they must rely upon Divine guidance over individual understanding: "...because no prophecy ever came by human will, but men and women moved by the Holy Spirit spoke from God" (v. 21).

Psalm 2 is a royal Psalm that affirms God's authority in the heavens and bestows universal rule on Israel's king. Verse 7 introduces the theme of Divine adoption: "You are my son; today I have begotten you." And so the hope of a future ideal monarchy is suggested, and "Happy are all who take refuge" in the Lord (v. 11b).

POINTS TO PONDER

1. Imagine that you are one of the disciples who accompanied Jesus up the high mountain. How would you describe what happened? What did you see, hear, and feel? What is the significance of the appearance of Moses and Elijah with Jesus?

2. Why did Jesus take three of his disciples with him when he went up the mountain? Why do you think he warned them not to tell anyone about what they had witnessed until later (Mt. 17:9)?

3. Why do you think Peter was inspired to suggest that they build three dwellings on the site (v. 4)?

4. When the heavenly voice was heard from the cloud, the disciples were afraid and fell to the ground (v. 6). When have you felt that you were in the presence of the Divine? What was your reaction at the time?

5. Compare the experiences of Moses (in Exodus) and Jesus on the mountain in his Transfiguration. How were Moses, Jesus, and the others around them affected by these two events?

_____

_____

_____

_____

_____

TEMPTATION IN THE WILDERNESS

Genesis 2:15-17; 3:1-7; Psalm 32; Romans 5:12-19; Matthew 4:1-11

It is written that when God created the earth and the heavens, the "Lord God formed man *[adam]* from the dust *[adamah]* of the ground, and breathed into his nostrils the breath of life; and the man became a living being" (Gen. 2:7). Here we read that humankind is not only *made in the image of God* (Gen. 1:27), but that the first human is brought to life by the very breath of God. From the beginning, God is intimately involved with and invested in humanity.

God then places the man in a garden in Eden "to till it and keep it" (v. 15). In this garden there are two trees: the tree of life and the tree of the knowledge of good and evil.

A tree of life is mentioned in Proverbs (3:18; 11:30; 13:12; and 15:4), where it generally refers to the fruit of joy. The tree of the knowledge of good and evil is not mentioned anywhere else in Scripture.

The polar opposites of good and evil are used to represent the totality of higher knowledge. The man is told that he is not to eat the fruit of this tree, or he will die (v. 17). Humanity was to obey the Lord and not aspire to know more than God.

In the verses not appointed for today (2:18-24) creation is completed when God makes a woman and brings her to the man. Just as there is fellowship within the Being of God, so humanity is given opportunity for an exchange of love on a human level. The man and woman "were both naked, and were not ashamed" (2:25).

The mood of the narrative shifts in chapter 3 with the introduction of the serpent, whose shrewdness is in marked contrast to the innocence, *i.e.,* nakedness, of the man and woman. The woman is enticed to eat of the fruit of the forbidden tree by the guiles of the serpent, who promises that her eyes will be opened to know good and evil as God does (v. 5). In turn, she gives the fruit to the man. "Then the eyes of both were opened, and they knew that they were naked" (3:7).

Through disobedience, the harmony that once reigned in creation was replaced by alienation between God and humanity and between the man and woman. There would now be toil, suffering, pain, exploitation, and death. Yet even as they are cast out of the garden, God's grace is evident, as "the Lord God made garments of skins for the man and for his wife, and clothed them" (3:21).

The Apostle Paul, in his letter to the Romans, contrasts human sin with God's gift of salvation through Christ Jesus. One man transgressed, and so sin and death became realities in the world (5:12a). As a result, "death exercised dominion from Adam to Moses, even over those whose sins were not like the transgression of Adam" (v. 14). Paul did not say that the entire race inherited guilt in the person of Adam; rather, death came to all humanity because everyone sinned.

Then, mercifully, by one sinless man's obedience, grace displaced death, and those whose sin was taken away were made righteous (v. 18). As much as sin had abounded before the coming of Christ, now grace simply overwhelmed it, bringing eternal life to all. Thus the pain of condemnation was replaced by the status of righteousness.

PRAYER FOR THE DAY

O God, just as Jesus was led by the Spirit to be tempted of Satan in the wilderness, come to us in our own temptations, and deliver us for your purposes, to live and serve you, through Jesus Christ our Lord. *Amen.*

To this truth, Paul added that the Law, which had given definition to transgression, was also swept away so that grace might "exercise dominion through justification leading to eternal life through Jesus Christ our Lord" (v. 21b).

Psalm 32 proclaims the joy of one who has been forgiven (v. 1). Just as King David had experienced the burden of sin, confessed his guilt, and been forgiven, anyone who turns to God in faith in the midst of trouble will be surrounded with shouts of deliverance (v. 7b).

The Gospel reading for the First Sunday in Lent is always an account of Jesus being tempted in the wilderness. After Jesus' Baptism in the Jordan by John, the Spirit led him into the wilderness to be tested by the devil. This testing serves to illustrate the true meaning of the baptismal proclamation that *Jesus is the Son of God* (3:17). This episode is reminiscent of the trials of the wilderness wanderings of Israel, as well as recalling the fasts of Moses (Deut. 9:18) and Elijah (1 Ki. 19:8), and therefore sets the experience of Jesus in the context of Israel's history. It is the Spirit who leads Jesus into the wilderness, with the devil assuming the role of the tempter (cf Job 1-2; Zech. 3:1-2; 1 Chron. 21:1) rather than the personification of evil.

Jesus, after fasting for forty days and forty nights, was famished. Fasting was understood to be a means of opening oneself to receive God's guidance; but in his hunger Jesus was now vulnerable to the first temptation: "If you are the Son of God, command these stones to become loaves of bread" (Mt. 4:3).

Jesus replies here with a reference from Deuteronomy 8:3 that "One does not live by bread alone, but by every word that comes from the mouth of God" (v. 4). This temptation also recalls God's faithfulness, when the Lord provided Israel with manna in the desert (Ex. 16:1-4).

ON REFLECTION

Like the rest of us, Jesus heard two competing voices. The first had been the Voice of his Father-God at his Baptism: "You are my Beloved in whom I am well pleased." But the Jordan River water had barely dried before Jesus heard another voice. This voice started every interaction: "If you are the Son of God ..." In other words, *Prove yourself, Jesus*. Verify your vocation according to a justification by something other than God.

It is a temptation we face daily.

When it comes to the Devil, C. S. Lewis said Christians make two mistakes. The first is to fixate on "purposeful evil." We see the Devil under every rock. Satan is behind every ache and pain—or behind anyone who disagrees with us, especially in matters of theology.

Sound theology reminds us that Satan is not the opposite of God. *God has no opposites.* Lucifer is an *angel,* albeit a fallen one. And the only time evil is mentioned in the New Testament is in the context of being a defeated enemy.

The other mistake is to underestimate the power of evil—attributing it to primitive, unenlightened superstition—and be easily blindsided by it.

For as bone-chilling an account of the reality of satanic power around, read Malachi Martin's *Hostage to the Devil*—the work that inspired William Blatty's *The Exorcist.* In the end, the way to defeat evil is to give it to God, as Jesus did in the wilderness—and then, ultimately, and for all time, on Calvary's Cross.

—H. King Oehmig

In a reversal of the order of the second and third temptations as presented by Luke, here the devil takes Jesus to a high point of the temple in Jerusalem. He declares that if Jesus is truly the Son of God, he can jump down and not be harmed—God's angels will protect him.

In verse 6b the devil demonstrates his own knowledge of Scripture with words from Psalm 91:11-12. Jesus in turn replies by referring to the warning in Deuteronomy 6:16 not to put the Lord to the test (Ex. 17:1-7).

As the final temptation, the devil takes Jesus to a high mountain and shows him "all the kingdoms of the world and their splendor" (v. 8). Jesus is told that if he will fall down in worship, he will have dominion over all that is before him. Jesus again refuses, saying, "Away with you, Satan!" (v. 10). Jesus continues by paraphrasing Deuteronomy 6:13, "Worship the Lord your God, and serve only him" (v. 10).

Jesus decisively rejected the lure of the powers of the world in favor of uncompromising obedience to God the Father. Thus "the devil left him, and suddenly angels came and waited on him" (v. 11). Through this testing, the true nature of Jesus as the beloved Son of God becomes manifested.

POINTS TO PONDER

1. As you read the Gospel passage, try to imagine what it might have been like for Jesus to be alone in the wilderness for forty days and nights. Why was this period of time necessary for him?

2. How would you characterize the temptations of Jesus? What are some of the tactics used by the devil to tempt Jesus? What do Jesus' responses tell us about right relationship with God?

3. Read the Old Testament Lesson for today in Genesis 2:15-17; 3:1-7. What were the temptations faced by the first man and woman? How do these temptations compare with those of Jesus? What are some of the temptations in our own lives that distort our understanding of and response to God's call to us?

4. Refer to today's Epistle in Romans 5:12-19. How have the consequences of Adam's sin been altered because of Jesus Christ? What is the "free gift" of which Paul speaks in verse 15, and how do we receive this gift?

5. How would you define "sin" in light of today's passages?

THE RISK OF FAITH

Genesis 12:1-4a; Psalm 121; Romans 4:1-5, 13-17; John 3:1-17

In the Old Testament passage, the history of the nation of Israel begins with the call of Abram, who is told by God to leave everything he knows and go "to the land that I will show you" (Gen. 12:1).

This command is issued along with three promises. First, God declares that "I will make of you a great nation" (v. 2a). Abram is also told that he will be blessed and become a blessing to the world (v. 2b). Finally, those that would bless or curse Abram or his descendants will also be blessed or cursed by the Lord (v. 3).

The trust Abram placed in God's call was demonstrated by his obedience. In faith, Abram goes forth, not knowing where God will lead him, but trusting that the promises he has received will not fail.

Here we see that, through Abram and his descendants, God promises to create a new future out of the creation that has gone astray. The hope of a transformed world depends upon an aging man and his barren wife!

These promises will be tested again and again, but Abram embraces the call and puts his trust in God alone. This puts him in right relationship with God, and the Lord accounts it to him as righteousness (15:6).

This understanding of the relationship of faith to righteousness was especially important to the Apostle Paul, as he explained to the Christians in Rome what it meant truly to follow Christ.

Abraham did in fact obey the commands of God; but the Lord's acceptance of him as righteous was not based on his performance, but on faith. Paul then refers to Psalm 32:1-2, which states that *the people whose sin the Lord forgives are truly blessed* (4:7-8).

This holds true for all who believe, and does not depend upon circumcision—Abraham obeyed God's call when he was 75 and was not circumcised until he was 99 (Gen. 17:24) as a seal of God's righteousness. Thus Paul could argue that all who share the same trust in God without being circumcised can also claim Abraham for their father.

It was through righteousness, not the law that the promise of inheritance came to Abraham. Paul goes on to proclaim that God's grace is not limited, but is extended to all who "share the faith of Abraham" (v. 16b) and put unfailing trust in God (v. 17).

In today's Gospel we read of the Pharisee Nicodemus who came to Jesus early in the ministry of Jesus, following the call of the first disciples, the miracle of the wedding at Cana, and the cleansing of the temple. Nicodemus is a "leader of the Jews" (Jn. 3:1), and his behavior is above reproach. He is also a cautious man who knows the value of the position he holds. Thus he comes to Jesus "by night."

Nicodemus addresses Jesus as "Rabbi," honoring him with the title reserved for those learned in Torah (v. 2b). Nicodemus recognizes from Jesus' signs and good works that he is commissioned from God (v. 2c).

PRAYER FOR THE DAY

O Lord, we confess that we have not obeyed your commandments or walked in your ways, and we need your forgiveness. Bring us again with penitent hearts and renewed faith to cling closely to the unchangeable truth of your Word, Jesus Christ your Son. *Amen.*

Jesus then tells Nicodemus what is most necessary for salvation: "No one can see the kingdom of God without being born from above" (v. 3). This signifies a transformation from the inside out, a reorientation of the self toward God.

As a spokesman for orthodoxy, Nicodemus provides an answer firmly rooted in this world. When one has reached maturity, the thought of a genuinely fresh start is as difficult to imagine as reentering the womb. But this rebirth refers to a *spiritual* experience, not a physical birth.

Jesus continues by saying that "no one can enter the kingdom of God without being born of water and Spirit" (v. 5). That is to say, everyone who would enter the Kingdom of God must be sealed with water on profession of belief and repentance as represented in John's baptism. Birth from above by the Spirit is the gift of faith that enables one to believe, along with the empowerment of grace to persevere.

Birth from flesh, the acceptance of personal identity on a purely earthly level, cannot bring anyone into this experience.

Jesus here compares the Spirit to the mystery of the wind: one can observe the effects of the wind but no one can control it. Both in Greek *(pneuma)* and Hebrew *(ruach),* the word that means spirit may also stand for *wind.* Like the wind, God's Spirit cannot be predicted or fit into human categories.

Nicodemus still remains confused, and cannot move beyond his literal understanding and into the world of the Spirit. He asks, "How can these things be?" (v. 9). Jesus chides him by asking how can one who is a "teacher of Israel" (v. 10) not comprehend what Jesus is telling him. If Nicodemus is not able to believe the evidence of the "earthly things" Jesus has told him, how can he even begin to imagine "heavenly things" (v. 12)?

ON REFLECTION

He stood for respectable religion at its best. His behavior must have been above reproach. His reputation must have been built around an array of theological degrees that were the envy of many. He was a man who knew the importance of the position he held, and did not want to jeopardize it. Perhaps that is why Nicodemus comes to Jesus by night—the only person in the Gospels said to have done so.

Call it the "Gospel by flashlight." When his wife and kids are fast asleep, and the dogs are put up for the night, Nicodemus tiptoes down the hallway and out the door—hopping on a bicycle and heading into the dark. Whatever the consequences of being seen with a renegade rabbi—and one from a hick town, out of which nothing good can come (Jn. 1:46)—Nicodemus is not deterred. He takes the "leap of faith."

Oscar Wilde once remarked that there were two tragedies in life. One was not to get what one wanted. The other was to get it. Maybe that is why Nicodemus came to Jesus. He had gotten all he wanted in life—and found himself asking, "Is this it?"

Later, Nicodemus would come "out of the closet" and contribute, along with Joseph of Arimathea, a hundred pounds of myrrh and aloes to anoint the dead body of Jesus (19:38-41). Which leads one to believe that whatever happened that night between him and Jesus, it must have been enough for Nicodemus to find out what it meant to be "born again."

—H. King Oehmig

To properly grasp such heavenly realities, one must go up to heaven itself, but only the One who has come down from heaven can claim this privilege (v. 13). Just as Moses lifted up the bronze serpent in the wilderness in order to heal the people who could see it (Num. 21: 9), so must Jesus be lifted up on the healing cross for all the world to behold.

Thus God's boundless love for the world, for all of human existence, is expressed in the familiar words of verse 16. Through the selfless giving of the Son, the way to eternal life is opened for those who believe in his Name.

Indeed, we have the promise that the Son came *to save* and not to condemn the world. What we do know is that *Jesus as the Word* brings light and life to the world (1:4).

Psalm 121 is an expression of confidence in God's care: "From where will my help come?" (v. 1b). The answer is that *we can be assured that help comes from the Lord* who is the Creator of heaven and earth. The Lord does not slumber and is our keeper both day and night, protecting us from evil "from this time on and forevermore" (v. 8).

POINTS TO PONDER

1. What are some of the issues Nicodemus might have struggled with as he made his decision to see Jesus? We read that Nicodemus came to Jesus by night (Jn. 3: 2). What is the symbolic significance of darkness in this passage?

2. Why does Nicodemus have difficulty understanding what Jesus is trying to tell him? What prevents Nicodemus, as well as us today, from fully comprehending the words of Jesus?

3. What do you think Jesus means when he speaks of being "born from above" (v. 3b) and being "born of the Spirit" (v. 6b)? How would you compare the Spirit to the wind?

4. Refer to the Old Testament and Epistle readings for today. Discuss what these passages suggest to us about *faith* and *our relationship with God.*

5. John 3:16 is one of the most familiar passages in Scripture. In light of your discussion of today's readings, what do these words mean for you?

THE WATER OF LIFE

Exodus 17:1-7; Psalm 95; Romans 5:1-11; John 4:5-42

As the activities of Jesus and his disciples come under increasing scrutiny, they travel north from Judea to Galilee through Samaria, and stop near Sychar. When they arrive at noon at a place known as Jacob's well, the disciples go on into the city to buy food. Jesus is weary from traveling and remains at the well.

As he is resting there, a Samaritan woman comes to the well to draw water, and Jesus asks her to give him a drink. The woman is surprised that a Jewish man would converse with her (Jn. 4:9). The antipathy between the Jews and Samaritans had begun centuries earlier when the Samaritans had refused to participate in the restoration of Jerusalem after the return from Exile.

According to Jewish law, such contact between Jews and Samaritans was prohibited, and Jesus could risk being considered ritually unclean. Jesus also breaches another social barrier in addressing a woman in public.

Jesus indicates that he can give the woman refreshment far better than the water he asks of her (v. 10). The woman points out that he cannot give her a drink of any kind since he has no vessel to lower into the deep well. Besides, she asks, "Where do you get that living water?" (v. 11b).

Jesus replies that all who drink of the water from the well will be thirsty again, but this water "will become in them a spring of water gushing up to eternal life" (v. 14b).

The woman receives the words of Jesus on a literal level and responds that she would be glad to be relieved of her daily trips to the well to carry water if she could find a substitute for its life-giving power.

Then Jesus tells the woman to call her husband (v. 16), and reveals what he knows about her past relationships when she replies that she has no husband (v. 18). Jesus does not condemn her, but the fact that he knows so much about her catches her attention.

The tone of the conversation shifts. She begins to believe that she can trust Jesus and exclaims, "Sir, I see that you are a prophet" (v. 19).

She then asks him a question. The Samaritans believed that Mt. Gerizim and not Jerusalem was the proper place for worship. Jesus replies that true worship is characterized by total giving of one's life to God, worshiping God in spirit and truth (v. 24).

To this the woman responds by affirming that when God's Messiah comes, he will reveal all truth. Jesus answers her with an affirmation of his identity: "I am he, the one who is speaking to you" (v. 26).

In verses 27-38, the disciples return with supplies and are astonished to see Jesus speaking with the woman, but they say nothing. In the meantime, the woman departs, leaving her water jar by the well. She rushes back to town to invite her neighbors to "come and see" (v. 29a).

PRAYER FOR THE DAY

Heavenly Father, we do not have the power within ourselves to protect ourselves, inwardly or outwardly. Defend us, we pray, from all dangers in this mortal life to both body and soul, through Jesus Christ our Lord. *Amen.*

Jesus tells the disciples that he has food of which they are yet unaware. His mission—his sustenance—derives from completing the work of the Father (v. 34).

God's harvest is now ready to be reaped, as manifested by the approach of the Samaritans. The disciples are to bring in the crop that others have labored to grow (v. 38). In this work, the sower (Jesus) and the reaper (disciples) will rejoice together (v. 36).

In the final verses, people from the city come to see Jesus because of the testimony of the woman (v. 39). Jesus and the disciples stay for two more days teaching in Sychar, and many more come to believe that Jesus is truly the Savior of the world (v. 42).

Water also features prominently in the Old Testament reading, as the Israelites demand that Moses provide them with water in the Sinai.

Slavery in Egypt had provided them with a measure of security, food, and water; but now in their discomfort they quarrel with Moses. Moses responds by asking, "Why do you test the Lord?" (Ex. 17:2).

As they persist in their complaints, Moses turns to the Lord for help in avoiding a revolt that endangers his own life (v. 4). God answers Moses by instructing him to take some of the elders and go on ahead of the people. He is to take his staff which he had used to strike the sea (14:16) and use it to strike a rock at Horeb to bring forth water.

Moses did as the Lord commanded and called the place Massah (to put to the test) and Meribah (to quarrel or contend) because the Israelites had tested the Lord, saying, "Is the Lord among us or not?" (v. 7).

ON REFLECTION

John Sanford, Episcopal priest and author of *The Kingdom Within* (HarperSanFrancisco, 1987), tells a story that has deep resonance with the readings today about the "water of God."

The "old well" Sanford writes about was situated outside the front door of his family's 150-year-old farmhouse in New Hampshire. The house had never been modernized, and did not have the benefit of electricity or plumbing. The well was the family's only source of water, and, as Sanford described it, "had unusually cold and pure water and was a joy to drink." It never ran dry, even during the most severe droughts.

When the family fortunes improved, running water was installed in the house. The old well was sealed over, and stayed boarded over for years. One day, Sanford decided to uncover the well. Expecting to see the dark, cool water of his youth, he was shocked to witness a bone dry well. What happened?

Sanford wrote: "A well of this kind is fed by hundreds of tiny, underground rivulets, along which seep a constant supply of water. As water was drawn from the well, more water moved in along the rivulets keeping the tiny apertures clear and open. But when the well was not used and water no longer was regularly drawn over so many years, it went dry—not because there was no water, but because it had not been used."

Sanford concluded that the soul of a person is like this old well. What happened to the well can also happen to our souls—if the living water of God does not flow into us and through us. It may seem that "God is dead," but it is our own dry, barren souls that have been boarded over, and we no longer draw from "that spring which wells up to eternal life."

—H. King Oehmig

The Apostle Paul also teaches that the Lord supplies all our needs through the saving grace of Christ: "Since we are justified by faith, we have peace with God through our Lord Jesus Christ" (Rom. 5:1). Because of this redeemed state, Paul is able to boast of his suffering, which leads to the hope of sharing in God's glory. We are thus recipients of God's love that is "poured into our hearts through the Holy Spirit" (v. 5).

Paul goes on to say that even while we were sinners, *Christ died for us* as the ultimate proof of God's love. Therefore we are "justified by his blood" (v. 9) and saved from God's wrath. We are reconciled to God in the present, which makes salvation in the future possible.

Assured of this reconciliation before God, we can sing to the Lord in Psalm 95: "Let us make a joyful noise to the rock of our salvation!"

POINTS TO PONDER

1. How would you characterize the Samaritan woman? Why do you think Jesus chose to have this prolonged discussion with her? How do you think she was changed by this encounter?

2. Jesus tells the woman that he will give her "living water" (Jn. 4:13-15). What do you understand this *living water* to be?

3. Jesus and the woman also discuss the meaning of true worship. What do you think it means to worship in "spirit and truth" (vv. 23-24)?

4. When the woman returned to her village, others came to believe that Jesus was the Messiah because of her testimony. How do you come to believe that Jesus is the Son of God?

5. In talking openly with this woman, Jesus overstepped a number of social, cultural, and religious barriers. What are some of the barriers in our own world that we must overcome in order to see Christ in all persons?

THE BLIND SEE

1 Samuel 16:1-13; Psalm 23; Ephesians 5:8-14; John 9:1-41

In our Old Testament passage today, the Prophet Samuel is called to anoint a new king to replace Saul, who had disobeyed the Lord (1 Sam. 15). Although "the Lord was sorry that he had made Saul king over Israel" (15:35b), Samuel still grieves over the Lord's rejection of Saul. Nonetheless, he follows the Lord's command to travel to Bethlehem to anoint a new, obedient king from among the sons of Jesse.

Since Saul is still king, Samuel fears for his life if Saul discovers what he is about to do. Thus the Lord tells Samuel to proceed under the pretext of performing priestly duties. When Samuel arrives in Bethlehem, the people are afraid until he assures them that he comes to offer a sacrifice to the Lord, and invites them to participate.

As the sons of Jesse come before him, Samuel is sure that Eliab is the chosen one; but the Lord tells him that God does not see as mortals see (v. 7b). Seven of Jesse's sons pass before Samuel, but none are the chosen.

When Samuel asks Jesse if all his sons are here, Jesse replies that his youngest son is keeping the sheep. When this son, David, arrives, the Lord commands Samuel to "Rise and anoint him; for this is the one" (v. 12b). Although David had not yet reached maturity, the spirit of the Lord "came mightily upon David from that day forward" (v. 13).

Today's Psalm, the familiar Psalm 23, brings us the comforting image of God as Shepherd of the human flock. But the Psalm goes on from describing green pastures and still waters, to tell of a table well prepared and a cup that is more than full. It also promises goodness and mercy and predicts our ultimate rest in "the house of the Lord" (vv. 5-6).

In the Gospel story, the disciples ask Jesus, "Rabbi, who sinned, this man or his parents, that he was born blind?" (Jn. 9:2). Their question comes from a long-held, but mistaken assumption that misfortune and illness are the result of sin.

Jesus replies that although sin is not the cause of the man's blindness, his condition provides an opportunity to display the life-changing power of God. Moreover, the disciples are now to be included in doing this work (v. 4a).

Jesus demonstrates God's power as he applies mud to the man's eyes (v. 6). In the ancient world, spittle was commonly believed to have medicinal properties (Mk. 7:33; 8:23).

Jesus then tells the man to go and wash in the pool of Siloam. The man does as Jesus instructs him and is able to see. However, the blind man's neighbors discount the healing, saying that this is not the same man (vv. 8-9). Nevertheless, the man declares that he is the same person they had seen begging, and describes how Jesus gave him sight.

After this, the man is taken before the Pharisees to tell his story again (vv. 13-17). The religious authorities take issue with the fact that the healing took place on the Sabbath, as no one who treats the Sabbath in such a casual way can be from God. In the progression of his understanding, the healed man now declares to the Pharisees that *Jesus is a prophet* (v. 17).

PRAYER FOR THE DAY

Our Father, who sent your blessed Son Jesus Christ to be the true Light of the world, grant us always to live in his Light, as he lives in us, with you and the Holy Spirit, one God, now and forever. *Amen.*

The Pharisees are concerned that the testimony of the man and his healing may set a dangerous precedent. Although the man's parents affirm that he was born blind, they do not know how he has been given sight. They are afraid of the Jews and refuse to become involved.

In verses 24-34, the Pharisees again question the man in hopes of discrediting him. They insist that glory should be given to God alone, and not to Jesus. When asked yet again to describe what happened, the man unsettles his questioners by asking if they wish to hear the story again because they too wish to follow Jesus (v. 27b). The Pharisees reply by reviling the man and claiming to be disciples of Moses, whom they know to be God's true spokesman.

The healed man marvels at the obtuseness of the religious leaders and points out that no one could perform such a miracle without being from God (vv. 30-33). The Pharisees decide that the former blind man is a sinner because he defends this healer, and they drive him away.

When Jesus hears this he seeks out the man and asks, "Do you believe in the Son of Man?" (v. 35). When the man asks for further clarification, Jesus replies with words similar to his self-revelation to the Samaritan woman (4: 26). "You have *seen* him, and the one speaking with you is he" (v. 37.) The man responds, "Lord, I believe" (v. 38a), and demonstrates his belief by worshiping him.

Jesus goes on to say that he brings judgment because there are those who choose to believe—to see—and those who do not. He points out that the Pharisees' refusal to admit to their own spiritual blindness was worse than actually *being* blind. "Now that you say, 'We see,' your sin remains" (v. 41b).

The letter to the Ephesians makes the contrast between darkness and light very clear by reminding the followers of Jesus that they no longer live in darkness "but now in the Lord you are light. Live as children of light" (Eph. 5:8).

ON REFLECTION

A marvelous little story is told about the mighty 16th-century mystic, spiritual adept, and social activist, Teresa of Avila. While attempting to ford a pothole filled with water after a thunderstorm, her wagon hit a big bump—and tossed her headlong into the puddle. The jarred saint looked heavenward, raised her arms in exasperation, and shouted, "Do you always treat your friends this way?" Sputtering and dragging herself out of the mud hole, she looked up again to the heavens and answered her own question: "No wonder you have so few of them!"

"@!^#* happens" the bumper stickers declare—and why not, when insurance companies call natural disasters of all kinds, from deadly tornadoes to hurricanes to earthquakes, "acts of God"? If this is the way God treats people of faith—or anyone else—why bother? Who wants to worship a Fiend? But, contrary to all deuteronomic thinking—that suffering is payment for sin—Jesus dispels this horrendous theology. If God thought sickness and suffering was the Divine will, why did Jesus and the Apostles spend almost all their time *healing* people and *undoing* the will of God?

Jesus proclaims anything but a "monster God." While the mystery of iniquity is never explained in Scripture, the answer to it is displayed in the Cross, death, and Resurrection of Jesus himself. The Paschal Mystery says that no suffering—not even the unspeakable death of God's Beloved, when turned over to God in faith—cannot be redeemed and used for the benefit of others.

—H. King Oehmig

Thus they are to discover what is pleasing to the Lord, associating themselves with what is "good and right and true" (v. 9), while rejecting and exposing the "unfruitful works of darkness" (v. 11). Through their faithful lives, such disobedience in the world will be exposed and ultimately redeemed (v. 14a).

POINTS TO PONDER

1. Put yourself in the place of the man born blind and try to imagine how he might have felt as the events of the Gospel story unfolded. How does he describe Jesus in John 9:11, 17, 33, and 38?

2. Jesus tells his disciples that the man's blindness was an opportunity for God's works to be revealed (v. 3). How do you see God working in all aspects of life—in bad as well as good circumstances?

3. As you read this passage, why do you think no one, including the blind man's parents, acknowledged the healing miracles that had taken place? Who are the truly blind people in this story, and why?

4. Refer to the Epistle for today in Ephesians 5:8-14 and reflect on what it means to come out of darkness into the light.

5. In the Old Testament passage in 1 Samuel 16:1-13, we read that "the Lord does not see as mortals see; they look on the outward appearance, but the Lord looks on the heart" (v. 7). As you reflect on today's readings, what new ways of seeing are we called to understand and practice in our lives?

THE RESURRECTION AND THE LIFE

Ezekiel 37:1-14; Psalm 130; Romans 8:6-11; John 11:1-45

On this last Sunday in Lent, the Lectionary foreshadows the Resurrection, as the public ministry of Jesus comes to a dramatic conclusion with the raising of Lazarus.

We also read of Ezekiel's experience of the valley of dry bones. Ezekiel was a sixth-century B. C. prophet and priest during the Exile. The Lord gives Ezekiel a vision of dry bones and asks if they can come to life again. When Ezekiel replies that he does not know, God commands him to prophesy to the bones that *they shall live again and "know that I am the Lord"* (37:6).

When Ezekiel spoke as the Lord commanded, the bones came together with sinews, flesh, and skin, "but there was no breath in them" (v. 8b). Then the prophet was commanded to call on the wind or breath of God (v. 9). As in Genesis (2:7), here also *God breathed life,* "and the breath came into them, and they lived ... a vast multitude" (v. 10).

The bones are a symbol of the nation, dead in sin and scattered by involuntary exile. However, just as God could call together the bones and breathe life into them, so God will bring new life to Israel (v. 12). God's Spirit will be upon them and they shall live again in their own land—and know that the Lord is God (v. 14).

The story of Jesus' power in raising Lazarus opens the way for the Passion narrative (Jn. 18-19). After the healing of the man born blind (9:1-41), Jesus describes himself as the good shepherd who will give his life for his sheep (10:11). In coming to the aid of his friend Lazarus, these words are fulfilled. And Jesus sets in motion the events that will lead to his own death and Resurrection (11:45-57).

Because of the open hostility of the religious authorities toward Jesus, he and his disciples had left Judea for the other side of the Jordan where his ministry began (10:39-40). Here a message from Martha and Mary reaches Jesus, telling him that their brother Lazarus is ill. Although Lazarus and his sisters are beloved friends, Jesus delays going for two days, saying that "This illness does not lead to death" but is for the glory of God and the Son (11:4). When Jesus is finally ready to depart for Bethany, his disciples try to stop him, reminding him of the attempts on his life in Judea (v. 8). Jesus responds with a saying about the necessity of walking in the daylight.

When Jesus goes on to say that he is going to awaken Lazarus, who has fallen asleep, the disciples take his words too literally (v. 12). Jesus then moves from the metaphorical to the literal to make his point: *Lazarus is dead.* Moreover, he is glad that he was not there to heal him of his illness, as this death will provide an opportunity for faith (v. 15).

Thomas takes his stand with Jesus, saying: "Let us also go, that we may die with him" (v. 16). It is better to walk with Jesus and be in danger than to find safety in separation from him.

PRAYER FOR THE DAY

O God, we need the blessed guidance of your will. Help us to love what you command and desire what you give, so that, within this ever-changing world, our hearts may remain fixed on you, through Jesus Christ our Lord. *Amen.*

After two days, Jesus arrives in Bethany where he is met by Martha. She asserts that if Jesus had been there, Lazarus would not have died. But she says, "Even now I know that God will give you whatever you ask …" (v. 22).

When Jesus declares that "Your brother will rise again" (v. 23), Martha takes this as the fact that the righteous will be raised on the last day (v. 24). Jesus then answers that *he himself is the resurrection* and those who believe in him will never die (vv. 25-26).

When Jesus then asks Martha if she believes that in him death is conquered, Martha cannot yet quite own such faith; but she believes Jesus is the Messiah, "the Son of God" (v. 27).

Martha returns home and tells Mary that Jesus is calling for her. Mary kneels at his feet, as she asserts that if Jesus had been here, her brother would not have died. Here we read that Jesus "was greatly disturbed in spirit and deeply moved" (v. 33). He weeps as he approaches Lazarus' tomb.

When Jesus asks that the stone in front of it be rolled away, Martha reminds him that there will be a stench, since Lazarus has been dead four days. Contemporary Jewish belief held that the soul of the dead remained in the vicinity of the body for three days and then departed.

Jesus reassures Martha by reminding her that she will "see the glory of God" (v. 40). As the stone is removed, Jesus prays in thanksgiving. Then he calls: "Lazarus, come out!" (v. 43). Lazarus emerges from the tomb fully alive and restored with no lingering decay of death. Jesus calls his friends to remove the funeral wrappings so that he is free to resume his life.

Thus there were many that day who believed in Jesus (v. 45). This fulfills what Jesus said earlier: "Very truly, I tell you, the hour is coming, and is now here, when the dead will hear the voice of the Son of God, and those who hear will live" (5:25).

ON REFLECTION

Dietrich Bonhoeffer once said that Christianity plunges into many different dimensions of life simultaneously. Nowhere is that truer than in the story of the raising of Lazarus—the crowning of "seven signs" in the Fourth Gospel.

A man named Lazarus has died prematurely. Grief blankets the air around Bethany. Mary and Martha are deeply upset—and let Jesus know that his decision to stay two days longer where he was cost their brother his life: "Lord, if you had been here, my brother would not have died," Martha put it bluntly (11:21).

There is a wonderful saying among African American Christians: "Jesus may not be on time, but he's never late." He isn't too late for Lazarus. After himself weeping, Jesus calls forth the unimaginable. The unfathomable. A four-day dead Lazarus emerges from the tomb. According to John, *this* hair-raising event is what leads to the arrest and execution of Jesus—rather than the hurling of the moneychangers out of the temple (11:47-53).

"Unbind him, and let him go, " Jesus commands the onlookers (11:44), and they do. Presumably the power that raised a dead man to life could also have undone his burial linens; but Jesus calls humanity to be part of the miracle. Calls you and me to be a part of the healing. God will not do for us what we can do for ourselves—Jesus is showing us. And that will beg the question: what "Lazarus" out there is God calling *us* to unravel, and to set free with Gospel power?

—H. King Oehmig

In the letter to the Romans, this promise of the defeat of the power of death is confirmed as Paul contrasts two ways of living: those who live in the flesh conform to the world; while those who live in the Spirit have their minds and hearts set on God. This Spirit is God's gift, which brings eternal life (8:11).

The Psalm for today is the plea of one who knows firsthand separation from God: "Out of the depths I cry to you, O Lord" (v. 1). Yet even in the pit of alienation, it is possible to believe that God will hear and show compassion (v. 2).

My soul waits for the Lord more than those who watch for the morning, more than those who watch for the morning (v. 6).

POINTS TO PONDER

1. As you read today's Gospel passage, imagine that you are present as the events unfold. Focus on the thoughts and feelings of the sisters Mary and Martha throughout the story. Although they have faith in the healing powers of Jesus (Jn. 11:21, 32), what keeps them from fully understanding who Jesus truly is?

2. Jesus knew that he would raise Lazarus, so why was he "greatly disturbed in spirit and deeply moved" as he approached the tomb (v. 33)? What else do we learn about Jesus from this passage?

3. What do you think life might have been like for Lazarus after Jesus called him out of the tomb?

4. This dramatic event of the raising of Lazarus is the climax of Jesus' earthly ministry in the Gospel of John. How does this story prepare us for the events of Holy Week and Easter?

5. Also refer to the Old Testament reading for today in Ezekiel 37 and discuss what this passage meant for the nation of Israel at the time. What message do these words have for us today, especially in light of the Gospel passage?

THE PALMS AND THE PASSION

Isaiah 50:4-9a; Psalm 31:9-16; Philippians 2:5-11; Matthew 26:14—27:66

Liturgy of the Palms (Mt. 21:1-11; Ps. 118:19-29)

Jesus has repeatedly told his followers that he must go to Jerusalem, where he will undergo great suffering at the hands of the religious leaders, be killed, and rise again (cf Mt. 16:21; 26:1-2).

As they approach the city, Jesus sends two disciples into Bethphage for a donkey and her colt. As Jesus enters the city riding the donkey, a large crowd greets him by spreading garments and tree branches on the road.

Their acclamation of "Blessed is the one who comes in the name of the Lord!" (v. 9b) echoes Psalm 118:26. His arrival puts the city in turmoil as the people question who this man might be. What they know is that he is a prophet from Nazareth.

Liturgy of the Passion. This moment of triumph ends quickly as the Liturgy moves to the Passion and the cries of "Hosanna!" become "Crucify him!" The Old Testament and Epistle readings further illuminate the themes of the entry into Jerusalem and set the stage for the Passion itself.

The Third Servant Song of Isaiah evokes the Passion of *Jesus as the Servant obedient to the Lord* (50:5), who endures insults and abuse for the Lord's sake. But the servant knows that God will be with him to vindicate him. "It is the Lord God who helps me; who will declare me guilty?" (v. 9a).

The hymn in the letter to the Philippians declares that "at the name of Jesus every knee should bend ... and every tongue should confess that Jesus Christ is Lord, to the glory of God the Father" (2:10-11). By emptying himself to experience death on a cross, Jesus was fulfilling the Divine intent.

Jesus as God incarnate is one with the Father; but his equality with God did not consist in grasping a prize. Instead, he has made God known to us by taking on our humanity. Thus God will greatly exalt Jesus so that all the world will acknowledge him as Lord.

The Passion narrative begins in chapter 26, as Jesus once again predicts his coming crucifixion (vv. 1-2); the religious leaders plot his death (vv. 3-5); an unidentified woman anoints Jesus' feet (vv. 6-13); and Judas Iscariot makes arrangements with the chief priests to betray him (vv. 14-16).

As Jesus shares the Passover meal with his disciples and institutes the Eucharist as a foreshadowing of the final giving of his body and blood, he announces that one of them at the table will betray him (vv. 17-29).

As they depart for the Mount of Olives after the meal, Jesus further predicts that in fulfillment of Scripture they will all desert him. When Peter vigorously protests, Jesus tells Peter that he will betray him three times before morning comes (vv. 31-35).

PRAYER FOR THE DAY

Everlasting God, in your great love you sent your Son, our Savior Jesus Christ, to take our nature, to suffer death upon the Cross, giving us the example of his great humility. Have mercy on us, we pray, in this life: that we may walk in the way of his suffering, and share in his marvelous Resurrection, for your honor and glory. *Amen.*

As Jesus prays in the garden at Gethsemane, he takes Peter, James, and John with him. These disciples had also been present at the Transfiguration (17:1-8); but they fall asleep as Jesus agonizingly submits himself to the Father's will (vv. 36-46).

Judas then appears, accompanied by an armed crowd, and Jesus is arrested. When one of Jesus' followers draws a sword, Jesus rebukes him and again renounces the way of power and violence, as he did at the temptations in the wilderness (vv. 47-56).

Jesus is taken before the High Priest Caiaphas (vv. 57-67), where false witnesses are brought to testify against him, convicting him of blasphemy. In answer to the question of whether or not he is the Messiah, Jesus replies that "From now on you will see the Son of Man seated at the right hand of Power and coming on the clouds of heaven" (v. 64).

Verses 69-75 recount Peter's denial and his subsequent grief over his cowardliness. In a passage that is unique to Matthew, Judas also manifests remorse over his actions. He returns the money he received for his betrayal to the chief priests and hangs himself (27:3-10).

When Jesus is taken before Pilate (27:11-31), the Roman governor of Judea, Pilate is "greatly amazed" that Jesus does not defend himself. Pilate does not want to become involved in the political maneuverings of the religious authorities, so he concedes to the demands of the crowd to release another prisoner, Jesus Barabbas, and to execute Jesus. As he hands Jesus over to be beaten and mocked, Pilate washes his hands to disassociate himself from the execution (27:24).

As Jesus is led to Golgotha, Simon the Cyrene is compelled to carry the cross. As was customary, a sign was placed on the cross with the charge against the condemned. Ironically, the sign read, "This is Jesus, the King of the Jews" (27:37).

ON REFLECTION

An eminent scholar of African American literature in the United States was asked why Martin Luther King, Jr., had not become a Marxist—and why those in the Civil Rights Movement had accepted his philosophy of nonviolence. The scholar answered right away: "Because of the overpowering force of the figure of Jesus, that is why."

The overpowering force of the figure of Jesus: that is what we are to immerse ourselves in during this holiest of weeks, and on this strangest of days. First, let us join the parade—with palms in hand and hosannas on our lips. Let's join in the whirlwind as enthusiastically as we can—one in which the very stones are crying out with excitement.

The overpowering force of the figure of Jesus: but then we will also plunge to the depths of the Suffering Servant ... feel the weight of the Prince of Peace being arrested by a SWAT team, and being executed in the most heinous, ignominious way imaginable—utterly refuted by his people, and seemingly also by the God he proclaimed.

This Sunday of the Passion is a two-part creation that, in miniature, testifies to the height of human nature, and to the depths of human depravity: from the praise of God incarnate to the torture and death of God incarnate. Throughout the ordeal, we will come more deeply to realize the astonishing nature of God, who loved the world this much: to the point of giving up the Beloved to the horror of the Cross. Here, most of all, do we observe the "overpowering force of the figure of Jesus."

—H. King Oehmig

When the soldiers cast lots for his clothing, the crowd, the religious authorities, and two bandits crucified with Jesus continue to mock Jesus, challenging him to prove that he is the Messiah by coming down from the cross (27: 32-44).

As darkness descends over the land, Jesus cries out words from Psalm 22: "My God, my God, why have you forsaken me?" (27: 46). Some in the crowd think Jesus is calling to Elijah for help when he cries out again and breathes his last (27:50).

Jesus' death is accompanied by apocalyptic disturbances that lead a terrified Gentile centurion and others with him to confess, "Truly this man was God's Son!" (27:54).

Although his disciples had deserted him, there were women who remained throughout the ordeal (27:55-56). That evening, Joseph of Arimathea received permission from Pilate to take the body of Jesus and prepare it for burial in his own tomb. A stone was placed at the entrance, while Mary Magdalene and the other Mary kept watch.

Matthew shows that the life and death of Jesus have taken place in fulfillment of the Scriptures and in accordance with God's plan for the salvation of the world. Throughout his ministry, and especially at his Passion, the life of Jesus has reflected the words from the Psalm for today: "But I trust in you, O Lord; I say, you are my God" (31:14).

POINTS TO PONDER

1. As you read the Gospel Lesson for the Liturgy of the Palms in Matthew 21:1-11, try to imagine the scene as Jesus enters Jerusalem at the beginning of Holy Week. What kinds of persons today receive similar "red carpet" treatment? What do these choices tell us about the values of our culture?

2. As you listen to the Passion story, choose one of the characters in this drama and imagine the event through his or her eyes. What added insights do you have about what happened?

3. Pay particular attention to the words and actions of Jesus himself (26:64; 27:11; 27:46-50). What picture of Jesus emerges for you?

4. In 27:54, why do you think the centurion and his cohorts declare that Jesus was truly the Son of God?

5. Read the Epistle for today in Philippians 2:5-11. How is the meaning of the life of Jesus expressed in this hymn?

RESURRECTION!

Acts 10:34-43; Psalm 118:1-2, 14-24; Colossians 3:1-4; John 20:1-18 or Matthew 28:1-10

In all of the Easter accounts, it is the women who are the first to arrive at the tomb. Matthew tells us that on Friday the body of Jesus had been temporarily placed in the tomb of Joseph of Arimathea, since final burial was delayed until after the Sabbath.

At the request of the religious authorities, the Roman governor Pilate had ordered that the tomb be securely sealed and guarded so that the followers of Jesus could not steal the body and then claim that he had been raised from the dead (27:57-66).

We read that, when Mary Magdalene and the other Mary arrived at the tomb at dawn on the Sabbath, there was a great earthquake. An angel of the Lord appeared and rolled back the stone at the entrance.

The soldiers standing guard were terrified at the angel, whose "appearance was like lightning," and whose clothing was "white as snow" (28:3). The angel reassured the women that Jesus "is not here; for he has been raised" (28:6), just as he had foretold. As proof of this astonishing news, he told them to see for themselves that the tomb was empty, and gave them a message to take back to the other disciples. "He has been raised from the dead, and indeed he is going ahead of you to Galilee; there you will see him" (v. 7).

As the women ran "with fear and great joy" (v. 8) to tell the others, Jesus appeared. The women immediately bowed down and held his feet, *worshiping him.* Jesus told them not to be afraid and repeated the message that the disciples were to meet him in Galilee (28: 16-20).

In John's account, Mary Magdalene comes to the tomb alone, and when she sees it is empty, runs to tell the others that the body of Jesus has been stolen. At her announcement, Peter and the beloved disciple run to the tomb (Jn. 20:3).

Both men observe the linen cloths lying in the tomb with no body there. The beloved disciple perceives the truth of what has happened and believes, although he was not aware of the scriptural affirmation of the Resurrection: "As yet they did not understand the scripture, that he must rise from the dead" (v. 9).

After the two disciples return to their homes, the focus returns to Mary, who stands weeping outside the tomb. As she looks inside, two angels ask her why she weeps. Mary still does not comprehend what has occurred and believes that the body of Jesus has been stolen.

As she turns around, Mary sees an unknown person who also asks why she weeps. Mary assumes that this man is the gardener, and she asks if he is the one who has disturbed the grave.

Only when Jesus calls her by name does Mary finally recognize him and call him "Rabbouni!" In love and joy she embraces the Lord, who admonishes her to cease, since he has not yet ascended to the Father (Jn. 20:17a).

PRAYER FOR THE DAY

Heavenly Father, who through your only-begotten Son Jesus Christ overcame death and opened to us the gate of everlasting life: we praise you with joy and thanksgiving on this day of the Lord's Resurrection, with honor and blessing now and evermore! *Amen.*

Jesus tells her to go to the others and say, "I am ascending to my Father and your Father, to my God and your God" (v. 17b). Here is another change in relationship: the God and Father of Jesus is now the God and Father of Jesus' followers, whom he here calls "my brothers."

Mary returns to the disciples with the stupendous news that "I have seen the Lord" (v. 18). Mary has moved from the darkness of grief to joyous faith in the Risen Christ and is compelled to tell others.

During the Easter season, the first Lesson comes from the Book of Acts. Here the Apostle Peter delivers the first proclamation of the Gospel to the Gentiles in the home of the Roman centurion Cornelius. As a witness to the life, death, and Resurrection of Jesus, Peter had come to understand in a dream (10:9-16) that no one should be called profane or unclean (10:28).

Thus Peter accepts the invitation of Cornelius and declares that the Gospel is for all people, uniting them to God and to one another. "...God shows no partiality, but in every nation anyone who fears him and does what is right is acceptable to him" (vv. 34-35).

God's message of peace was sent to the world through Jesus Christ, who is *Lord of all* (v. 36). Empowered by the Holy Spirit, Jesus went about doing good and healing those oppressed by the devil. However, there were those who were threatened by such power, and Jesus was crucified. But God raised him from the dead on the third day, and he appeared to his chosen disciples, with whom he ate and drank.

Those who saw the Risen Christ are now called to testify to the world that Jesus is the one foretold by the prophets and ordained by God as "judge of the living and the dead" (v. 42).

ON REFLECTION

The two most esteemed pillars of civilization in the ancient world—Roman law and Jewish piety—presided over the execution of Jesus of Nazareth. With the unspeakable death he endured, Jesus had been utterly refuted. The "seducer of the people" had been silenced. Law and order had won. Jesus, the blasphemer, had been "counted among the wicked" (Mk. 15:28). Anyone hanged from a tree was considered cursed by God (Deut. 21:23). Jesus died, on the tree, cursed of God. That is the story about Friday.

What about the story of Sunday? The story that the Discovery Channel could never begin to explain—no matter how many ossuaries they uncover. As theologian Hans Kung has written: "How did a new beginning come about after such a disastrous end? How did a community emerge in the name of a crucified man? How did a condemned heretical teacher come to be known as Israel's 'Messiah' or known as 'Savior'?"

Henri Nouwen said that perhaps the greatest challenge of the Easter message is not in trying to explain the Resurrection. It lies in something more human and less esoteric. It consists in getting the world to *accept a gift for which we can give nothing in return.* For murdering the Son of the Most High, we do not get a holocaust of revenge. We are given instead the definitive disclosure of *eternal life,* God's most precious gift. Rather than retaliation, we are given the witness of what our final healing, our final destiny will be: *Resurrection.*

—H. King Oehmig

Furthermore, through Christ, sin will be forgiven. Thus Peter proclaims the Easter message that everyone who puts faith in Christ Jesus will find eternal life and forgiveness of sins.

In the letter to the Colossians, Paul further explains what it means to live as Easter people. Not only are we to proclaim that Christ is risen, but our *life in the Risen Christ* also calls us to a new set of values and actions centered on God—and not on the world that rejected Jesus.

Now that we have died to our old life, we are to set our minds on things above rather than on earthly things (3:2). Our new life is to be defined by actions that are in conformity with the life of Christ. Therefore, when Christ appears in glory, at the end of all things, we shall be included and be revealed with him in glory (v. 4).

Today's Psalm, 118, reminds us to give thanks for this Divine revelation and love of which we are recipients: *I thank you that you have answered me and have become my salvation* (v. 21).

POINTS TO PONDER

1. As you read John 20:1-18, put yourself in the place of Mary Magdalene, Peter, or the "other disciple" as they came to the tomb. What did they expect to find, and how do you think they might have felt when the tomb was empty?

2. In verse 8, why do you think the "other disciple" believed? We are told in verse 10 that the disciples returned to their homes. How do you think they might have explained what they had just discovered to the others?

3. This story continues in verses 11-18. As you read this section, discuss how Mary was finally able to identify the Risen Jesus.

4. The meaning of the Resurrection for the early Church and for Peter is expressed in today's reading from Acts 10:34-43. How would you explain the truth of the Resurrection to someone else?

5. How do you think Mary and the other disciples were changed by their experience of the empty tomb? How is your life different because of the events of Easter morning 2000 years ago?

"PEACE BE WITH YOU"

Acts 2:14a, 22-32; Psalm 16; 1 Peter 1:3-9; John 20:19-31

The Gospel passage for today, which records two post-Resurrection appearances of Jesus, is always read on the Second Sunday of Easter in all three years of the lectionary cycle. In the first appearance (20:19-23), the mission of the Church is defined, and the disciples are empowered. In John's earlier account, Peter and the beloved disciple had seen the empty tomb, and Mary Magdalene had told the disciples that she had seen Jesus alive (20:1-18). However, none of the disciples had imagined a bodily resurrection, and they were not ready to believe Mary's report.

Because Jesus had been executed on charges of sedition, his followers had reason to believe that their lives might be in danger by association with Jesus. Thus the frightened disciples gather behind locked doors. Jesus' sudden appearance within the room shows that he is no longer subject to physical restrictions.

Jesus greets the disciples with the words, "Peace be with you" (v. 19), and then shows them the wounds on his hands and side. The disciples react with joy as they recognize Jesus. The message Mary had brought them earlier, that *she had seen the Lord* (20:18), is now confirmed. There is rejoicing in the midst of the sorrow and turmoil of the day.

Jesus' familiar words of peace are also words of forgiveness, as he reconciles to himself the followers who abandoned him at the cross.

Once again Jesus repeats his message of peace and entrusts his followers with a mission: "As the Father has sent me, so I send you" (v. 21). This is at the very heart of John's Gospel. Just as the Son has revealed the Father, now the disciples are to reveal the Son to the world (17:18).

But the disciples cannot accomplish this on their own, so the Lord breathes on them (just as God had breathed life into Adam in Gen. 2:7), and says "Receive the Holy Spirit" (v. 22). The gift of the Spirit will empower them to be *witnesses to the world of the saving power of Jesus.*

Jesus adds a further charge: "If you forgive the sins of any, they are forgiven them" (v. 23). Likewise, they have the authority to "retain the sins of any." Thus the Church is empowered by the Holy Spirit and sent out as Jesus himself was sent by the Father.

The second appearance of Jesus occurs a week later and focuses on the basis of faith. The Apostle Thomas, who had been absent the week before, is now present. When told of the Lord's previous appearance, Thomas expresses the need to *see for himself* the physical wounds of Jesus.

When Jesus once again appears, he offers Thomas the proof, saying, "Do not doubt but believe" (v. 27). Thomas' disbelief is immediately turned into a profound declaration of faith as he proclaims: "My Lord and my God!" (v. 28). Jesus is indeed the Risen Christ. There is no need for Jesus to breathe upon Thomas, for through the representative acceptance by the others, he has already received the Holy Spirit.

PRAYER FOR THE DAY

Almighty God, who through the mystery of Jesus' Passion gave to us the new covenant of reconciliation: may we who have been reborn into the fellowship of Christ's Body continue to show forth in our lives what we profess by faith, through Jesus Christ our Lord. *Amen.*

Jesus goes on to declare the blessedness of those who come to faith without the need for physical proof (v. 29b). These words are a rebuke to Thomas but an affirmation that the generations to come—those who read John's Gospel—must rely on these words and not on physical proof.

The passage concludes with a statement of purpose for the Gospel of John. There are many more stories about Jesus, but these are told to bring belief that *Jesus is the Messiah, God's Son,* so "that through believing you may have life in his name" (v. 31).

In the reading from Acts, we see Peter carrying out the mission entrusted to the disciples by the Resurrected Lord to *bear witness to him,* in this impassioned speech to the Jerusalem crowds on the Day of Pentecost. The central fact of the Resurrection forms the core of the address, which begins on an eschatological tone with words taken from the Old Testament Prophet Joel (2:28-32) in Acts 2:17-21, followed by a statement of the Gospel in verses 22-24.

Although Jesus performed signs and wonders among them, he was crucified by lawless men. But all of this was a part of God's plan. God raised Jesus from death "because it was impossible for him to be held in its power" (v. 24).

In verses 25-28, Peter refers to Psalm 16:8-11 as David's prophecy of the Lord's Resurrection, for it is obvious that David himself is dead. *It is Jesus whom God has raised up* (v. 31). As first-hand witnesses, Peter and the others can proclaim God's continuing work in the world through the Resurrection of Christ Jesus (v. 32).

The Epistle readings for the Easter season in Year A are taken from the first letter of Peter, which was addressed to Christians in five Roman provinces in Asia Minor (1:1). The letter encourages followers of Jesus to imitate Christ by doing good and enduring sufferings.

Here the Resurrection is seen as the link between present faith and future hope, as the fruits of the Resurrection are proclaimed, offering a "new birth into a living hope" (v. 3).

ON REFLECTION

Thomas wasn't the only reluctant believer in the Resurrection. All eleven Apostles were doubters. According to Luke, they think the message of Mary Magdalene, Joanna, and Mary the mother of James—breathlessly testifying to the empty tomb of Jesus—is simply an "idle tale" (24:11). In Matthew, some disciples, even after seeing Jesus, still do not believe (28:17). Thomas, known as the "Doubter," can hardly have had a monopoly on Easter unbelief.

And why shouldn't these followers of Jesus have had doubts, be skeptics? No one was expecting anything like "resurrection." No one saw it happen. No one had a category of thought to put it in—it was an act wholly other, and totally unprecedented. If nothing else, the way the disciples reacted should tell us that faith does not come only where there is proof—but smack dab in the middle of doubts and questioning. As Frederick Buechner has so aptly said, "Doubts are the ants in the pants of faith—they keep it alive and moving."

Like the rest of us, Thomas is from Missouri, where "seeing is believing." Thomas was lucky—this time. Maybe the capacity for Thomas to take in the Resurrection of Jesus was less in seeing and touching his healed scars than it was in his having had the Holy Spirit released on him through the other Apostles. As the New Testament makes clear, it is only through the presence of the Holy Spirit that one can call Jesus "Lord" (1 Cor. 12:3).

—H. King Oehmig

The message for believers is that they too will inherit salvation and God's victory over death and the grave. In this hope of union with the Risen Christ, they can rejoice, even while they suffer. Peter reminds them that they need have no fear, as the trial of their faith simply proves it genuine (vv. 6-7).

In words that remind us of the Gospel story of Thomas, Peter commends the faith of these disciples who love and believe in Jesus *even though they have not actually seen him,* for they shall receive salvation through their faith.

In all of the readings for today, God's ongoing work in the world is manifested in the *Resurrection of Jesus,* which brings the promise of salvation, forgiveness of sins, and eternal life.

POINTS TO PONDER

1. Try to imagine that you are among those gathered behind closed doors on Easter evening. How would you describe the atmosphere in the room? How do you think the disciples might have felt when Jesus suddenly appeared among them? Why do you think he showed them his wounds?

2. In John 20:19, 21, and 26, Jesus says, "Peace be with you." Why do you think he repeats this greeting? What effect do you think these words had on the disciples? How are they important to us today?

3. What is the mission that Jesus gives to his followers in verses 21b-23, and how are they empowered for this? How are we as individuals and as the Church to fulfill this mission today? How are we enabled to do so? In particular, what does it mean that we are to forgive and retain sins?

4. As you read the exchange between Thomas and Jesus in verses 24-29, how would you characterize the words and actions of both Thomas and Jesus here? What do you think moves Thomas to declare that Jesus is Lord and God? What do we learn from this passage about doubt, faith, and belief?

5. All of the readings for today proclaim the reality and implications of the Resurrection. Read the Epistle for today in 1 Peter 1:3-9 and reflect on your understanding of the implications of the Resurrection in your own life.

THE ROAD TO EMMAUS

Acts 2:14a, 36-41; Psalm 116:1-3, 10-17; 1 Peter 1:17-23; Luke 24:13-35

On this Third Sunday of Easter we hear a Post-Resurrection story that is unique to the Gospel of Luke. This appearance also occurs on the Day of Resurrection. But unlike the earlier one in John, this episode does not include frightened disciples hiding behind closed doors. Here the Risen Lord appears to those outside his inner circle of followers.

Early on Easter morning when Mary Magdalene and the other women found the tomb of Jesus empty, two men appeared and told them that *Jesus was not there* because he had risen. When they told the others, their news was perceived by the disciples as an "idle tale." However, Peter went back to the tomb to see for himself, and came away amazed (Lk. 24:1-12).

It is now later in the same day, and two followers of Jesus are on their way to Emmaus, a village about seven miles outside Jerusalem. They had heard the report of the empty tomb and were in deep conversation about what might have happened—when *Jesus himself joined them.* However, they were kept from recognizing him (24:16)—as was Mary in the garden (Jn. 20:14).

When Jesus asks what they are discussing, one of them, Cleopas, seems amazed that this stranger does not know what has transpired in Jerusalem in the past few days. As Jesus urges him on, Cleopas tells him about Jesus of Nazareth, the great prophet who was crucified three days ago by the religious leaders. They had hoped that Jesus was the one who would liberate Israel—but now it seems unlikely.

It has been three days since the death of Jesus, but now they have heard the astounding news from some of the women that *his tomb was empty* and that angels appeared telling them that *Jesus is alive.* Others had verified this, but no one had actually seen Jesus.

Jesus reproves them for their inability to believe the prophets who had foretold that *it was necessary* for the Messiah to undergo these things before being glorified. He goes on to tell them all the things concerning himself in the Scriptures.

As they draw near their destination, the two travelers urge Jesus to stay with them that night. As they gather for their evening meal, Jesus assumes the role of host: he "took bread, blessed and broke it, and gave it to them" (v. 30), words that recall the feeding of the five thousand (9:16) and the Last Supper (22:19).

Immediately, "their eyes were opened" (v. 31), and they recognized Jesus through the eyes of faith. But just as they realized this, he vanished—showing again that his Resurrected body is not subject to physical limitations.

Amazed, they remarked how their hearts were set afire—"burning" within them—as Jesus opened the Scriptures to them (v. 32). It is only in the light of the Resurrection and Jesus' teaching about it that the story of God's purpose is fully revealed.

PRAYER FOR THE DAY

O God, whose blessed Son made himself known to his disciples in the breaking of bread: open the eyes of our hearts that we truly may know him and experience his redeeming work, now and forever. *Amen.*

The interpretation of Scripture is accompanied by the breaking of bread: word and worship.

In their excitement they immediately return to Jerusalem, where the remaining eleven Apostles and others are gathered. They also now believe, as they give their own witness to the Lord's Resurrection, adding that Jesus had appeared to Simon (v. 34).

Luke does not tell of a separate Resurrection appearance to Peter, but Paul does make reference to an event (1 Cor. 15:5). The travelers from Emmaus relate their own experience and tell how Jesus was "made known to them in the breaking of the bread" (v. 35).

The reading from Acts is a continuation of Peter's Pentecost speech from last Sunday. In the conclusion to his address, Peter tells his listeners that Jesus, whom they crucified, was the one that God had made "both Lord and Messiah" (2:36). Because God *acted,* the one who was crucified *was raised* (v. 32), and is now Lord and Messiah.

As Lord, Jesus is Divine; and as Messiah, he is the one who brings in God's Kingdom.

Upon hearing these words, the crowd find themselves "cut to the heart" (v. 37) with remorse, asking what they can do. Peter tells them—Jew and Gentile alike—to repent and be baptized in Jesus' name to receive forgiveness of sins and the gift of the Holy Spirit. Peter exhorts the crowd to "save yourselves from this corrupt generation" (v. 40) through belief in Christ. Three thousand were baptized that day and born into the family of God.

The passage today from 1 Peter not only emphasizes this transforming power of the Resurrection, but also sets forth how the newly converted are to live their lives. Peter describes them as exiles who are to leave behind the futility of their former ways and live in reverent awe of God, who can be trusted to judge one's actions impartially.

ON REFLECTION

Rather than attempting to understand the Resurrection, we would be better off simply seeking to experience it—as the Emmaus Road disciples did. They experienced Resurrection power through the same means of grace that we do, week after week, year after year—that is, through the exposition of Scripture and the breaking of bread. *Word needs Sacrament,* and *Sacrament needs Word* for the full Gospel of Jesus to be entered into.

Paul Tillich maintained that the Christian message for our time could be summarized in two words: NEW BEING. And then the noted theologian went on to say that the New Being of Jesus comes about in our lives in three ways. 1). *Re-conciliation:* This is the reversal of hostility. Forgiveness and acceptance heal the wounds of "exile." Estrangement, in the New Being, is overcome by love that manifests itself in peace—peace with God, with oneself, and with the world. 2). *Re-union:* This means the acceptance of reconciliation. Grace through Jesus is offered all along; only when it is accepted in faith does it become efficacious. Forgiveness can be offered, but only when it is accepted—and returned—can the New Being manifest reunion with God, self, and neighbor. 3). *Re-surrection:* This is not dead bodies coming out of the grave—it is the life of the Holy Spirit, poured out upon the believing community, to do the work of Jesus in the world. Wendell Berry calls it "practicing Resurrection." By intention, we decide to live in the power of Jesus' Resurrection—we practice it day by day—and become God's change agents, radiating a "new way of being."

—H. King Oehmig

They have been ransomed by the self-sacrifice of Christ, whose destiny was determined before creation itself (Eph. 1:4), and is now manifested to them. Thus they can confidently place their faith and hope in God who raised and glorified Jesus.

They have been cleansed through their acceptance of the truth of the Gospel, and thus are to respond by loving one another "deeply from the heart" (1 Pet. 1:22). Their genuine love and care for one another will be a further manifestation of this new community God has called into being.

They have received new life—been "born anew"—through the "imperishable seed" of the Gospel, which is the "living and enduring word of God" (v. 23). It is God who grants this new life, and they are to respond by manifesting a new way of being in the world that is in keeping with the Gospel message.

Thus, by the action of God, Jesus was raised from the dead and is revealed to us through Word and Sacrament. Our response to this redeeming action of God in Christ Jesus is to live a new life characterized by mutual love and care. This is true Easter joy.

In the words of our Psalm, 116, we can praise God who has "loosed" our bonds (v. 16a) and brought us life!

POINTS TO PONDER

1. As the two travelers walk along the road and talk with the stranger (who is actually Jesus), how do they describe the events of the previous three days?

2. What is their understanding about Jesus and the recent happenings in Jerusalem? How do they feel about their prospects for the future?

3. As Jesus walks with them, how does he explain the things about himself as revealed in the Scriptures? Why was it important for him to interpret these things to them?

4. In addition to the revelation of Scripture, Jesus is recognized through the breaking of the bread (Lk. 24:35). How do you feel the presence of Christ in the Eucharist and in other ways in your own life?

5. In the Epistle reading (1 Pet. 1:17-23), what is expected of those who belong to the new community of believers in Christ? How do we carry out these responsibilities today?

THE GOOD SHEPHERD

Acts 2:42-47; Psalm 23; 1 Peter 2:19-25; John 10:1-10

Today is Good Shepherd Sunday. The figure of the shepherd is one of the most enduring metaphors in Christianity, originating in the Jewish tradition, in which many significant characters in the Hebrew Bible were keepers of flocks.

Joshua is commissioned to be "shepherd" of Israel (Num. 27:16-23); and David is called to be "shepherd of my people Israel" (2 Sam. 5:2; 1 Chron. 11:2).

No other human leader of Israel is given the title. *God* is the shepherd *par excellence,* who not only leads the flock, but also nurtures, feeds, protects, and defends it (Ps. 23; 28:9; 80:1; Is. 40:11).

In the New Testament, the title of shepherd and the shepherd's responsibilities are applied to Jesus. In Mark and Matthew, Jesus compassionately reaches out to the crowds, who followed him because they were "like sheep without a shepherd" (Mk. 6:34; Mt. 9:36), a phrase used in the Hebrew Scriptures to express the absence or failure of leadership (Num. 27:15-17; 1 Ki. 22:17).

In today's Gospel, Jesus has come to Jerusalem for the Feast of Tabernacles. After healing the man born blind (Jn. 9:6-41), he is embroiled in a heated discussion with some Pharisees. Jesus makes a shift from images of light and darkness to sheep and shepherds.

At night, shepherds would herd their sheep into a common enclosure or sheepfold. Usually the fold had a single entrance, and the owners of the flocks would take turns sleeping at the entrance to keep out predators. In the morning the shepherd would lead the sheep out to pasture, calling each sheep by name and piping or singing a tune. Since each shepherd had a distinct call, the sheep would not follow a stranger.

The Pharisees are confused by Jesus' figurative language, so he explains that he is "the gate" who provides protection for the sheep. However, no matter how well the door may be protected, a robber may climb up some other way and seize the sheep.

These thieves and bandits come to steal and destroy and exploit the sheep for their own gain. They are like the messianic pretenders and false prophets who would mislead the flock; whereas those who follow the voice of Jesus will find salvation, since *he has come to bring abundant life.*

As the gate, Jesus is the way to eternal life—a familiar theme in John's Gospel. As shepherd, he guides and protects his followers. The imagery of Psalm 23 beautifully describes the abundant life that is promised by Jesus. With the Lord as our shepherd, we can trust in God's unfailing love and protection.

The Epistle of 1 Peter continues to provide encouragement to the faithful, offering another perspective in which *the sacrifice of the shepherd* makes possible the return of straying sheep. This portion of the letter is addressed specifically to slaves in a household (1 Pet. 2:18) whose behavior is held up as an example.

PRAYER FOR THE DAY

We praise you, Risen Lord, the good shepherd of your people, who knows us each by name. Guide and correct us by your Holy Spirit, that your people, prone to err and stray like lost sheep, might be brought into the sheepfold of the Father, where true joys are to be found in glory everlasting. *Amen.*

This letter refers to Christians as a community of outsiders who face hostility and risk in holding on to their beliefs. Thus they are urged to endure their suffering, unjust as it may be. Such undeserved suffering is approved by God (v. 19); whereas to submit oneself to the due penalty of wrongdoing is no more than one ought to do (v. 20).

In fact, it is to just such behavior that we have been called. Christ died for us, leaving us the example of how to live and "follow in his steps" (v. 21). We are to conduct our lives in the pattern set down by the sinless Christ *who made no complaint* against those who caused his suffering. Instead, he relied totally upon the justice of his Father in heaven. Verse 22 cites an example from Isaiah 53:9 in which the Servant suffers despite his innocence. However, the suffering of Jesus brings life, forgiveness, and healing for others (v. 24). Thus Jesus the shepherd is the guardian of our souls and of the community of faith.

The reading from Acts for today comes after the end of Peter's Pentecost sermon (2:14-36). Here life in the new Christian community is described as an ideal fellowship characterized by devotion to the Apostles' "teaching and fellowship, to the breaking of bread and the prayers" (v. 42).

The "wonders and signs" (v. 43) of the Apostles were evidence that God's Spirit was working through them as in Jesus. They all sold their possessions and held "all things in common" (v. 45), as a response to the increasing growth of the Spirit among them and their mutual love for one another. Luke emphasizes not only the work of the Spirit in the community, but also their fellowship in worship as they attended the temple and "broke bread at home" (v. 46). The breaking of bread is also mentioned in verse 42, and calls attention to the emerging role of the Eucharist in the community.

ON REFLECTION

A cartoon from *The New Yorker* said it all about leadership. A flock of sheep is facing a sheepdog out on the grasslands. Depicted are comments on the dog's performance. One such musing says, "Autocratic." Another reads, "Would be better if more decisive." Yet another says, "Doesn't take criticism well at all." "Not open to suggestion," another sheep muses. The last one reads, "Good on ideas, but not so good on follow-through."

The Fourth Sunday of Easter is always "Good Shepherd" Sunday. The Gospel text is from the 10th chapter of John. William Temple (1881—1944), Archbishop of Canterbury, translated "good shepherd" as "the shepherd, the beautiful one." Interesting. Temple wanted to show that "good" here does not simply refer to "moral rectitude." It means evocative "beauty" as well—having the ability to attract. Jesus embodies *the beauty of holiness,* the splendor of love that draws people to him. Temple would go on to say that Christians are to practice this same kind of "goodness"—to be in the world in a way that is not morally superior, or repulsive, but in a way that draws people to God.

With Jesus as the "beautiful shepherd," we need to be reminded that all of us are to be under-shepherds to the Shepherd. With graciousness, we are to show the way to still waters, to revive souls, to lead others to green pastures, and to steady them through the valley of the shadow of death. Daily, we are to emit the scent of the Gospel—a fragrance of goodness and mercy—in such a way that others are drawn to Jesus, not repelled by what they smell.

—H. King Oehmig

Their worship at the temple is evidence of continuity with their Jewish tradition; but such worship in their homes represents a new way of *being in community* that recognizes Christ in their midst (Lk. 24:35).

Finally, this was a community characterized by joy, generosity, and thankful praise, earning them "the goodwill of all the people" (v. 47). As a result of devoting themselves to teaching, fellowship, and worship, this new community flourished, and "day by day the Lord added to their number those who were being saved" (v. 47).

Luke's description here of the Christian community is an idealistic one, but it is a vision of what is possible through the transforming power of God's Spirit in the Resurrected Christ.

POINTS TO PONDER

1. How would you describe the relationship between the shepherd and the sheep in John 10:1-10? What does this suggest about our relationship with Jesus?

2. What are the dangers faced by the sheep as described by Jesus? In verses 3-4, Jesus says that the sheep follow the shepherd because they know his voice. How do you hear and recognize the voice of Jesus in your own life?

3. In verse 7, and again in verse 9, Jesus says, "I am the gate." Why do you think Jesus calls himself "the gate" in this passage? How do we enter into his life?

4. In the final verse Jesus says that he came that "they might have life, and have it abundantly." What do these words mean for you?

5. As you read the familiar words of Psalm 23 for today, how are the life and ministry of Jesus reflected here? As followers of Jesus, how are we called to be shepherds for others?

UNTROUBLED HEARTS

Acts 7:55-60; Psalm 31:1-5, 15-16; 1 Peter 2:2-10; John 14:1-14

Few passages in Scripture have brought as much comfort and assurance as Jesus' farewell address to his disciples (Jn. 13:1—17:26). It is the evening of the Last Supper. Jesus has washed his disciples' feet (13:3-17), and Judas has left to do what he must do (13:18-30).

As Jesus tells those who remain with him, "I am with you only a little longer" (13:33), he reveals that *where he is going, the disciples cannot follow* (13:36b). But as he prepares them for his absence, he offers the assurance: "Do not let your hearts be troubled" (14:1).

In 14:1-4, Jesus promises *his eternal presence* will be with them. However, "to believe" (v. 1) involves committing the whole self to the care of God. If Jesus goes to prepare a dwelling place for them "in my Father's house" (v. 2), there will be room for all of them.

Although Jesus will no longer be with them as an earthly physical presence, he will nonetheless stay with them. This sense of *abiding* or *staying* with Jesus is the focus of discipleship. Eternal life begins when we "abide in the Son and in the Father" (1 Jn. 2:24-25). This is the promise of Jesus: everlasting, mutual indwelling.

Thomas speaks for the rest of the group when he asks *how can they know the way to this place* when they don't know where Jesus is going (v. 5)? Jesus answers with some of the most familiar words from John: "I am the way, the truth, and the life" (v. 6).

As "the way," Jesus is the one who leads to the Father. In addition, his life and teachings exemplify "the way" his followers are to live. He has, from the beginning of the Gospel, been identified with "the truth" (1:14, 17). And Jesus is the answer to Pilate's question, "What is truth?" (18:38).

Throughout the Gospel, Jesus is also identified with *life:* "...in him was life, and the life was the light of all people" (1:4). Those who believe in Jesus have eternal life (3:15-16, 36); Jesus is "the resurrection and the life" (11:25).

"No one comes to the Father except through me" (14:6b). This exclusive claim is provided at this time as an assurance to the disciples, who face an uncertain future. It is not meant to be used as an attack on other ways, but is the community's affirmation of their faith in Jesus as the Messiah.

With the response of Jesus to Philip's demand to "show us the Father" (v. 8), the focus turns in verses 8-11 to a discussion of the relation between Jesus and God. Jesus replies that "Whoever has seen me has seen the Father" (v. 9).

To know Jesus is to know the Father; to see Jesus is to see the Father. In all that Jesus has said and done *it is the Father who has spoken and acted,* because Jesus and the Father are never separated.

PRAYER FOR THE DAY

Come, Holy Spirit, and pour upon us your continual wisdom, that we may know Jesus to be the way, the truth, and the life, the One who leads us to the Kingdom of God. Give us grace so to follow your path day by day, that our believing may result in doing, and become a means of grace for all to whom we are sent, through Jesus Christ our Lord. *Amen.*

Nor will the disciples ever be separated from Jesus. In fact, they will be empowered to do the very works that Jesus has done, when Jesus is no longer with them (v. 12).

This ongoing work of the community will be possible because *prayers made in the name of Jesus will be answered.* However, these prayers are not to be asked in self-interest, but in order that the Father be glorified by the Son. Whatever is needed to accomplish that will be given to the disciples through Jesus—they only have to ask.

In the Epistle in 1 Peter, encouragement is offered to the new Christian community as it attempts to follow Jesus as "the way" and to live their faith. First of all, there is no room for destructive behavior, and they are to rid themselves of malice, envy, and slander. As newborns in the faith, they are to strive for the "spiritual milk" of the Gospel (2:2), which will bring salvation.

Verses 4-8 refer to a number of Old Testament texts (Is. 8:14; 28:16; Ps. 34:8; 118: 22) that point to Jesus as the source of this new way of life. Though he was rejected by the world, Christ is the "living stone" (v. 4), and is now the foundation or cornerstone of the faith.

Believers need not fear to be identified with Jesus. For when they are truly united with Christ, they too become "living stones" (v. 5), built into a living temple in order to offer acceptable spiritual sacrifices.

In verses 9-10, Old Testament references are used once again (Ex. 19:5-6; Is. 43:20-21; Hos. 2:23) as the fledgling Christian community is called to be God's chosen, proclaimers of the Gospel. Once they were scattered individuals, but now they have become a holy community, called out of darkness into light.

The passage from Acts gives a dramatic example of the risks and suffering faced by the first Christians as they lived out their faith.

ON REFLECTION

Wherever "the way, the truth, and the life" passage comes up, THE QUESTION quickly follows: Are only Christians saved? What about my next-door neighbor who is Jewish? What about the Eskimo of the 4th century B. C.? Have all the Aborigines from pre-recorded history burned in hell? The Muslims? The Hindus and Buddhists? And what about garden variety atheists—are they condemned too?

The passage does not have to be read that way at all. Yes, Jesus is the way, the truth, and the life, and no one comes to the Father except through him. Exactly. No one ever taught about "God" the way Jesus did. By following Jesus, the seeker comes to know God in the way that Jesus did—uniquely as *"Abba"*—a toddler's word for "Daddy" in Aramaic. To speak to the Holiest of Holies in this highly intimate, perhaps irreverent form of address was unique to followers of the Way.

The passage does not mean that those who do not follow Jesus are hell-bound and do not come to know God at all. Buddha. Mahatma Gandhi. Moses. Sarah. They all knew God, just not in the unique way Jesus did. When Jesus said: "And I, when I am lifted up from the earth, will draw all people to myself" (Jn. 12:32), he meant what he said. It will not be only Christians that are drawn to him—but all people, for all time, in all places. Some might be more resistant than others, but no matter. In the end, no one will be able to refuse the Way, the Truth, and the Life. Or will want to.

—H. King Oehmig

The verses in today's reading are from the final words of Stephen as he is stoned to death by an angry mob.

Stephen "did great wonders and signs among the people" (6:8). However, his energy and eloquence soon made him a marked man among the community's opponents.

He was arrested on false charges of blasphemy and brought before the council in Jerusalem, where he gave a fiery speech (7: 2-53), reviewing Israel's history as one of unrelieved rebellion against God. He accused the people of Jerusalem of consistently resisting the Holy Spirit, persecuting God's prophets, disobeying the law, and murdering Jesus.

His words were met with outrage from the crowd, and they dragged Stephen outside the city and stoned him. As he was struck down, he was filled with the Holy Spirit and proclaimed that he saw a vision of Jesus standing at the right hand of God. His words further angered the crowd. Then, as he died, Stephen prayed just as Jesus had, for God to receive his spirit and forgive those who executed him.

Stephen's vision of heaven as he died was an affirmation of the victory over death promised by the Resurrection of Jesus, and proclaimed as well by the Psalm for today: "Into your hand I commit my spirit: you have redeemed me, O Lord, faithful God" (31:5).

POINTS TO PONDER

1. In his farewell sermon, how does Jesus begin to prepare his disciples for his absence in John 14:1-4? What specific assurances does he offer them?

2. In verses 5-7, Jesus responds to the questions of Thomas. What does it mean that Jesus is the way, the truth, and the life? How does Jesus, in his response to Philip in verses 8-11, describe his relationship to the Father?

3. What are the fruits, as well as the responsibilities, of belief as described in verses 12-14? What do these words suggest to us about our prayer life?

4. What are the promises and assurances found in the words of Jesus to his disciples? What specific challenges for the mission of the Church, as well as for us as individual disciples, are given here?

5. In the reading from Acts for today (7:55-60) we see Stephen following in Jesus' steps even to martyrdom. How does the vision of Jesus offer us courage to face hostility and rejection in the world today?

THE LAW OF LOVE

Acts 17:22-31; Psalm 66:7-18; 1 Peter 3:13-22; John 14:15-21

The Gospel reading is a continuation of last week's passage from Jesus' farewell address to his disciples. In it he prepared them for his absence and promised that God the Father would send an Advocate to be with them in his stead.

The central theme here is *God's love, which is manifested for us in Christ.* For the disciples, the proper way to respond to this love is to keep the Lord's commandments (14:15). To enable them to carry out this command, Jesus will ask the Father to send them "another Advocate" (v. 16).

The word "Paraclete" can be literally translated as *one who is called alongside.* Throughout the course of his ministry, Jesus has been the *Paraclete* or Advocate for the disciples—their guide, counselor, intercessor, teacher, sustainer, help, and comforter.

Now as Jesus goes to the cross, and prepares to ascend in glory, he will not leave his disciples alone as *orphans* to face rejection, persecution, and possible martyrdom. He will pray to the Father to send them another Advocate to be with them forever.

Jesus goes on to describe this other Advocate as the "Spirit of truth" (v. 17). This Advocate is a gift for the community of faith. But the world will not be able to accept the Advocate, since the Spirit of truth serves to reveal all falsehood.

Yet the Advocate can remain with the disciples, since Jesus has taught them to recognize and value the truth. Thus the Spirit will abide with and in them.

When the disciples can no longer see the human Jesus, he will nonetheless continue to be with them everywhere and at all times, since the Advocate dwells or abides in everyone who loves Jesus and keeps his commandments.

Moreover, the Advocate or Spirit is far more than a substitute for the absent Christ, and will prepare the disciples for God's continued revelation.

The Spirit's total activity, as seen by the disciples, has been in the ministry of Jesus. Now that Jesus is going to the Father, the Spirit will act in those who believe in him. Thus God will continue *through them* the work that has begun in Jesus, and all of this will glorify the Father.

This is true for us today as well, as Jesus continues to be present in and through us. Thus we can rejoice with the Psalmist, who blesses the Lord "because he has not rejected my prayer or removed his steadfast love from me" (66:20).

Just as Jesus was preparing his disciples to become his presence in the world after he returned to the Father, the words of 1 Peter can give further instruction on suffering among the followers of Jesus.

PRAYER FOR THE DAY

O gracious God, in whom we live and move and have our being, so clothe your people in your love, that we may desire what you command, so that through the abiding presence of the Spirit of Truth we may know the Resurrected Lord, and the power of the new creation, through Jesus Christ our Savior. *Amen.*

First of all, those who do good in the world are not likely to be targets of deliberate harm; but even if they do suffer, they are ultimately blessed and should not be intimidated (3:13-14).

As followers of Jesus, they should always be ready to explain, gently and firmly, why they believe. When Christian conviction prompts good conduct, even when one is subjected to persecution, this will honor Christ and shame the persecutors.

The disciples are followers of the sinless one who suffered for the unrighteous in order to bring us to God. *Christ the righteous* gave up his life for the sins of the unworthy. That ultimate suffering was vindicated when Jesus was made alive again in the spirit.

The redemptive suffering of Christ serves for all humanity—even those who lived too early to receive it. It is explained in 1 Peter that when Jesus was taken down from the cross, he "descended into hell" to deliver the message of salvation to imprisoned spirits who had not been granted the opportunity to learn God's truth (vv. 19-20a).

Being put to death physically, Jesus now gives spiritual life to all. Through baptism we are united with Christ. Noah's deliverance from the flood serves as an example or symbol of deliverance from the powers of evil and death. This baptism is not a removal of dirt from the body, but "an appeal to God" (v. 21), which God hears and answers.

All of this is made possible because of the Resurrection of Jesus, who now sits at the "right hand of God" in heaven "with angels, authorities, and powers made subject to him" (v. 22).

The speech of the Apostle Paul in Acts invites his listeners to share in this indwelling life with God through Christ. Previously Paul had fled crowds in Thessalonica and Beroea, and he was now in Athens clarifying teachings about the Resurrection.

ON REFLECTION

The author of *The Prophet,* Kahlil Gibran, once said: "If love is not always growing, it is always decaying." One does not have to be a prophet to know the truth of this truism. Just as soon as a relationship is taken for granted, left unattended, or treated as a "possession" rather than an organic, living entity—love begins to atrophy. Over a period of time, love can vanish altogether: How many loveless marriages testify to the fact that relationships can decay unto death?

The same is true for our relationship with God. We lapse. We stray. We neglect. We take God for granted. We turn to busy-ness, to doctrines, ideologies, or power struggles instead of Holy Love on which to build our lives. God does not leave us; we leave God. But if we pay attention to our relationship with God—love flowers. Love blooms. All other relationships are put into their proper perspective when this primary connection is tended to—and when it is kept first in the life of the believing community. It seems so simple, yet it is infinitely hard for us earthlings to maintain.

So how best to keep the flame of love alive with God? The primitive Christian community held that doing four things was crucial: "They devoted themselves to the apostles' teaching and fellowship, to the breaking of bread and the prayers" (Acts 2:42). Maybe after all is said and done, this is the best prescription ever written—the simplest roadmap handed down to us—on how to grow in love with God and one another.

—H. King Oehmig

Speaking in front of the Areopagus, site of the advisory council to Athenian kings, Paul begins by noting how "extremely religious you are in every way" (17:22). And to make sure that no genuine spiritual power should be slighted, he notes the altar where sacrifices are offered to an "unknown god" (v. 23).

In verses 24-28, Paul describes what they already instinctively know and revere about God. God is the Creator of all that is who gives breath and life to all humanity. God is "Lord of heaven and earth" (v. 24) and is not dependent on human endeavor as are the Greek deities.

Just as people of every nation share a common ancestor, they also search for God, who is nearer than they imagine. Indeed, Paul affirms, alluding to the poet Epimenides, "In him we live and move and have our being" (v. 28).

In the same verse, Paul borrows from another poet, Aratus, when he says that we are all God's offspring. Thus we should not think of God in terms of images of metal or stone.

Whereas God once overlooked such human ignorance, it is now time to repent. Now judgment has come through the righteousness of a man appointed by God and raised from the dead (v. 31). Jesus' sacrifice is the central act of salvation history, which brings new life to the world.

POINTS TO PONDER

1. What are the promises that Jesus makes in the Gospel passage to those who follow him? How do these promises continue to be manifested in our lives?

2. Jesus uses the word "love" several times. How would you define love as it is expressed in these verses? What is the relationship between love and obedience?

3. Jesus promises to send an Advocate to be with the disciples forever. What is the role of this Advocate? How do we experience the Advocate in the world today?

4. Why is it that the world cannot receive the Spirit of truth? What enables the disciples to receive this Spirit?

5. What is the relationship between Jesus and the Father as expressed here? How does this relationship extend to us as well?

THE HOUR OF GLORY

Acts 1:6-14; Psalm 68:1-10, 33-36; 1 Peter 4:12-14; 5:6-11; John 17:1-11

Today we read a portion the great intercessory prayer—the "High Priestly Prayer" of Jesus—which forms the point of transition to the difficult days ahead.

In this prayer in John 17, Jesus sums up the significance of his earthly life. He has finished the mission he was sent to do, and he asks that God's glory now be revealed through him. He also prays for God's protection for his disciples, who are understandably confused and frightened of the future. Even though they will fail badly when Jesus is arrested and executed, their internal commitment and outward witness to the Gospel will survive.

Christ's revelation of himself to the world is now complete, and as he looks up to heaven, he declares that his "hour" of self-offering has come (v. 1). It is through that offering that he will come to glory. Thus Jesus asks the Father to glorify the Son, so that the Son may in turn glorify the Father.

The earthly ministry of Jesus has given glory to the Father by accomplishing God's work. Now that the tasks are completed, the Father will glorify the Son. Indeed, Jesus possessed this glory prior to the creation.

Making God's true name and nature known to the disciples is the central element of Jesus' mission. Those individuals belonged to the Father, but God entrusted them to the Son, who has enabled them to obey the Father's Word.

Those so given to the Son have recognized that the Father is the source of everything the Son has received. Therefore, the Son has been able to transmit the knowledge that he himself has received. This has been possible because they have trusted in him as sent by the Father, and *Jesus is further glorified in them.*

Jesus offers this prayer specifically for his disciples, and not for the world (v. 9). Jesus has overcome the world (16:33), but persecution will still threaten to divide his followers. Therefore, Jesus prays that they remain united, and that their unity reflect the oneness of Jesus with the Father. "Holy Father, protect them in your name that you have given me, so that they may be one, as we are one" (v. 11).

The disciples for whom Jesus prays are our representatives. As the Lord prayed for them and as he sent them, so he does for us. As the truth was entrusted to them, and as it conferred on them Jesus' holiness, it now confers holiness upon us. Our Great High Priest intercedes also for our protection, giving us the power to *resist evil* and to *remain faithful* to the end.

Today's Epistle also warns of the need for protection for the followers of Jesus in a hostile world. Believers have already experienced certain "fiery ordeals" (1 Pet. 4:12). In living triumphantly through these trials, Christians are to be tested and found trustworthy.

PRAYER FOR THE DAY

Glorious God, of majesty unbounded, you have exalted your only Son Jesus Christ to reign over all: send us your Holy Spirit, the Lord and Giver of Life, that we may not remain comfortless, and that we may be strengthened daily to do your will, with a whole-hearted commitment and with a single-minded conviction. *Amen.*

Indeed, to share Christ's suffering is a privilege, for it is a promise that one will also share in his glory (v. 13a). To enter into Christ's life in this way is possible because the Spirit of God rests upon believers.

Suffering in itself brings no merit, and it is only the suffering that one endures as a disciple that can glorify God (v. 13b). Furthermore, believers who are reviled in the name of Christ are blessed "because the spirit of glory, which is the Spirit of God, is resting on you" (v. 14).

In addition to assurances of God's presence, the letter also offers ways that believers are to respond and resist in the face of their suffering. First, they are to humble themselves before almighty God, who will triumph over all adversity and exalt them (cf Lk. 14:11).

Humility is not servility, but an acknowledgment of dependence upon God and God's grace. Thus they can cast their anxiety upon God, who cares for them with compassion and concern.

They will need to discipline themselves and be alert in order to resist evil, which is like a prowling lion out to devour them (5:8). Knowing that their fellow believers in other places endure the same ordeals will provide a sense of solidarity. They can have faith that God will "restore, support, strengthen, and establish" them (v. 10), as their suffering brings eternal glorification.

This Sunday between Ascension and Pentecost is sometimes referred to as "Expectation Sunday." Following the Ascension, the followers of Jesus wait in expectation for empowerment by the Holy Spirit.

They know that something important is to happen, but they are still uncertain about what it is to be, so they ask Jesus if *now is the time* that he will "restore the kingdom to Israel" (Acts 1: 6). But if they were expecting a declaration of the restoration of the Davidic throne, Jesus reminds them that the timing of God's plan for the Kingdom is known only by the Father.

ON REFLECTION

Our Gospel depicts an interesting, perhaps unnerving, time in the life of the earliest Christian community. Jesus has ascended to heaven, and the Holy Spirit has yet to come. The disciples must have found themselves in that place where we often find confusion: that is, in the time between times. They have left one shore, but have yet to arrive on the other shore. The "good old days" lie behind them; a "brave new world" awaits them. And they inhabit this perplexing flux of a post-Ascension, pre-Pentecost dilemma for ten days.

The time in between times. How do we modern Christians deal with the "twilight zone" of transitions? What do we do with our in-between-ness? In his work *Transitions: Making Sense of Life's Changes* (Addison-Wesley, 1988), William Bridges, Ph. D., maintains that three things need to be recognized. 1) Every change begins with an ending. This does not mean finality, but it does mean that we recognize that there has been an ending. Once out of denial, we can mobilize our resources to move on, to change. 2) We enter the neutral zone. It is a time in which we often feel confused and disconnected. We feel lost. But if we can persist through this "disorientation" to "reorientation," we have done the hardest part. 3) New beginnings. We start over, energized and excited about the future, knowing that God's creativity has not been exhausted in the past. Full of hope, we reach the other shore of new life—just as the Jesus people did when the Holy Spirit fell on them at Pentecost.

—H. King Oehmig

He speaks instead of personal transformation through the Holy Spirit, which will empower them to become witnesses to the Resurrection—in Jerusalem, Judea, Samaria, and to the ends of the earth.

As Jesus ascends into heaven, "two men in white robes" (v. 10) appear and ask why they continue to stand there gazing up into the sky. The figures further promise that *just as Jesus has so miraculously left them, he will come again.*

Thus they are given charge to spread the Gospel in Jesus' stead. As they now anticipate the coming of the Spirit, they return to Jerusalem for a time of reflection and devotion to prayer.

Just as Jesus prayed for his disciples—for the Church—in John 17, here the disciples as the *nucleus* of that Church pray likewise for their coming mission.

Our Psalm for today reminds us that we can choose to be on God's side: "Let the righteous be joyful; let them exult before God" (68:3).

POINTS TO PONDER

1. How is the total life and ministry of Jesus expressed in this prayer?

2. The words "glory" and "glorify" are used several times in the Gospel as well as in the Epistle (1 Pet. 4:12-14). How are we called to glorify God in our own lives?

3. In the final verse, Jesus asks that the unity of his followers reflect the oneness that he himself has with the Father. How is this oneness manifested? How do you experience a sense of oneness with God? How does it feel to know that Jesus prays for each one of us even today?

4. What challenges for the Church, and for us as individual followers of Christ, are implied in these words of Jesus? What does this passage suggest about our own ministries?

5. As you look at all of the readings for today, what promises and reassurances are offered for the followers of Jesus?

THE FEAST OF THE HOLY SPIRIT

Acts 2:1-21; Psalm 104:25-35, 37b; 1 Corinthians 12:3b-13; John 20:19-23

At the Ascension, Jesus had promised his followers that they would "receive power when the Holy Spirit has come upon you" (Acts 1:8). Thus they waited in prayer for the time when this promise would be fulfilled (Acts 1:14).

In the Hebrew liturgical calendar, Pentecost was also known as the Feast of Weeks, in which the community offered thanksgiving for the early grain harvest (Ex. 23:16; 34:22). But by the first century, Pentecost had become a commemoration of the giving of the Law to Moses on Mt. Sinai, celebrated fifty days after Passover.

The followers of Jesus were gathered together in Jerusalem on the Day of Pentecost when God's empowering Spirit came upon them *like the sound of a mighty rushing wind* accompanied by tongues of fire settling on each one of them.

They were immediately filled with the Holy Spirit, and burst forth in words of praise in languages the disciples did not know, which were recognized by others. The crowds were "amazed and astonished" (Acts 2:7) to hear these Galileans proclaiming "God's deeds of power" (v. 11) in their own tongues.

However, some mocked the disciples, saying they were drunk. But Peter stood up and proclaimed that this was the fulfillment of the prophecy of Joel (2:28-29), in which God pours out the Divine Spirit upon all flesh.

The universal mission of the Church is symbolized here with the specific naming of the nations (vv. 10-11). The confusion of the Tower of Babel (Gen. 11:1-9) had been overturned by the power of the Holy Spirit in which all humanity was brought together—both Jews and proselytes.

Thus the promise of Jesus had been kept, and the community of faith had been empowered with *new ways of speaking and hearing* that the world had never before experienced.

Jesus was empowered by the Holy Spirit at his Baptism (Jn. 1:32-33). Throughout his ministry, all of his actions were performed together with the Spirit. In the chronology of John's Gospel, even before the Day of Pentecost, Jesus bestowed this same Spirit upon his chosen Apostles on the Day of Resurrection.

Earlier in the day, Mary Magdalene had reported to the others that she had seen the Lord (20:11-18). Now it is that evening, and the disciples are gathered together behind locked doors from fear of possible enemies. Then Jesus suddenly appears among them. This was no ghost or spirit of Jesus, but Christ in his physical body.

Jesus greets them by saying, "Peace be with you" (v. 19b)—and the peace that Jesus brings is an assurance of God's transforming love to a lost world.

PRAYER FOR THE DAY

Eternal and loving God, on this day you poured out on your people the gift of the Holy Spirit, so that every race and nation may come to know you as Father, and Jesus Christ as Lord. May the Holy Spirit forever bind us together in perfect love, give us right judgment in all matters, strengthen us to do your will, and finally bring us to our eternal home in Light everlasting. *Amen.*

Jesus then shows his friends the marks of his wounds. The disciples rejoice that Jesus has overcome death and the grave, as he stands in their midst as the bearer of peace.

Again Jesus repeats the assurance of God's peace and adds, "As the Father has sent me, so I send you" (v. 21). The mission that had been entrusted to Jesus by the Father is now to be carried out by the disciples (cf 13:20).

Jesus breathes on them and says, "Receive the Holy Spirit" (v. 22). This action recalls Genesis 2:7 when the Lord God breathed life into Adam, as well as the dry bones that live again in Ezekiel 37:3-6.

This empowerment is accompanied by the charge to *forgive* or *retain* sins just as Jesus had done. However, this endowment was not for the Apostles as individuals, but as the Church. The Holy Spirit would work through the disciples to pronounce the assurance of God's forgiveness through repentance and faith.

Although the Book of Acts and the Gospel of John present differing accounts of the giving of the Holy Spirit, the significance of our commemoration of Pentecost is to show that the Church has been *empowered by God's Spirit* to carry on the ministry of Jesus as witnesses to the Gospel.

In the first letter to the Corinthians, Paul describes the manifestations of the Spirit that give life to the community of faith, as well as the power to carry out its mission.

The church at Corinth was beset by conflict among dissenting factions, which Paul attempted to dispel by emphasizing the need for unity. To do this he called attention to the gifts of the Spirit apportioned to the community.

Paul reminds his readers that it is the gift of the Spirit that enables them to confess that "Jesus is Lord" (12:3b). The Church is created by the Spirit, which gives its members the faith to believe.

ON REFLECTION

At the beginning of her masterful work *The Eighth Day of Creation: Gifts and Creativity,* Elizabeth O'Connor told a story about Michelangelo. On a blistering hot day in Rome, Michelangelo was pushing a huge rock down a street to his studio. An onlooker, lazily sitting on his porch, was taken by the sight of this old man wheezing and sweating to move the nearly immovable. "Hey, down there," the onlooker shouted, "why break your back for a worthless piece of stone?" Michelangelo stopped, wiped his brow, looked up at the scoffer, and replied, "Because there is an angel in that rock that wants to come out."

Perhaps the major work of the coming of the Holy Spirit at Pentecost was to "release the angel from the rock"—for the disciples and for the world they would die for. No sermon was preached, no one was healed, no one was baptized, no evangelism ever went on until the Holy Spirit was released on the disciples. Only in the Spirit's power could they set free the "angel" in the lives of the people who would accept them. And they could do that only because the "angel" in them had been liberated from the rock of their previous lives. Conversion is contagious.

Only as we ourselves are "clothed with power from on high" (Lk. 24:49) can we become a new people, a new community in the image and likeness of Jesus. Only then can the "angel come out of the rock," and we can become, in the words of St. Catherine of Siena, "another Christ."

—H. King Oehmig

He goes on to say that there are varieties of gifts, services, and activities, but it is the same Spirit, the same Lord, the same God who bestows and activates all the gifts for the common good. The gifts are derived from God's generosity, and are intended for service to God, not competitive use.

The gifts are many, and God perceives exactly what is needed to serve the needs of the entire community. Every individual is granted specific gifts, but no one can expect to receive all the gifts. Nor can anyone boast that any gift is superior to another.

The inventory of gifts (vv. 8-10) includes the wisdom to declare truth, as well as knowledge that might be needed in a particular situation.

There are gifts of faith, healing, miracles, prophecy, and discernment. There are those who are gifted with ecstatic speech, such as was evident on the Day of Pentecost. This gift is to be accompanied by the interpretation of that speech for the community.

All of these gifts are given freely by the Spirit to the corporate body. And the Church needs all of them, just as the physical body requires all its parts. All are one in Christ, since all were "baptized into one body ... all made to drink of one Spirit" (v. 13). Old divisions of Jew, Greek, slave, or free are cast aside in this new life of unity in the Spirit.

POINTS TO PONDER

1. As you read the passage from Acts, try to imagine the scene, as wind and fire appear to the disciples on the Day of Pentecost. What do you think some of their thoughts and reactions might have been at this time? Why do you think a tongue of fire rested on each individual present?

2. As you read all of the passages appointed for today, consider the following questions: What different aspects of the Holy Spirit are revealed in these readings? How is the Spirit received?

3. How are those who receive the Spirit empowered? What are those who receive the Spirit called to do as a result?

4. Today's Gospel is also about the giving of the Spirit. How would you define or describe the Holy Spirit? How have you experienced the Spirit in your own life?

5. In today's Epistle, Paul describes gifts of the Spirit. What are the gifts that you have received? How have you used these gifts?

HOLY, HOLY, HOLY

Genesis 1:1—2:4a; Psalm 8; 2 Corinthians 13:11-13; Matthew 28:16-20

"O Lord, our Sovereign, how majestic is your name in all the earth!" (Ps. 8:1). Our Psalm for today begins with a wonderful affirmation for Trinity Sunday—the only time in the Church Year when we commemorate a *doctrine.* Today we celebrate *one God in three Persons:* Creator, Redeemer, and Sanctifier.

The doctrine of the Trinity forms the foundation of our confession of faith expressed in the Nicene and Apostles' Creeds. Although it is implicit in the Scriptures, the Trinity as a doctrine never appears explicitly in the Bible. Rather, it grew out of the Christian experience of God as *Father, Son,* and *Holy Spirit.*

Ultimately, the Trinity is a mystery and a paradox—an awareness of how much more God is than we can ever begin to comprehend.

The Old Testament reading for today celebrates the actions of God the Father, Creator, and sustainer of the universe (1:1). But there are also allusions here to the Son and Spirit.

When God speaks, the Divine Word causes life to be. Jesus himself is God's *Word,* who was with the Father from the beginning (Jn. 1:1-3). The "wind from God," or *ruach* (v. 2) that swept over the unformed creation to give it coherent being, is understood as God's *Spirit,* active in creation.

God creates order out of the primal chaos on the first day by creating light to separate the day from the night (vv. 3-5). On the second day (vv. 6-8), God creates a dome called Sky to separate the waters above and below.

On the third day, God divides the dry land, Earth, from the waters of the Seas, so that the earth can bring forth vegetation and replenish itself (vv. 9-13).

The celestial lights are then set in the sky on the fourth day to order the days and nights, as well as to be signs for the seasons (vv. 14-19). On the fifth day, sea creatures and birds are created with God's blessing to multiply (vv. 20–23). Then the other living creatures, "cattle and creeping things and wild animals" of every kind, are added to the earth on the sixth day (vv. 24-25).

Also on this day, male and female human beings are created in God's image. As the last to be created, they are the crown of creation (v. 28). Everything in creation has been given into the care of humanity; but "dominion" has to do with insuring the well-being of the other creatures, not with exploitation or domination.

Then God viewed everything in creation and declared it *very good* (v. 31a). We are told that God "rested" on the seventh day: "So God blessed the seventh day and hallowed it" (2:3). The creation itself is a work of love.

The familiar Trinitarian understanding is expressed clearly in the disciples' command, or "Great Commission," in Matthew: "Go therefore and make disciples of all nations, baptizing them in the name of the Father and of the Son and of the Holy Spirit" (28:19).

PRAYER FOR THE DAY

Holy God, who by your gracious will have given us the confession of a true faith in the glory of the eternal Trinity: keep us steadfast in the Unity of Three Persons that we may forever continue in your service, O Father, the Creator; O Son, the Redeemer; and O Holy Spirit, the Sustainer, one God, now and forever. *Amen.*

On the Day of Resurrection, the angel at Jesus' tomb instructed Mary Magdalene and the other Mary to tell the disciples that *Jesus was raised from the dead* and that "he is going ahead of you to Galilee; there you will see him" (Mt. 28:7). Thus the eleven remaining disciples go to the mountain in Galilee to which Jesus had earlier directed them (Mt. 26:32).

Then when the disciples saw Jesus, they worshiped him; but there were some for whom the sight of the Risen Lord did not eliminate all uncertainties.

Jesus declares that "all authority in heaven and on earth has been given to me" (v. 18). He has repeatedly proclaimed his authority (9:6, 8; 11:27; 21:23-27), but here he does so as a prelude to this command. In the name of the authority that God delivered to Jesus, the disciples are to *go forth*.

And what are they called to do? First, they are to "make disciples of all nations." In the early ministry of Jesus, they were to go only to the "lost sheep of the house of Israel" (Mt. 10:6). But now the mission is to extend to the Gentiles as well.

They are to baptize in the name of the triune God, as the baptized confess their relationship to Father, Son, and Holy Spirit. They are to continue the teaching ministry of Jesus to the baptized, stressing obedience to the words of Jesus.

Finally, Jesus promises his continued presence with them as they carry out their mission. Jesus is always "Emmanuel"—*God with us* (Mt. 1:22-23).

In many ways this passage is a summary of the teachings on discipleship in Matthew's Gospel. God has given Jesus universal authority to commission the disciples to witness to the coming of God's Kingdom to the world.

The Apostle Paul, at the close of his second letter to the Corinthians, also uses the Trinitarian formula in the form of a blessing.

As the founder of the community at Corinth, Paul now serves to defend himself against those who attack his authority and his ministry.

In this portion of the letter he attempts to set the record straight about his apostleship, to end the dissention before he comes among them again. Thus Paul exhorts the Corinthians to reject wrongdoing and to do the will of God.

ON REFLECTION

One of the characteristics of the medieval Church was that certain feasts came to honor doctrines—rather than events in Scripture, or saints of high notoriety. The feast of the Holy Trinity became one such "festival of dogma." It came to be during the exile of the papacy in Avignon by Pope John XXII in 1334. Preachers ever since have been trying to figure out what to say on the subject. How can God be three, yet one—neither confounding the Persons nor dividing the substance of the Divine Being?

The conundrum brings to mind the story of a philosopher and a theologian who sit down on a park bench. The two immediately get into a dispute about the meaning of the universe. The theologian, in great frustration, tells the philosopher: "You resemble a blind man in a dark room looking for a black cat—which isn't there." "That may be," the philosopher replied, "but a theologian would have found it."

The word "God" for the early Church simply was not adequate. In Jesus, the believers experienced God—in a way that extended beyond simply his being a holy man or a prophet. He acted like God; he did things only God could do. Jesus then promised an "Advocate" or Comforter who would mediate to the community the powers of the coming age (Heb. 6:5). The Holy Spirit then comes as God's continuing, directing, sustaining Presence among the believing community. *God over us. God with us. God among us.* Yet one and the same God.

—H. King Oehmig

In this final paragraph of the letter, he encourages them "to put things in order" (13:11) and to live in peace and harmony with one another. To do so will be to realize the gift of God's love among them.

The closing verse invokes the grace of Jesus, the love of God, and the communion of the Holy Spirit. Paul's intent here is not to make a doctrinal statement, but to call attention to the healing, reconciling gifts of grace, love, and fellowship that come through faith in Jesus Christ.

POINTS TO PONDER

1. As you begin your discussion, read together the Apostles' Creed, the Nicene Creed, and the Athanasian Creed. What does our tradition tell us about the doctrine of the Trinity?

2. In Matthew 28:17, what was the response of the disciples when they saw Jesus? Why do you think "some doubted"?

3. The words that Jesus speaks in verses18-20 are known as the Great Commission. What does Jesus command the disciples to do here? By what authority are they to carry out this mission? How will they be empowered for these tasks?

4. How is the Church called to carry out this commission today? What is your own part in this ministry?

5. In the Old Testament reading for today (Gen. 1:1—2:4a), God is revealed as Creator. In the life of Jesus, we see God as Redeemer; and through the Holy Spirit, God is Sanctifier. How do you experience these various aspects of God in your own life?

Proper 1: See Epiphany 6; Proper 2: See Epiphany 7; Proper 3: See Epiphany 8

THE IMITATION OF CHRIST

Genesis 6:9-22; 7:24; 8:14-19; Psalm 46; Romans 1:16-17; 3:22b-28 (29-31); Matthew 7:21-29

In our Old Testament passage in Genesis 6 we read that God's judgment took the form of a devastating worldwide flood. This wiping out of all of humanity, except for one family, would be the seminal event leading to the advent of a new people under covenant with God.

"And God saw that the earth was corrupt" and filled with violence—how is it any different today? Here Noah is told the way to preserve himself and his wife, three sons, and their wives by building a survival ark of cypress wood. He is directed by God as to the exact measurements, creation of rooms, and the covering of pitch to keep it waterproof.

Into this ark of safety they are to place two of every living creature from upon the earth, and they are to store up food to keep them alive through the ordeal.

Noah, it is written, did all that God required of him. And at God's command the waters "swelled on the earth for one hundred fifty days" (7:24).

In the second month, on the twenty-seventh day of the month, the earth was again dry (8:14). Then God told Noah, "Get out of the ark, you and your wife, and your sons and your sons' wives." Then they were to bring out every living thing as well.

We read further on that Noah built an altar there to the Lord, offering burnt sacrifices of the correct animals, and thereby found God's favor, and received the promise that never again would the Lord God destroy the living creatures on the earth.

Barry J. Robinson writes: "When God finally says in this story, 'Never again!' it is not because of any change that the flood has wrought in the world that has made him say it, not because the terrible devastation it has caused has forced him to take pity on us. It is not even for the sake of one good man named Noah and all his family. It is because God has decided to act in a new way toward us, and, in short, to indulge his own grief and trouble for the sake of loving us as his very own no matter what."

The Psalmist in Psalm 46 expresses confident faith in God's protection: "The Lord of hosts is with us; the God of Jacob is our refuge" (vv. 7, 9). In the face of cosmic upheaval and natural catastrophe, the Lord is "our refuge and strength, a very present help in trouble" (v. 1).

When there is strife among the nations of the world, the Lord will make wars cease "to the end of the earth" (v. 9) and will destroy the weapons of destruction. Thus the people can rest assured: "Be still, and know that I am God!" (v. 10)—for all the earth exalts the Lord.

In today's Epistle, the Apostle Paul affirms that he is *not ashamed* of the Gospel—because it is the power of God for salvation to everyone who has faith. In fact, "The one who is righteous will live by faith" (1:17).

PRAYER FOR THE DAY

Almighty and all-loving God, you call us to be related by faith with you and through love with our neighbor: give us the inspiration not only to worship you, but also to do your will in the image and likeness of Jesus Christ, who, with the Holy Spirit, lives and reigns with you, one God, now and forever. *Amen.*

The way of life that follows God cannot be defined simply as performance of commandments. So Paul insists that God's way of putting people right with the Divine will has been revealed; and it has nothing to do with law.

"The righteousness of God through faith in Jesus Christ for all who believe" (v. 22a)—this is the Way. Try as we may, we fail to meet any proper standard of behavior. So Paul, like the prophets before him, declares that all of us have sinned, and that we make of our sin and failure a barrier that keeps us from God our Father.

But salvation comes to us in the person of Jesus. He came to endure the death that brings forgiveness—for all the sin that ever was or ever will be. This is God's free gift, if only we accept it.

How then can anyone boast? And how can anyone declare that he or she is justified by keeping the law, no matter how well? There is no law but the law of faith (v. 27b).

God is the God of all peoples through the same faith—not by keeping the letter of the law. Yet the law is still to be upheld in faith and obedience as our gift back to God.

Matthew's collection of the Lord's teachings, and the rather shorter compilation of Luke, conclude in much the same way. Human words have no real value unless the speaker lives in obedience to God's commandments.

To call Jesus Lord, to claim him as personal Savior, to declare that he is God's Anointed One—even to perform miracles in his name—is no passport into the Kingdom of heaven. The only way we can recognize Jesus as Lord is to act in accord with his teachings.

Jesus' Sermon on the Mount sets forth the requirements and the cost of discipleship. In Matthew's arrangement these sayings show the character of our Lord's ministry.

The value of performing miracles, such as prophesying or preaching in Christ's name, or casting out demons or performing miracles in his name, must be evaluated.

ON REFLECTION

The social critic, H. Richard Niebuhr, maintained that the Gospel always calls for love-in-action—what Jesus taught: "Not everyone who says to me, 'Lord, Lord,' will enter the kingdom of heaven, but only the one who does the will of my Father in heaven" (Mt. 7:21). "God nowhere commands love for its own sake," Niebuhr said.

It is not just for the sake of our neighbors that Jesus tells us to have a verb-centered faith. Bruce Barton in his book *The Man Nobody Knows* (Bobbs-Merrill, 1952) illustrates the point by citing two seas in Palestine. One sea is fresh and clear. Greenery lines its banks. Wildlife of all sorts and conditions live around this sea, and it teems with fish. People come to enjoy its beaches and take delight in the emerald waters for recreation. This is the Sea of Galilee. To the north, the Jordan River flows into it, and to the south, the River Jordan flows out of it.

Further south, there is another sea. The Jordan River empties onto it as well. But in this sea no fish can live, nor can wildlife thrive around its banks. Greenery is sparse. What accounts for the difference between the two bodies of water? The Sea of Galilee receives—but does not keep—the water that flows into it. In contrast, the other sea keeps every drop of water that reaches it. One is potent and alive—the other is stagnant. It keeps everything and gives nothing. It is called the Dead Sea.

—H. King Oehmig

They receive what worth they have from the manner of life of the prophet or exorcist who performs them.

Verses 22-23 present an imaginative description of the religion of those whose talk was without performance, whose worship was without work, and whose reliance was on what Dietrich Bonhoeffer called "cheap grace." Jesus told what these people might expect in their final judgment.

To call Jesus "Lord" means nothing unless the person who speaks of him thus is doing the will of Jesus' Father in heaven.

There follows here in Matthew 7 what many describe as a parable: the contrast between a house built on solid rock and one constructed on shifting sand. A house built on sand might stand until the rainy season came. But the wind and floods would then provide a true test of endurance. The house built on a rock stands for the performance of God's will, the activity that makes discipleship stable and secure amid the fluctuations of life.

POINTS TO PONDER

1. How did Noah's trust and obedience become woven into God's plan for humanity? How are we ourselves part of a new covenant of obedience toward God?

2. According to St. Paul in Romans, how is it that we are able to be in right relationship with God? What does this mean in the context of our daily life with Christ?

3. As you read the Gospel passage and Psalm 46, reflect on the imagery of the house built on a rock, and God as our refuge and strength. How do these metaphors (as well as other images in the Psalm) connect with your own experience of God?

4. According to the Gospel reading, who will be allowed to enter the Kingdom of heaven, and on what basis?

5. As you reflect on all of today's passages, what would you say are the foundations of your own belief?

THE POWER OF FAITH

Genesis 12:1-9; Psalm 33:1-12; Romans 4:13-25; Matthew 9:9-13, 18-26

Today's Gospel reading begins with the call of the tax collector Matthew, and the subsequent exchange between Jesus and the Pharisees on the appropriateness of *eating with so-called sinners*. Mark (2:13-17) and Luke (5:27-32) include similar accounts, but give the man's name as Levi, son of Alphaeus.

In Roman-controlled Palestine at that time, tax collecting was considered traitorous, as taxes supported the Roman occupation. For Jews, the practice was also considered blasphemous because a portion of the money collected was used to build pagan temples.

At each level, the contractor or collector expected to make a profit by charging whatever he wanted above what the Romans expected to collect from him. Thus these tax collectors were much despised and regarded as sinners.

All three Gospels place the call of Levi or Matthew immediately after the account of the paralyzed man who was brought to Jesus, and to whom the Lord's first word of healing was, "Your sins are forgiven" (Mt. 9:2). This leads to the declaration that "the Son of Man has authority on earth to forgive sins" (v. 6). Thus, the calling to God's service of a man considered to be among the worst of sinners is an obvious example of that right to forgive sins.

Jesus sees Matthew sitting at the tax booth and calls him to "Follow me" (Mt. 9:9). Matthew is a social and religious outcast. So it is seen as a disgrace that Jesus and his disciples share a meal with Matthew and *many* tax collectors and "sinners" (9:10).

To be at table with those considered to be sinners was to thwart religious custom and become ritually impure. Thus the Pharisees ask Jesus' disciples why their teacher eats with outcasts. Jesus replies that only the sick need a physician. Similarly, nobody needs God as much as those who have been lost or have separated themselves from the Lord.

By readily accepting the Lord's call to discipleship, Matthew can be seen in direct contrast to the members of the religious establishment who are offended by the offering of God's grace to all. Jesus presents a radically different understanding of forgiveness, and thereby redefines acceptable social boundaries.

The reading continues with two healing miracles which are also told in Mark 5:21-43 and Luke 8:40-56. However, in Matthew's version the accounts are shortened, and this serves to put more emphasis on the faith of the two main characters.

As Jesus finished speaking, a leader of the synagogue came with an urgent plea for Jesus to lay hands on his daughter who had just died. He expressed confidence that Jesus could restore her to life.

PRAYER FOR THE DAY

Gracious Lord, whose will is human well-being in its totality, open our hearts and minds to receive your never-failing love, that we may know the healing power of Jesus Christ, and be made well in mind, body, and spirit, in the peace of the Holy Spirit, who lives and reigns with you in glory everlasting. *Amen.*

As Jesus and his disciples departed with the distraught father, a woman in the crowd, who had suffered with hemorrhages for twelve years, touched his cloak. Her physical condition would have made her ritually unclean and unable to enter the synagogue. She knew that Jesus had healed others, and believed that if she could touch even the hem of his garment, his healing power would reach her.

When she touched him, Jesus assured her that her faith had made her well, and she was immediately healed. Being "made well" (v. 22) meant that spiritual healing had also taken place, and she could take up her place in the community again.

As Jesus approached the leader's house, flute players and a crowd had already gathered to begin the mourning. They laughed when Jesus told them they should go away, as the child was not dead. Once inside, Jesus took the girl by the hand, and she got up. "And the report of this spread throughout that district" (v. 26).

The Old Testament reading today also focuses on faith, with the call of Abram. This story marks the beginning of the saga of the patriarchs in Genesis that will continue through Proper 15.

God calls Abram to leave his ancestral home and kindred to go "to the land that I will show you" (Gen. 12:1). Abram's descendants will become a great nation and a light to the rest of the world. Furthermore, the other nations will be blessed or cursed by the Lord, depending upon their treatment of Abram and his descendants.

Abram does as God commands and takes his family to the land of Canaan, which the Lord promises to Abram's offspring. In response, Abram there built an altar and "invoked the name of the Lord" (v. 8).

The erection of the altar is an indication that this land belonged to God and not to the Canaanite gods. By calling upon the name of the Lord, Abram further acknowledged his faith and allegiance to God.

ON REFLECTION

Theologian Paul Tillich maintained that "faith" was not a belief in something based on a low degree of evidence. He said that "faith" was a consequence of being "grasped by God." By this definition, "faith" reached beyond reason. It was an experience of the New Being, mediated through Jesus, the Christ.

Matthew must have been grasped by God to follow Jesus—why else would he have left a good living and followed an itinerant, penniless rabbi? Tax collectors and sinners must have been "grasped by God" to sit at dinner with him when they would not be caught dead doing so with other religious figures. The leader of the synagogue must have been "grasped by God" to put his reputation on the line to ask a healer accused of being in league with the devil (Mk. 3:22) to come and heal his daughter. The woman with the issue of blood—who clearly violated social and cleanliness laws to touch the hem of his garment—must have been "grasped by God" as well, to be so bold.

"Those who are well have no need of a physician," Jesus tells the righteous, "but those who are sick" (Mt. 9:12). And these "sick" seem to be the ones who are "grasped by God" in the Gospels. They enter the New Being of the Kingdom of heaven.

In spite of everything they had done, they found Jesus' love unmotivated and spontaneous—and having nothing whatsoever to do with merit. Maybe that is why Jesus called these "sick ones" strangely blessed (Mt. 5:1).

—H. King Oehmig

The promises made to Abram came purely as an act of God's grace. Abram's faithful obedience in response was an enormous risk; but his actions resulted in future hope for the world, and served as a model for the generations to come.

The Apostle Paul, in today's portion of his letter to the Romans, writes of the nature of faith in terms of the *relationship between faith and the Law*. After his conversion, Paul came to understand that Torah cannot be a substitute for personal goodness and obedience to God.

The promise to Abraham centuries earlier depended upon faithful obedience rather than on a system of rules. Abraham received the promise because he trusted God, and that put him in right relationship with God. If being right with God depended upon Law, there would be no promise at all.

Law alone brings wrath. Faith or trust confirms the promise as God's gift of grace. Because Abraham had that kind of trust, he is the spiritual ancestor of all others who have that trust.

Abraham did indeed become the ancestor of many nations, as well as the father of all who trust in God. Thus, just as Abraham's faith "was reckoned to him as righteousness" (4:22), those who believe in the *Resurrection of Jesus Christ* for the *forgiveness of sins* will also be considered righteous.

The Psalm for today celebrates God's goodness and power with music and song. The word of the Lord is the source of life itself, and the Lord is faithful, righteous, and just. All the inhabitants of the earth stand before the Lord in awe. *Happy is the nation whose God is the Lord.*

POINTS TO PONDER

1. The first part of the Gospel reading focuses on the call of the tax collector Matthew to be a disciple of Jesus. Why do you think Jesus chose Matthew, and why do you think Matthew so readily responded to the call to "Follow me"?

2. Jesus openly socialized with those who were characterized as sinners by the leaders of the religious establishment, explaining that he came "to call not the righteous but sinners" (Mt. 9:13). What do these actions tell us about the ministry of Jesus?

3. The second part of the Gospel reading records two healing miracles. How are the leader of the synagogue and the woman with hemorrhages models of discipleship for us? How do these two incidents relate to the call of Matthew?

4. As you reflect on the call of Abram in the Old Testament reading, what are God's promises to Abram? How do you think Abram and his extended family might have felt as they left their homeland?

5. The Apostle Paul in his letter to the Romans praises Abraham as a man whose faith put him in right relationship with God. What do we learn about faith and trust in God from today's readings?

SENT OUT FOR MINISTRY

Genesis 18:1-15 (21:1-7); Psalm 116:1, 10-17; Romans 5:1-8; Matthew 9:35—10:8 (9-23)

The story of Abraham is centered on God's promises of land and descendants (Gen. 17:1-8). But Abraham's only son is the child of the slave girl Hagar. Furthermore, Abraham's wife Sarah is barren, and they are both past childbearing age.

Here the Lord appears to Abraham in the guise of three strangers who arrive at the entrance to his tent during the heat of the day. Although Abraham does not realize that his guests are heavenly beings, he immediately goes out to greet them and attends generously to their needs.

Sarah bakes cakes, and Abraham has his servants prepare a calf. Hospitality was an important social obligation in the ancient Near East, and God's people were to welcome strangers as a response to the hospitality shown by God.

As the three guests are eating, one of them makes a startling announcement: "I will surely return to you in due season, and your wife Sarah shall have a son" (18:10a). Sarah's response, as she listens from inside the tent, is to laugh at this ridiculous idea.

The word *laughed* here echoes *Isaac,* the name that will be given to her son. When the guest overhears her laughter he asks, "Is anything too wonderful for the Lord?" (18:14a).

Sarah's laughter echoes that of Abraham earlier (17:17); but Sarah is rebuked for her laughter, which is interpreted as a lack of faith.

But *the Lord's promise is fulfilled,* and Sarah does indeed bear a son. Isaac is circumcised in accordance with the covenant made between God and Abraham (17:9-14). Once again Sarah laughs, but this time in joy and thanksgiving for the miracle of the birth of her son.

In the Gospel passage, Jesus commissions the twelve disciples. The ministry to which he calls them is to be an extension of the preaching, teaching and healing ministry of Jesus himself (9:35).

As Jesus turns his attention to the crowds that follow him, he describes them as "harassed and helpless, like sheep without a shepherd" (Mt. 9:36). They are lost, vulnerable, and confused.

But here, as elsewhere in Matthew, Jesus has compassion for the crowds (14:14; 15:32; 20:34) and sees an opportunity for the message of God's Kingdom to be received. Indeed, the people are like a harvest waiting to be reaped. However, as there are not enough laborers, Jesus calls for prayers to the "Lord of the harvest" (9:38) to provide workers.

Thus Jesus summons his disciples and grants them authority over "unclean spirits" and the power to cure disease (10:1). Matthew then names the Apostles (10:2-4) as an indication that the circle of the Twelve is complete and that they are now ready for this ministry. An "apostle" is one who is sent, and this is the only time that this word appears in Matthew's Gospel.

PRAYER FOR THE DAY

Gracious God, so incline our hearts to follow where you lead, so fill us with your unfailing power and love, that we may boldly express the Gospel of Jesus Christ: that a great harvest of followers may come through the wisdom and winsomeness of your Holy Spirit, to your glory. *Amen.*

Other lists of the Apostles are found in Mark 3:16-19; Luke 6:14-16; and Acts 1:13, and are essentially the same, except that Luke-Acts includes Judas, son of James, instead of Thaddaeus. Matthew's listing is distinctive because the names are arranged in six pairs.

"Simon, also known as Peter" is always named first in recognition of his preeminent role as spokesman for the Apostles, as well as his initial calling along with his brother Andrew (4:18-20). Matthew's designation as "the tax collector" indicates that even though he was chosen by Jesus to serve as a disciple, he would still be considered a sinner and social outcast.

Simon the Cananaean is referred to as Simon the Zealot by Luke, which can mean he was part of a radical, suspect political revolutionary group. Finally, Judas Iscariot, identified as Jesus' betrayer, is always named last. All are fallible men with tremendous challenges ahead.

Jesus continues the commissioning with instructions in this "missionary discourse" (10:5-42). First he tells them that they are to minister only "to the lost sheep of the house of Israel" (10:6). Later, in his encounter with the Canaanite woman, Jesus will also tell her that he has been sent only to the "lost sheep of the house of Israel" (15:24).

In Matthew's Gospel the mission to the Gentiles begins with the "Great Commission" of the Risen Lord in 28:19. For Matthew the restoration of Israel was primary, from both historical and theological perspectives.

Like Jesus and John the Baptist (3:2; 4:17), the Apostles are to "proclaim the good news" of the nearness of the Kingdom (10:7). Likewise, they are to follow the example of the healing ministry of Jesus (10:8) as a manifestation of God's care and compassion for the world.

They are to give of these gifts without expecting pay. Furthermore, they are to go out into the world without supplies or spare

ON REFLECTION

There are three questions to ask when reading Scripture: what does the text reveal about the character of God; what does the reading say about human nature; and, finally, what happens when God's activity and human nature intersect?

Judging from the Gospel reading for today, we can see through the ministry of Jesus—as he goes about to all the cities and villages teaching and healing—that God's nature is active, not passive. In Jesus, God is "on the make." The Divine does not wait for people to show up, but pursues us like "the hound of heaven."

What does the text tell us about human nature? This doesn't go down so well with us moderns. Jesus says that the crowds were like "sheep without a shepherd." Who today wants to be known as a "sheep"—defenseless, passive, helpless—and eventually mutton for the slaughterhouse? Who doesn't want to be independent, in control, in charge? No wonder it was the least, the lost, and the last who, for the most part, responded to Jesus.

And what does the text tell us about the intersection of the Divine and human spheres? Annie Dillard perhaps said it best: "Religion is for outcasts and victims; Jesus makes that clear ... our lives are complex. There are many things we must consider before we go considering any lilies. We are in charge; we are running things in a world we made. We are no one's little flock." The work of the Gospel, then and now, is never finished.

—H. King Oehmig

clothes, expecting food and shelter from those who heed their message.

Where their message of God's peace is not received, they are to shake off the dust of that community and move on. And there is a dire warning for those who reject the word (vv. 14-15). Jesus warns that they will encounter resistance, division, and persecution.

But they can trust that God's Spirit will be with them and that they will triumph in the end, since they will not have carried out their mission throughout Israel "before the Son of Man comes" (10:23).

In the letter to the Romans, Paul addresses the question of the suffering endured by those who follow Jesus. Because we are justified—are in right relationship with God—through *faith,* we therefore live in God's grace and peace. Thus we can be assured—can boast—that *God will grant salvation.*

And our suffering will ultimately bring hope "because God's love has been poured into our hearts through the Holy Spirit" (5:5). This love is manifested in Christ's saving death at a time when we were "weak" to accomplish liberation from the power of sin and death. Thus we can see ourselves too as the "ungodly" (v. 6).

Paul goes on to say that it is rare to give one's life for a righteous person; but God's boundless love is demonstrated by the fact that Jesus died for us "while we still were sinners" (v. 8).

In Psalm 116, the Psalmist says that, while it is not possible to repay the Lord for the Divine help, he is God's servant. He will offer the sacrifice of thanksgiving in the name of the Lord and fulfill his vows in the Lord's house. *Hallelujah!*

POINTS TO PONDER

1. In Matthew 9:36, we read that Jesus had compassion on the crowds who followed him. How are these people described, and how can we identify with them in our daily lives?

2. Jesus tells the disciples that "the harvest is plentiful, but the laborers are few" (v. 37). What is the harvest that Jesus speaks of here?

3. As Jesus sent the disciples out, what did he commission them to do (10:1, 5-8)? In the further instructions in verses 9-15, how were they to prepare for this ministry?

4. How do you think the disciples might have felt as they set out on their mission? How does their calling relate to the ministry of Jesus himself?

5. Carefully read the names of the Apostles in 10:2-4 and imagine them as individuals. What do you think the joys and challenges of these followers of Jesus might have been? What do we continue to learn from them today?

TEACHINGS ON THE KINGDOM

Genesis 21:8-21; Psalm 86:1-10, 16-17; Romans 6:1b-11; Matthew 10:24-39

The Lord promised Abraham a legacy of land and descendants (Gen. 17:1-8); but when Abraham's wife Sarah did not bear a child, Sarah gave him her Egyptian slave girl, Hagar. In the ancient Near East, surrogate pregnancy was an accepted practice, and the offspring of Hagar would be considered Sarah's. Thus Hagar conceived and bore a son named Ishmael, who was also promised future descendants (Gen. 16:1-15).

But there was jealousy between Hagar and Sarah, and when Sarah finally bore her own son, Isaac, the tension increased. To insure that Isaac would be Abraham's sole heir, Sarah went to Abraham and demanded that he cast out Hagar and Ishmael.

Abraham was greatly distressed by Sarah's demand, but the Lord told him to do as Sarah asked, adding further assurance that *Abraham's offspring will be named through Isaac, but Ishmael will also share in the promises* made to Abraham and become the father of a great nation. Isaac was the son of the promise, but God would insure the well-being of Ishmael as well.

Thus Abraham gave Hagar provisions of bread and water and sent her and Ishmael out into the wilderness of Beer-sheba. When their provisions ran out, Hagar and her son faced certain death. Hagar could not bear to witness the suffering of her child, so she laid him in the shade and waited a short distance away.

As she wept in her despair, an angel of the Lord called to Hagar not to be afraid for the life of her son, for " … I will make a great nation of him" (21:18). Then Hagar's eyes were opened, and she saw a well nearby.

God continued to be with the child as he grew into manhood, and Hagar found him a wife in Egypt. Thus the Lord's promises to both Hagar and Abraham were fulfilled; and through Isaac and Ishmael, Abraham became the father of two great nations.

In today's Gospel, Jesus has commissioned the disciples to carry out the ministry that he himself began, to *proclaim the Good News* of God's Kingdom, cure the sick, and raise the dead (Mt. 10:7). He now continues his charge to them by warning of the suffering and persecution that lies ahead because they are his followers.

Jesus declares in these words from the "Missionary Discourse" that the disciples can expect the same trials he has endured, since "a disciple is not above the teacher, nor a slave above the master" (v. 24). Therefore, if the enemies of Jesus accuse him of acting on behalf of Satan, how much more will they slander his disciples?

This is the hard reality of discipleship; but the disciples are not to be intimidated. The truth will prevail, and the lies of enemies will ultimately be exposed. The teachings that Jesus has given them in private are to be proclaimed "from the house-tops" (v. 27) so that all can hear.

PRAYER FOR THE DAY

Gracious and everlasting God, who in Jesus Christ came not to be served but to serve, and to give his life as a ransom for many, so clothe us in your Holy Spirit that when we face adversity or persecution for the sake of the Gospel, we may remain love bearers and faithful servants of your unfailing goodness until the Day of the Lord. *Amen.*

Jesus adds a further assurance: "Do not fear those who kill the body, but cannot kill the soul" (v. 28a). Instead, they are to be in awe of God, who alone controls both body and soul, and who loves them so that even the hairs of their head are numbered (v. 30).

Thus they are not to be afraid in times of trial, for they can always depend upon God's care. The Lord knows when a sparrow falls to the ground, and they are of more value than "many sparrows" (v. 31).

Jesus says that he will acknowledge before the Lord those who have been loyal to him. Likewise he will deny those who do not follow his example and give wholeheartedly of themselves for God's Kingdom.

When Jesus declares "I have not come to bring peace, but a sword" (v. 34), he is not calling for armed conflict. The radical message of the Gospel challenges the established order, resulting in dissention and conflict.

Such divisions will be felt most severely among family members. Alluding to Micah 7: 6-7, Jesus calls for complete loyalty to him, for salvation comes from the Lord alone.

Those who follow Christ in single-minded devotion must understand that such a choice may result in a painful rending of family ties. To honor one's parents was a primary commandment (Ex. 20: 12; Deut. 5:16); however, Jesus raises the question of priorities. One must not love family over Jesus.

Jesus also warns that the decision for discipleship must include the possibility of suffering and death; therefore his followers must be willing to "take up the cross" (v. 38). These words took on added significance after the death and Resurrection of Jesus.

Jesus tells them not to be afraid (vv. 26, 28, 31) and holds out the promise of God's presence and care. Ultimately, those who lose their life for the sake of the Gospel will find true life—now and for eternity.

ON REFLECTION

Conventional wisdom says that, in general, clergy see people at their best. Lawyers see people at their worst; and doctors see them as they are. Maybe for that reason a lawyer friend knew what he was talking about when he said: "No good deed goes unpunished." Help somebody out, and they try to sue you—or do you in. Give someone a compliment, and they bite your head off. We all know about "biting the hand that feeds you"—as the one doing the biting or as the one being bit.

The disciples are sent out by Jesus to do nothing but make present God's liberating power among the populace. They heal the sick, preach release to the captives, and offer liberation to the oppressed. And what should they expect in return? A never-ending litany of alleluias? High-fives at every stop? A nice, comfortable retirement? Hardly. Jesus had already told them that he was sending them out as "sheep among wolves" (Mt. 10:16) … and now they are finding out firsthand how "a disciple is not above his teacher" (10:24). They will be rejected, flogged, vilified, called workers of the devil—just as Jesus was. No good deed goes unpunished for long.

So why did they do it? Why did they put up with so much pain and suffering to follow Jesus? Certainly they were not spiritual masochists. I suspect it was because the disciples had been grasped by a Divine love so wondrous and so powerful that whatever hardships came along paled in comparison to what St. Paul called "the riches of his grace that he lavished on us" (Eph. 1: 7-8).

—H. King Oehmig

Paul had proclaimed that through the sacrificial death of Christ we have all received the gift of God's grace and have "peace with God through our Lord Jesus Christ" (Rom. 5: 1).

This then raises the question of "Should we continue in sin in order that grace may abound?" (6:1b). Does it really matter what we do if God's grace and forgiveness are assured?

Paul's response is an emphatic no! We have been unified with Christ through our baptism, and to be baptized into Christ is to be baptized into his death.

This means the death of our old self, so that we are no longer slaves to sin and may partake of a new life in Christ. "But if we have died with Christ, we believe that we will also live with him" (v. 8).

Life in Christ is more powerful than death itself; and just as death no longer has dominion over the Risen Christ, sin also has no sway over the life of those who believe in him. Thus the reason that one should not continue in sin is found in verse 11. In our life in Christ we are in fact "dead to sin and alive to God in Christ Jesus."

Our Psalm today, Psalm 86, is an appeal for protection from affliction and from enemies. The suppliant acknowledges a need for Divine compassion, even while giving thanks for past deliverance.

God's greatness is more than might. No other god may be compared with the Psalmist's Lord, whose majesty is kindness and truth. "You, O Lord, have helped me and comforted me" (v. 17b).

POINTS TO PONDER

1. How does Jesus characterize the life of a disciple in the Gospel passage?

2. Although Jesus was clear about the perils of discipleship, he also told his disciples not to be afraid. What are the specific fears he identifies, and what assurances does he offer to calm their fears?

3. Jesus challenges his followers to "take up the cross and follow me" (Mt. 10: 38). What do you think these words might have meant to those who heard Jesus speak?

4. What do these words of Jesus suggest about establishing priorities in our lives?

5. Jesus speaks of losing and finding one's life (v. 39); and in the letter to the Romans, Paul writes of dying and living with Christ. What do we need to let go of in order to live fully in Christ?

_____

_____

_____

_____

_____

_____

ON WELCOMING GRACE

Genesis 22:1-14; Psalm 13; Romans 6:12-23; Matthew 10:40-42

The readings for today call attention to the tension between the costs and promises of following God's call.

When God called Abraham, he was promised a future of land and descendants (Gen. 17:1-8). Abraham trusted in God's promises by leaving his Chaldean homeland at God's command. Then, finally, Abraham and his wife Sarah had a son, Isaac. But their future was put in jeopardy as God called Abraham to do the unthinkable—to offer his beloved only son as a sacrifice.

God's command to take Isaac and go to a mountain "that I shall show you" (22:2) connects this story with God's original call to Abraham to go "to the land that I will show you" (12:1). Thus Abraham, the boy Isaac, and two servants set out on a journey. On the third day, they reached their destination.

From there, Abraham and Isaac went on by themselves, leaving the two servants behind (v. 5). By saying *"we"* will be coming back, Abraham either hides his purpose from his servants or expresses his inexplicable faith in God's promises.

As they walk along together, Isaac carrying the wood and Abraham bringing the knife and fire, Isaac asks "Where is the lamb for a burnt offering?" (v. 7). Abraham's response that God will provide the lamb (v. 8) is a crucial moment, as Abraham affirms his faith in the providence of God.

On Mt. Moriah, Abraham builds an altar and lays out the wood. He binds Isaac as one would bind a sheep, and lays his son on the wood. The text mentions no resistance from Isaac.

Only when Abraham raises his hand and takes up the knife to kill his son does the angel of the Lord call to Abraham to stop (v. 12). The word "fear" is used here in the sense of obedience to the Divine will.

Afterward Abraham sees a ram caught in a thicket and offers it instead of Isaac. Thus Abraham calls the place of sacrifice "The Lord will provide" (v. 14) in recognition of God's grace and generosity.

"God tested Abraham." In the rabbinic tradition, this was because God knew that Abraham would pass the test and that his faith would serve as an example for future generations. Later on the Apostle Paul would write that "God is faithful," and will not let believers be tested beyond their strength, but with the testing will also provide the way out—"so that you may be able to endure it" (1 Cor. 10:13).

Throughout Matthew's missionary discourse (10:1-42), Jesus has warned his Apostles of the costs of discipleship. In the conclusion to the discourse, Jesus speaks of rewards as well.

PRAYER FOR THE DAY

Wonderful and holy God, who has spoken through prophets and disciples to bring people out of darkness and into your all-embracing Light, clothe us with wisdom and boldness from on high to be effective agents of Jesus Christ, so that all people may know the Gospel by the working of the Holy Spirit, who lives and reigns with you, one God, forever and ever. *Amen.*

As the Apostles carry out their mission, they will be rejected in some places but welcomed in others. They will travel as emissaries of Jesus; thus, those who welcome the Apostles will welcome Jesus—and God. This comes from the tradition that accepting a king's emissary is the same as welcoming the king himself. The mission of the Apostles is inextricably connected to Jesus as the one who sent them.

As representatives of Christ today, we bring Christ to the world, reflecting all that Christ means as the revelation of the Father.

There are rewards for receiving Apostles, prophets, righteous persons, and "little ones." *Prophets* are those who speak for God. To welcome a prophet is to receive a prophet's reward.

Righteous people are mature in their faith, living in obedience to God. To welcome a righteous person is to reap the reward of the righteous.

The term *"little ones"* (v. 42) could have a variety of meanings; but as used later (18: 6,10, 14), the term could apply to new converts or new disciples. Thus the simple gesture of giving "even a cup of water to one of these little ones in the name of a disciple" is significant and will be rewarded.

Those sent out by God will be cared for by others, and they must learn to receive graciously, as well as to give. We must allow others to use their gifts with the knowledge that *all gifts come from God.*

Though the mission of the disciples as described by Jesus is fraught with danger, uncertainty, pain and dissention, there is also the promise of God's continual presence, sustaining and nurturing them.

In the Epistle, Paul continues his response to the question of "Should we continue in sin in order that grace may abound?" (6:1b).

ON REFLECTION

"Agentry" is a key concept in the understanding of discipleship. That is, the "agent" of Jesus, who went out in his name, was not just a "representative" of the Lord, but *the personal embodiment of him and his authority.* When someone met a disciple of Jesus, it constituted encountering Jesus himself. "Whoever welcomes you," Jesus said, "welcomes me, and whoever welcomes me welcomes the one who sent me" (Mt. 10:40).

For better or worse, for richer or poorer, in sickness and in health—Jesus is judged through his "agents." Our witness establishes not only who *we* are, but also who *Jesus* is—and what level of efficacy the Gospel has. Our level of commitment—our willingness to be transformed by the Spirit—validates Christianity in the world.

Next, Jesus shows us here that the Gospel is best communicated *relationally* rather than by *propositions.* The Gospel was "caught" naturally from person to person—a kind of "viral" model of evangelism through the Holy Spirit.

Think about it from the perspective of your own life, and it becomes obvious. Did a *proposition* get you out of bed, dress you, feed you breakfast, and drive you to church? Did dogma present you to be baptized? Did a proposition vow to support and uphold you throughout the peaks and valleys of your lifelong walk of faith? The point does not need to be belabored. If the church is to exist—or thrive—it will be through the agents of Jesus. Folks just like you and me.

—H. King Oehmig

In the verses for today, Paul declares that because of grace, sin will no longer have dominion over us (v. 14). For Paul, sin was a real and dangerous force; thus, to be freed from sin was more than just resisting negative inclinations (v. 12).

Paul's readers have a choice between being slaves to sin that leads to death, or slaves to obedience that leads to righteousness. Paul gives thanks that they "have become obedient from the heart to the form of teaching" to which they were entrusted (v. 17).

To be freed from sin and enslaved to God (righteousness) leads to sanctification and eternal life. "For the wages of sin is death, but the free gift of God is eternal life in Christ Jesus our Lord" (v. 23).

Psalm 13 laments God's apparent absence—but without any sense that the sins of the people have caused the separation. Rather it is the triumph of an enemy that has made it appear as though the Lord's face is hidden.

Surely God can give light to the eyes of those who seek God's truth. Therefore the Psalmist can be joyful because of God's saving help; he will sing to the Lord because God deals generously with those who are true servants. Thus "my heart shall rejoice in your salvation" (v. 5).

POINTS TO PONDER

1. What are the costs, as well as the rewards, of *discipleship* as expressed in today's Gospel passage?

2. What does it mean to "welcome" Jesus and the one who sent him?

3. What do you think is the "reward" that Jesus speaks of here?

4. What do these verses suggest to us about establishing priorities in our lives? How can we follow Jesus with single-minded devotion, and yet not neglect our other obligations to our families and community?

5. In the Epistle for today (Rom. 6:12-23) what does it mean to be "instruments of righteousness"? How do Paul's words relate to those of Jesus in the Gospel? How have you experienced this new life in Christ?

THE YOKE OF JESUS

Genesis 24:34-38, 42-49, 58-67; Psalm 45:11-18; Romans 7:15-25a;
Matthew 11:16-19, 25-30

The story of the second generation of the patriarchs continues with the quest for a wife for Abraham's son Isaac. Abraham's wife Sarah has died (Gen. 23:1-3), and Abraham himself is "advanced in years" (24:1). Thus he binds his most trusted servant to a solemn oath to find a bride for Isaac from among his kinsmen in Haran (24:2-9).

The unnamed servant faithfully sets out with an entourage of camels laden with gifts for the future bride and her family. When he arrives in Nahor, he stops at the well and prays that the woman who offers water to him and his camels will be God's chosen one (24:12-14).

When a beautiful young woman named Rebekah gives him a drink, with enough for all ten camels, he knows his prayer is answered. Moreover, she is the daughter of Abraham's nephew Bethuel. The generous hospitality that Rebekah offers the servant is similar to that of Abraham to the three strangers at the oaks of Mamre (Gen. 18:1-8).

The servant recounts the story of his meeting with Rebekah to her kinsmen and asks that she accompany him back to Canaan to become Isaac's wife. He emphasizes the prosperity of his master Abraham, whose wealth will now be inherited by his son.

When asked, Rebekah acquiesces to go with the servant. The blessing she receives from her family that she "become thousands of myriads" (v. 60) is reminiscent of the Lord's promise to Abraham of numerous descendants (Gen. 15:5). In the final scene, as Rebekah and her caravan approach her new homeland, they see Isaac in the distance. We read that Isaac took Rebekah for his beloved wife and "was comforted after his mother's death" (v. 67).

The story of Isaac is, in many ways, more about Rebekah than Isaac himself, who remains a passive figure. The saga comes full circle as Rebekah leaves her home to go to an unknown land, just as Abraham had done (Gen. 12:1). Here we see the generational repetition of the themes of blessing and prosperity, as well as the steadfast love, faithfulness, and guidance of the Lord.

Jesus, after giving instructions to the Twelve on discipleship (Mt. 10:1-42), continued his ministry of teaching, healing, and proclaiming God's Kingdom. However, Jesus and his message were attacked and opposed, especially by those in positions of power and authority.

He compares them to children who refuse to join in each other's games. When one group played the flute—i.e., music for a wedding—the other would not dance. When one group wailed, as at a funeral, the others refused to mourn.

When John the Baptist came, he was dismissed as being possessed by demons because of his ascetic lifestyle and message of repentance. Jesus himself was accused of gluttony and drunkenness because he shared table fellowship with those considered outcasts and sinners.

PRAYER FOR THE DAY

Immortal and holy God, you alone can order our unruly wills and infuse our souls with the law of love: grant that by the indwelling of your Holy Spirit we may know the yoke of the Gospel of Jesus Christ to be the light and source of true rest, that we may fulfill our callings with freshness and gladness of heart, to your honor and glory. *Amen.*

But eventually, Jesus will be vindicated by his deeds, and he offers a public prayer of thanksgiving to God who has hidden these things from the wise and the intelligent and "revealed them to infants" (11:25b).

For Matthew "these things" are the mighty acts and works of healing that Jesus has done (4:23; 9:35; 11:1). The disciples have also been given authority to do these things (10:1). However, it is not so much the works themselves that have been "hidden" but rather their source and significance. The comprehension of these actions is a matter of faith.

In contrast is the unconditional faith of those Jesus refers to as "infants"—his disciples and others who comprehend the significance of his ministry. (Compare his use of "little ones" in Mt. 10:42.) What counts is not their intellect and education or any other distinguishing features, but their belief, trust, and commitment. Jesus adds in verse 26 that this is all a part of God's gracious plan.

Jesus also declares that he is God's chosen delegate to whom "all things have been handed over" (v. 27). Jesus is the revealer of God. God alone knows the true character of Jesus, and only God can reveal him. Likewise, only Jesus can reveal God to human beings.

Jesus then extends an invitation to *"all* you that are weary and are carrying heavy burdens" (v. 28)—the weight of guilt residing in mind, body, and spirit. By responding to the call of Jesus, they will find "rest" or salvation in contrast to the heavy burdens of the teachings of the scribes and Pharisees (Mt. 23:4).

Jesus further invites them to "take my yoke upon you, and learn from me" (v. 29). The image here is of two animals harnessed together in order to make the heaviest burdens possible to bear.

In the Jewish tradition, the yoke also represented the wisdom of Torah (Sir. 51:26). In this way, Jesus calls his listeners to learn from him, for "I am gentle and humble in heart, and you will find rest for your souls" (v. 29).

ON REFLECTION

Woody Allen in his work *Without Feathers* (Ballantine Books, 1986) adds a note of "reality" to Isaiah's idealized state of the world reflected in the Day of the Lord, when the lion and calf would lie down together in oneness (11:6). Allen says, "The lion and the calf shall lie down together, but the calf won't get any sleep." How true.

Rabbi Joseph Telushkin in his work *Jewish Humor* (Harper, 1998) tells a similar tale. A man visits a zoo and stares into the lion's cage, where he sees a lion and a calf lying down together. Amazed, the man calls over an attendant and asks, "How long have you had a lion and a calf in a cage together?" The attendant says, "Over a year already." "How do you do it?" the incredulous man asks. "It's easy," answers the attendant. "Every morning we put in a new calf."

One way or another, by living in this world that has yet to experience the fullness of Isaiah's "peaceable kingdom"—where the unlike lie down together—we will get banged up. Everybody. So the question naturally ensues: where do we find comfort in the world? Food? Alcohol? Sex? Drugs? A sunny beach? A good movie? All can satisfy momentarily. But lasting comfort and rest that renews the body and feeds the soul—Jesus says that belongs to him.

Just come. You, worn out and beat up by the world, *come.* Learn from him and take on his yoke—and you will find a rest that Ambien cannot begin to touch.

—H. King Oehmig

The Apostle Paul speaks of a specific burden in Romans 7, and the description of his own internal conflict strikes a chord with believers in any age.

To an intense degree, Paul was aware of a struggle going on within him. It was a tug and pull between the *reason* by which his conscious mind sought to rule his life and *unconscious impulses* that demanded expression (v. 21). "I do not understand my own actions. For I do not do what I want, but I do the very thing I hate" (v. 15).

Sin is pictured here as a powerful force in which the individual is torn between what is known to be right behavior and the sin that is so compelling.

Although Paul acknowledges that he delights in the Lord inwardly (v. 22), his body can and will continually make him captive to the law of sin that is the condition of human beings on this earth. "Wretched man that I am! Who will rescue me from this body of death?" (v. 24).

Yet the answer also comes: it is God in Jesus Christ who brings deliverance from this form of slavery. Thanks be to God, Jesus provides us victory over evil.

POINTS TO PONDER

1. In verse 25 of Matthew 11, Jesus offers thanks for God's revelation to "infants." What is suggested here about the connection between worldly wisdom and true faith?

2. According to verse 27, how can we know God? How has God come to be a reality in your own life?

3. What is the relationship between God and Jesus as revealed here?

4. In verse 29, Jesus promises "rest" for those who are weary and carry heavy burdens. How would you describe this "rest"? Discuss the meaning of the "yoke" in verses 29–30. How is the yoke of Jesus easy? What does it mean to be gentle and humble in our world today?

5. Read the Epistle for today in Romans 7. What is the burden that Paul carries here? How does he find resolution for this conflict? How are Paul's struggles similar to your own?

SOWING THE GOSPEL EVERYWHERE

Genesis 25:19-34; Psalm 119:105-112; Romans 8:1-11; Matthew 13:1-9, 18-23

The story of Jacob, the third generation of the patriarchs, begins with the theme of barrenness, and is filled with deception and strife. Like Sarah before her, Rebekah is unable to conceive a child. Yet again it would seem that the Lord's promises to Abraham of land and descendants are in danger.

Finally, Isaac offered prayers to the Lord, and Rebekah became pregnant. New life comes from God, who once again insures the future of this family.

The pregnancy itself was not an easy one, foretelling the conflict that will pursue Jacob all his life. In fact, Rebekah was carrying two children who "struggled together within her." Thus she prayed to the Lord in despair: "If it is to be this way, why do I live?" (v. 22).

The response of God to Rebekah's plea in verse 23 is an oracle foreshadowing the entire life of Jacob. The two sons in Rebekah's womb represent divided nations, and the older son will serve the younger. The elder's entitlements are to be overturned, but no reason is given. And Jacob, despite his favored status, would employ lifelong deception to gain the upper hand.

The firstborn child was named Esau, indicating his relationship to Edom and Seir (Gen. 36:9). Jacob was born grasping his older brother's heel, already trying to gain his own advantage. Esau was a hunter, a "man of the field" (v. 27) who was favored by his father Isaac; while Jacob, a "quiet man, living in tents" (v. 27) was the favorite son of Rebekah.

The narrative moves abruptly to a scene in which the truth of the birth oracle is revealed (vv. 29-34).

One day Esau came in hungry from the fields and asked Jacob for some of the stew he was preparing. Jacob was willing to share his food, but first he bargained with Esau for his birthright. Esau was more concerned with fulfilling his present needs than keeping his future secure. The text tells us that Esau "despised his birthright" (v. 34)—treated this privilege as something of no worth.

Thus what was promised to Jacob by God in the oracle becomes a reality through the wiles of Jacob himself. This is a pattern that will be repeated throughout his life.

The Third Discourse of Matthew chapter 13 consists of a number of parables on why some hear and accept the Gospel, while others reject it. This was an issue during the ministry of Jesus and continues to perplex the Church even now.

Today's reading includes the Parable of the Sower (vv. 3-8) and its interpretation (vv. 18-23). Jesus describes four kinds of soil that illustrate the different responses to the good news of God's Kingdom fulfilled through him. Although it is referred to as the Parable of the Sower (cf Mk. 4:1-9; Lk. 8:4-8), the story is actually about the soil in which the seeds are planted.

PRAYER FOR THE DAY

O God, holy and mighty One, so incline the hearts of your people of faith to spread your message of healing love that those who do not know you, or love you, may come into the fellowship of grace through Jesus Christ our Lord, who with you and the Holy Spirit lives and reigns, one God, in life everlasting. *Amen.*

The seeds themselves are good and represent the teachings of Jesus. It is the soil in which they are sown that determines what kind of harvest they bring forth.

As the passage opens, Jesus was so pressed by the crowds that he retreated to a boat anchored on the shore of the Sea of Galilee. It was the Sabbath Day, and tensions with the guardians of a purified Judaism had earlier boiled over into open confrontation (12:1-45).

As he began to speak, Jesus employed the familiar image of a farmer sowing seed. As the seeds are scattered in a wide arc, some fall on the path to be eaten by the birds. This situation is akin to those who hear the Word of the Kingdom but do not understand it. Thus "the evil one" comes and snatches it out of their hearts (13:4, 19).

In the second illustration (vv. 5-6, 20-21), some seeds fall on rocky ground. These seeds spring up quickly; but without sufficient depth of soil to put down roots, the new plants are scorched by the sun.

They represent individuals who initially respond eagerly to the Gospel, but soon fall away "when trouble or persecution arises" (v. 21).

Then there are the seeds that fall among thorns, which choke them out (vv. 7, 22). These seeds are like those who hear the word, but outside concerns and the desire for riches soon lure them away.

Finally, there are the seeds that fall in good soil and bring forth an abundant harvest (vv. 8, 23). Hearing and understanding the good news of the Kingdom as proclaimed by Jesus results in bountiful lives of discipleship. The hundredfold yield calls attention to God's extravagance that will result from the Gospel message of Jesus. As Jesus declared earlier: "You will know them by their fruits" (Mt. 7:16).

Jesus ends the parable with an emphatic "Let anyone with ears listen!" (v. 9). Even when it seems that seed is being "wasted," the proclamation of the Kingdom of God *will* yield success.

ON REFLECTION

Jesus was not a theologian—at least in the way we moderns conceive of it. He held no advanced degrees in divinity. There was no record of his studying under a renowned rabbi such as Gamaliel in Jerusalem. He was not an expert on doctrine, nor was he a "scholastic" thinker. He had not been ordained—or authorized—by any established ecclesiastical body to teach. All of this brought forth the ire of those who had such authorization (Mk. 6:1-3).

Jesus was a public storyteller—an extraordinary one, at that. He used an economy of words and vividness of description to *show*, not *tell*, people about the Kingdom of heaven. All of these short stories were hardly spectral, but rather were drawn from ordinary life. A lost coin. Weeds in a field. A net full of fish. And then there is the one for today: the Parable of the Sower.

If there were ever any question about whether Jesus was something other than a carpenter, this should answer it. What farmer who wanted to stay in business would broadcast seed like this—flinging it helter-skelter over ground that offered no chance of germination?

Only a God of unlimited love, of overflowing abundance, of uncalculating grace would be so profligate, Jesus is telling us. And this God is doing so in Jesus. Which leaves the listener with the question that cuts to the chase: *What kind of ground are we?* Thorny? Stony? Arid? I suspect if we offer even a tiny bit of topsoil to Jesus, the seed planted will be a harvest beyond anything we could ask for or imagine.

—H. King Oehmig

In the portion of the letter to the Romans for today, Paul begins with a reminder of God's action in Christ Jesus, through whom humanity has been freed from sin and death. By becoming fully human, Jesus, once and for all, "condemned sin in the flesh" (8:3).

Paul goes on to draw a contrast between two opposing ways of life that reflect two different relationships with God. Those who choose to live "according to the flesh" are controlled by sin and are in rebellion against God and God's law. Such a life leads to death.

In contrast, those who live "according to the Spirit" are under the rule of God, which brings renewal of life and peace. God's life-giving Spirit dwells within them.

Through Christ's work of setting us free from the bondage of sin and death, we live no longer in the flesh but in the Spirit (v. 9).

Indeed, Paul declares that we cannot truly belong to Christ apart from the Spirit. "Anyone who does not have the Spirit of Christ does not belong to him" (v. 9b).

If we are in the Spirit, we have new life through Christ, and are enabled to renounce the ways of sin that rebel against God's will: "He who raised Christ from the dead will give life to your mortal bodies also through his Spirit that dwells in you" (v. 11).

While Paul calls us to live in God's Spirit, the verses of the Psalm for today proclaim the joy of following God's decrees, which provide protection and a moral guide to life. "Your word is a lamp to my feet and a light to my path" (119:105).

POINTS TO PONDER

1. As you read the Parable of the Sower in the Gospel passage, what are the hazards that prevent the seeds from growing?

2. What are some of the factors in your own life that interfere with your spiritual growth?

3. What constitutes good soil for growth? How can we help prepare rich, fertile soil for God's Word? What implications for evangelism and the mission of the Church do we find here?

4. In Matthew 13:18-23, Jesus gives an explanation for the meaning of the parable. What is the central message of this parable for you personally?

5. The Gospel parable speaks of how seeds come to life and bear fruit. In the Epistle reading for today, the Apostle Paul speaks in a similar manner of life in the Spirit. What are the fruits of life in the Spirit?

THE TEACHING ON WEEDS

Genesis 28:10-19a; Psalm 139:1-11, 22-23; Romans 8:12-25; Matthew 13:24-30, 36-43

Jacob, after cheating his older twin Esau out of his birthright (Gen. 25:29-34), plots with his mother Rebekah to steal Esau's paternal blessing (27:1-40). When Esau learns that he has once again been cheated by Jacob, he vows to kill him (27:41). Rebekah once again intervenes for her favorite son, warning him to flee to her brother Laban's in Haran, on the pretense of seeking a wife. Before he leaves, Jacob receives a blessing from Isaac in which God's promises to Abraham of land and descendants are again invoked (28:3-4).

Thus Jacob leaves Beer-sheba, and on the first night of his journey, he has a dream: he sees a stairway reaching from earth into heaven with angels of God ascending and descending upon it.

The Lord then speaks to Jacob (vv. 13-15) and confirms that the promises made to Abraham will be given to Jacob. Moreover, God will continue to be with Jacob and will bring him back to his homeland (v. 15).

When Jacob awakens, he exclaims: "Surely the Lord is in this place—and I did not know it!" (v. 16). Up until this point, Jacob has shown little recognition of God and has depended upon his own devices. Now he has had a direct experience of God: he has seen the gate of heaven opened before him (v. 17).

Jacob takes the stone he had used as a pillow to be a marker for this sacred place, naming it Bethel—the house of God. Bethel played an important role in Israel's history second only to Jerusalem (Jdg. 20:18, 26-28; 21:2-4; 1 Sam. 7:16).

Although Jacob does not forsake his crafty ways, he now lives with an awareness of God's claims on him. The saving actions of God are not dependent upon human faithfulness.

In the second of a series of parables in Matthew's third discourse, Jesus again uses the metaphor of sowing and reaping, as he speaks of unfaithful and fallen individuals. Here he takes a stand for including doubters and obvious sinners.

This is consistent with what Jesus has said earlier about judging others (Mt. 6:12; 7:1-5). The parable of the weeds among the wheat itself is told in Matthew 13:24-30, with an allegorical interpretation in verses 36-43.

Jesus begins by comparing the Kingdom of heaven to a planter who sows good seed in his field; but despite his care, weeds inevitably spring up. The text tells us that it was "an enemy" who sowed the weeds.

In the early stages of growth it is difficult to tell the difference between weeds and wheat. Thus as the crop grows, the weeds grow faster and choke out the wheat.

Since it is tricky to pull out the embedded weeds, there will be unwanted seeds in next season's crop as well. Thus it could take years for a farmer to completely eliminate them from his fields.

The farmer forbids his slaves to eradicate weeds because, in pulling them out, the wheat would also be uprooted. At the harvest the weeds will be reaped first, bound into bundles, and burned; but the wheat will be gathered into the barn.

PRAYER FOR THE DAY

Come, Lord Jesus, and pour upon us each day your grace to relieve our fears and guide us in the way of peace: that through the power of the Gospel, we may bear good fruit for the welfare of the world, to the glory of your name. *Amen.*

Later, the disciples come to Jesus and ask for the meaning of the parable. Jesus explains that the planter is the Son of Man; the field is the world; the good seed stands for the righteous, and the bad seed for the wicked. The enemy is the devil, and the harvest is the end of the age. The reapers are the angels who will destroy those who cause sin and evil. "Then the righteous will shine like the sun in the kingdom of their Father" (13:43a).

The prerogative of judging the quality of someone's relationship to God belongs to God alone. Matthew was not opposed to the use of discipline (18:15-20); but only God knows the depths of the human heart. We must not exclude difficult people from our fellowship. To do so would harm the fabric of the community.

But Matthew expected final judgment to occur sooner rather than later; and even though we do not know the exact time, what matters is that the One who loves us most fully is the One who judges us finally. So Jesus ends his explanation to the disciples with a resounding "Let anyone with ears listen!" (v. 43b).

The Apostle Paul is also concerned with issues of sin and final judgment. He proclaims that living according to the flesh—the ways of the world—leads to death; whereas living in the Spirit—the ways of God—brings life. We were not given this gift in order to return to the slavery of our former ways. Rather, the Spirit sets us free from past failures, and we become aware, through God's Spirit, of the *adoption* that enables us truly to know God as our Father.

ON REFLECTION

"The difference between the right word and the almost right word," said Mark Twain, "is the difference between lightning and the lightning bug." Something of the same thing could be said for the parables of Jesus—and the allegories spun off of them by the early Church.

The Parable of the Weeds is not the most electrifying parable; but neither is it a "lightning bug." It is a straightforward story about a parasite growing up among healthy grain as a result of sabotage—and then *what to do with the weeds*. In other words, it is a parable about the Church—holy and sinful at the same time.

So what should the farmer do? Run to the co-op and load up his tractor with Round-Up? Call in the local crop duster with the strongest herbicide available? Makes sense. But this "normal" reaction—practiced in countless Christian communities who claim to know "wheat" from "chaff"—is not the answer. "True believers" doing everything possible to rid the fellowship of those they claim are sabotaging the harvest of faith have not produced a pretty picture in Church history.

Maybe the most significant point of the parable is this: *Beware of sinners judging sinners.* Beware of fallible human beings "playing God" with other people. Watch out for well-meaning people wielding a Christian weed-eater in efforts to create their version of the Kingdom.

The mystery of the Kingdom's growing is wondrously underway, Jesus is telling us here. Be like the unfretful farmer who does *nothing* about the weeds. Look after your own harvest, hoe your own row, and leave the rest up to God.

—H. King Oehmig

Thus we accept suffering as part of our new life in grace (Rom. 8:17b). We can hold on to this wonderful truth through the trials of life, knowing that the victorious Christ also bears our suffering with us. For we are assured that whatever sufferings we must endure for the present time "are not worth comparing with the glory about to be revealed to us" (v. 18).

Moreover, this glory that is to shine forth is not for humanity alone, but for all creation, which has been subject to corruptibility. Now Paul speaks in expectation of recovery for the entire created order (v. 19), and likens this waiting of creation for redemption to the groaning of labor pains (v. 22).

Paul describes our hope as *waiting with patience for our complete healing in Christ*— which we do not yet see. Therefore, in this hope that *as yet does not appear,* we find both fullness now, and a foretaste of our future life with God.

The Hebrew people did not develop abstract language before the Exile. So when a Psalmist chose to meditate on God's knowledge, he did so in terms of human experience.

God knows us totally, discerning our thoughts before we are aware of them ourselves. God is aware of where we are, and of what we say and think. We cannot imagine such perception, let alone achieve it.

Psalm 139 spoke of God's Spirit in a way that would later help to develop the Christian faith in the Holy Trinity. We affirm that God's Spirit is present everywhere: in heaven, in the realm of the dead ... even in the farthest reaches of the sea.

Wherever we may be, we are still in the hand of God. There is no way to hide. Darkness and light to God are both alike. We are totally God's in any situation.

POINTS TO PONDER

1. As you read the Parable of the Wheat and the Weeds, what kind of world is described here?

2. In Matthew 13:36-43, Jesus offers an interpretation of the parable. What do the wheat and weeds represent for you?

3. What does this story tell us about final judgment and the presence of evil in the world?

4. Jesus begins by saying that this parable is about the Kingdom of heaven. What is the nature of the Kingdom as it is presented here?

5. What does this parable have to say to us today, particularly with regard to the many divisions and conflicts that exist in our world?

MORE KINGDOM PARABLES

Genesis 29:15-28; Psalm 105:1-11, 45b; Romans 8:26-39; Matthew 13:31-33, 44-52

After cheating his older brother Esau out of both his birthright (Gen. 25:29-34) and paternal blessing (27:1-40), Jacob fled from Beer-Sheba to Haran in fear for his life. Soon after his arrival, he met fellow kinsmen at a well, including Laban's daughter Rachel (24:4-14). Jacob fell in love with Rachel and agreed to serve Laban for seven years to claim her as his bride.

Jacob was surprised to learn on the morning after the wedding feast that his bride was not the beautiful Rachel, but her older sister Leah, whom Laban said must be married first.

Thus Jacob agreed to work another seven years for his beloved Rachel. Through his patience and endurance, Rachel finally became his wife. There is also the sense that he prevailed because he was chosen by God.

As seen in the story of Jacob, God's promises can always be trusted. Thus the Psalmist in Psalm 105 gives praise to the Lord for the mighty deeds God has done among the people of Israel—especially the everlasting covenant made with Abraham and his offspring throughout their generations.

Today we look at five parables in Matthew 13 that focus on the Kingdom of heaven. Except for the final one, the parables are told in pairs.

The first two are concerned with growth from seemingly modest beginnings. The analogy of the mustard seed (vv. 31-32) suggests rapid growth; in a single season, the tiny seed becomes a shrub large enough for birds to roost in its branches. The mustard seed is also used in Matthew's Gospel in a metaphor for faith (Mt. 17:20).

The community to which Matthew wrote expected an early end to human history, and thus people were not greatly concerned with long-term growth. What failed to happen within two or three years, they believed would have no chance to happen at all. Thus the point of the parable is that the arrival of the reign of God—the greatest event in the history of creation—is being ushered in through the humble ministry of Jesus. And it is a work with beginnings so small as to seem hardly perceptible. The expectation here is that God will intervene shortly, and that a substantial community of disciples will be prepared.

The comparison of the Kingdom of heaven to leaven or yeast (v. 33) emphasizes the hidden character of growth. Yeast works in dough to make it rise; thus a little yeast has the capacity to inflate the entire mass. This suggests that the workings of God's Kingdom are already in and among us in surprising ways, if only we could perceive them.

The next two parables focus on the infinite value of God's Kingdom. Individuals should be ready to exchange everything—wealth, power, reputation, even life itself—in order to enter the realm of the Spirit.

PRAYER FOR THE DAY

Gracious and eternal God, we praise you for the mystery of your Being revealed in the Gospel of Jesus Christ: grant us your Holy Spirit so that the eyes of our hearts may be awakened to your unseen but continual Presence. Bless us that we may be faithful witnesses of your holy Kingdom, until it arrives in its completeness on the last day. *Amen.*

First, the Kingdom is like hidden treasure (v. 44) in a field. Obviously the owner of the field knew nothing of it, or he would not have rented out the field. So the finder had every right to secure the field and its contents for himself. The point here is that heavenly treasure is to be secured regardless of the cost in earthly terms.

The story of the jewel merchant who will part with everything he owns to obtain one superlative pearl makes the same point (vv. 45-46). God's Kingdom is prized beyond any commodity or good fortune that it is possible to imagine.

The fifth parable (vv. 47-49) proclaims the inclusiveness of the Kingdom of heaven, and could be paired with the parable of the weeds among wheat (vv. 24-30). Both tell of a mixture of the bad and good that will be separated at the last judgment. Yet here a net thrown into the sea "caught fish of every kind" (v. 47); no mention is made of good and bad, indicating that all are included.

Since Jewish dietary laws forbade the use of anything without fins and scales, many species would be thrown back. The edible fish would be sorted and counted before being sold or consumed. The parable indicates that inclusiveness is to be found in God's call. A final judgment will reject the unfit.

The final saying of the parable connects this sorting with the climax of all things in 13: 42a. At the end of the age, God's true servants will be assigned their place in the heavenly Kingdom, while those who are false will be excluded. But as in the parable of the weeds, the message is that God will oversee such judgment.

Jesus then concludes with the image of scribes in the Kingdom of heaven who, like a householder, bring out both old and new treasures. These scribes would be knowledgeable about the Law as well as what is new in the teachings of Jesus. Therefore, both the old and the new have value in the Kingdom of heaven.

ON REFLECTION

Morton Kelsey in his book *The Other Side of Silence* (Paulist Press, 1976) wrote: "Jesus of Nazareth was the most democratic and down-to-earth of all the religious leaders the world has known. He offered a way for the common people to encounter and experience God. His way was not just for the intellectuals or full-time religious professionals. It was for everyone—particularly people like the publican who did not think he had a chance."

The Kingdom of heaven, Jesus tells us in his mustard-seed way today, is not a billboard reality. It won't be a sponsor of American Idol—or the Super Bowl. It is a *hidden* reality. In fact, it is no bigger than the size of a coffee ground—insignificant in a world that values everything "supersized"—yet it is nonetheless *the reality of realities.*

In the Gospel of Thomas, the disciples say to Jesus: "When will the Kingdom come?" Jesus tells them, "It will not come if you look for it. Nor can you say, 'It is here,' or 'It is there.' For the Kingdom of the Father is already spread out over the earth but people don't see it." As Thomas Merton said, when it comes to the Kingdom of God, "we are like a man riding on an ox looking for an ox." It is there in front of our noses. How simple—which is probably the reason Jesus said that we had to become as a little child if we were to enter the Kingdom's power and glory.

—H. King Oehmig

The Apostle Paul in Romans gives further insight about life in God's Kingdom regarding prayer. We may be confused about how to pray. Yet God knows both what and how, as God's Spirit both searches our hearts and comprehends our needs (8:26). We know that God is working everything out for the good for those who have been called into a genuine response of love (v. 28).

Paul depicts the Divine call as similar to the summons previously given to God's prophets. Those whom God calls are foreknown, foreordained, and so justified, with a final goal of being glorified.

With God acting on our behalf, even to the point of giving us the Son to redeem us, everything good will come to us. When God puts us in the right there can be no condemnation, since Christ Jesus, who died, *is risen* and makes intercession for us at God's right hand.

The passage ends in verses 38-39 with the emphatic proclamation that there is nothing now or in the future that can ultimately separate us from the love of God. No hardship is too great, no power too strong—not even death itself—that "will be able to separate us from the love of God in Christ Jesus our Lord" (v. 39).

POINTS TO PONDER

1. According to the five short parables in the Gospel passage, what are the characteristics of the Kingdom of heaven?

2. What do you find that is comforting as well as challenging in these "snapshots" of the Kingdom?

3. What do we learn here about our relationship with God and with others?

4. In these parables Jesus uses ordinary life experiences to describe the Kingdom. Which of the images used here are most meaningful for you, and why? How would you define the Kingdom of God?

5. According to the Epistle reading, what are the promises freely granted to us in our life in Christ?

THE MIRACULOUS FEEDING

Genesis 32:22-31; Psalm 17:1-7, 15; Romans 9:1-5; Matthew 14:13-21

After Jacob fled his homeland, he prospered in Haran and was blessed with wealth and a large family. But he still agonized over having cheated his brother Esau out of his birthright (Gen. 25:29-34) and patriarchal blessing (27:1-40). Thus he determined that the time had come to return to Canaan and be reconciled with his brother.

But when Jacob sent word to Esau of his impending arrival (Gen. 32:4-5), he was alarmed to learn that Esau was already on his way accompanied by four hundred men. Jacob feared for himself and his family (vv. 6-7a), as earlier Esau had threatened to kill him (27:41). Thus, the night before, he sent his family and herds ahead of him across the river Jabbok. Jacob himself stayed, and "a man wrestled with him until daybreak" (v. 24).

These two adversaries were each other's match, and as they struggled, Jacob demanded a blessing. Instead, the man conferred upon Jacob a new name, Israel: "For you have striven with God and with humans, and have prevailed" (v. 28). When Jacob asked for the man's name in return, he finally received the blessing. But the name demanded was not to be given until much later (Ex. 3:14).

Although the exact identity of his antagonist was not immediately clear, Jacob called the place Peniel: "For I have seen God face to face, and yet my life is preserved" (v. 30). However, Jacob, now Israel, did not escape unscathed. In the midst of the struggle, the man dislocated his hip.

The name Israel symbolizes that something new has happened, not only to Jacob, but also to the nation that will carry this name. This is a man, and a people, that has and will continue to struggle with and be blessed by God.

The reunion with his brother Esau (Gen. 33:1-11) gives Jacob another understanding of seeing God face to face. Esau has become successful and no longer harbors resentment against Jacob. Upon seeing each other, the brothers embrace, and Jacob exclaims that "to see your face is like seeing the face of God—since you have received me with such favor" (33:10).

The words of Psalm 17 reflect the experience of Jacob at Peniel, as the Psalmist expresses confidence in God's mercy, while he seeks deliverance from false accusations. For ultimately, he knows that "I shall behold your face in righteousness; when I awake I shall be satisfied, beholding your likeness" (v. 15).

The Gospel reading tells of the miraculous feeding of the five thousand, which is found in the other three Gospels as well (Mk. 6:35-44; Lk. 9:12-17; Jn. 6:1-15). Although the details of the various accounts differ, the essential message of God's loving care is foremost.

PRAYER FOR THE DAY

May your unending compassion, Holy God, be poured out on your people. Grant that this food that never perishes may nourish and sustain the proclamation of the Gospel of Jesus Christ. May all peoples of the earth be fed through the grace and mercy of your Holy Spirit, through you and our Lord Jesus Christ, one God, in glory everlasting. *Amen.*

This event foreshadows the Last Supper (Mt. 26:26-29), as well as the Eucharist.

As the passage for today begins, Jesus has withdrawn from Galilee in a boat and gone to a deserted place alone (14:13). This may have been prompted by word of Herod's execution of John the Baptist (14:3-12). Herod had acknowledged Jesus as a wonder worker and apparently regarded him as John the Baptist raised from the dead (14:2).

However, the crowds continue to follow after Jesus, and when he finally goes ashore, he is filled with compassion (cf. 9:36; 15:32; 20:34), and cures the sick among them.

When it became evening, the disciples came to Jesus asking that he send the crowds away to the nearby villages to buy food. Jesus replied that there was no need to send the people off because the disciples would give them something to eat.

When the disciples brought him the five loaves and two fish, Jesus pronounced a blessing and broke the loaves. In giving the blessing, Jesus performed the traditional role of the head of a Jewish household.

The disciples distributed the bread and "all ate and were filled" (v. 20). The disciples then collected what was left over in twelve baskets. Matthew tells us that more than five thousand were actually fed, as women and children were also present.

The disciples play a central role in this event. Jesus charges them with finding food for the crowd. Here the disciples (rather than a young boy, as in John's account in 6:9) bring forth the provisions.

This meal was not just a stopgap effort to tide the crowd over until they could get home for a complete meal. Rather, it was an extravagant, bountiful feast of God in which the people were genuinely nourished.

ON REFLECTION

The ministry of Jesus was characterized by a certain rhythm—call it engagement, disengagement. Encounter, retreat. Jesus refused to be burnt out by overexposure to the world, regardless of the cause. Today's Gospel reading starts with Jesus "withdrawing" from the world—but only to become more involved with the world later on. Self-care clearly was a Divine responsibility for the Son of man.

Rested, Jesus gets right back to Gospel business—this time dealing with hoards of people who are drawn to him like moths to light. "Compassion," said Frederick Buechner in *Wishful Thinking* (HarperSanFrancisco, 1993), "is the sometimes fatal capacity for feeling what it is like to be inside somebody else's skin. It is the knowledge that there can never really be any peace and joy for me until there is finally peace and joy for you too." Jesus knew what it was like to be hungry (Mt. 4:2). He knew the devil was using this human weakness to trick him in the wilderness, so he begged off turning stones to bread.

Here, however, he does virtually the same miracle—only on his time and his terms. Jesus takes what the disciples consider to be insignificant: a sack lunch. Rather than complaining about it, Jesus offers the food to God to be blessed, and then gives it away—feeding a whole ballpark of people in the process. In so doing, Jesus shows not only the compassion of God, but also the staggering abundance released when we share with others the blessings that have been given us by God.

—H. King Oehmig

The great feeding of the five thousand is in marked contrast to Herod's earlier banquet, described in the verses immediately preceding it. Herod's feast took place in a lavish court and was characterized by greed, deceit, and murder. The meal provided by Jesus is a foretaste of the messianic banquet of the age to come.

The fact that this event is recorded in all of the Gospels is evidence of its importance to the early Christian community. Many efforts are made to rationalize how the food was multiplied; but this incident serves primarily as a reminder of God's sustaining presence even when resources seem inadequate. In this, the event also provides a link to the mystery of the Eucharist.

In chapters 9-11 of the letter to the Romans, the Apostle Paul shows how the community of Jesus' followers is related to the history of Israel. In the verses for today, Paul confesses his "great sorrow and unceasing anguish" (9:2) for his ancestral community that has not embraced Jesus as Messiah. For to Israel belonged God's adoption in the call of Abraham, the deliverance from Egypt, the covenants, and the gift of Torah. Theirs was the worship of temple and synagogue, and to them had been given the promises to which the disciples of Jesus were heirs through the patriarchs.

From them had come the climax of God's self-revelation, Jesus the Messiah, who would come for all people to bring all things into wholeness: "the Messiah, who is over all, God blessed forever" (v. 5).

POINTS TO PONDER

1. Imagine that you are one of the people in the crowd in the Gospel story. How would you describe what happened? What do you think the significance of this miraculous meal might have been for those present?

2. How do you think the disciples might have felt when Jesus told them that they were responsible for providing food for such a large crowd? What kind of example do the disciples set for us in this story?

3. What is the picture of Jesus that emerges here? How does he relate to the crowd as well as to his disciples?

4. Matthew tells us that there were twelve baskets of food left over. How have you experienced God's extravagant abundance in your own life?

5. How are we called to respond to God's care and love that is set before us in the feeding of the five thousand?

THE FEAST OF THE TRANSFIGURATION

Exodus 34:29-35; Psalm 99; 2 Peter 1:13-21; Luke 9:28-36

Psalm 99 for today gives expression to the holiness and awesome power of the Lord that Moses and the Apostles experienced. The Lord, the Holy One, is to be exalted and worshiped above all others: "…for the Lord our God is holy" (v. 9).

The observance of the Transfiguration was celebrated as early as the fourth century in the Eastern tradition, and became a universal feast in the Western Church by the 15th century. Matthew, Mark, and Luke each provide a Transfiguration account (Mt. 17:1-9; Mk. 9:2-10; Lk. 9:28-36).

When August 6 falls on a Sunday, we turn to the Transfiguration passage in Luke, which replaces the sequential Sunday lections for that day.

The Gospel account begins with a reference to "sayings" that had occurred eight days earlier. Peter's confession of Jesus as "the Messiah of God" (9:20) was followed by Jesus' first prediction of his Passion (vv. 21-22) and teachings on the true cost of discipleship (vv. 23-27). This marks a turning point in the ministry of Jesus as he begins his journey to Jerusalem.

Luke's telling, unlike that of the other accounts, is set in the context of prayer (9: 28). Luke often depicts Jesus at prayer, but this time he takes Peter, James, and John with him. While he is at prayer, the appearance of his face changes, and his clothes become dazzling white (v. 29) as an outward manifestation of his divinity.

Then Moses and Elijah appear "in glory" and talk with Jesus about his coming "departure" ("exodus") or death in Jerusalem (v. 31).

Only Luke includes the detail that Moses and Elijah have a conversation with Jesus. As representatives of the law and prophets, their appearance is a further affirmation of the Messiahship of Jesus. The fact that they are glorified connects this event with the prediction of Jesus concerning the coming of the Son of Man in his glory.

Moses and Elijah had their own mountain experiences of the Divine (Ex. 24:13-18; 1 Ki. 19:8-13), and they are part of Israel's hopes for the future. Tradition said that the reappearance of these two prophets would be a sign of the coming of the Messianic age.

In another detail unique to Luke, we read that Peter and the others were "weighed down with sleep" (v. 32a). This contributes to the dream-like quality of the experience. Later on, these three men would once again fall asleep while Jesus prayed on the Mount of Olives before his crucifixion (22:45-46). Nonetheless, they saw the glory of Jesus with Moses and Elijah.

Peter, "not knowing what he said" (v. 33b), then proposes that they erect three dwellings to memorialize the site. These temporary shelters would be similar to those constructed at the harvest Feast of Booths, one of the three Jerusalem pilgrim festivals with end-time connotations.

PRAYER FOR THE DAY

Lord Jesus, the Light of the World, who revealed your glistening radiance to chosen witnesses on the holy mountain, so anoint us in the grace of your Holy Spirit, that we may know your eternal majesty as the Beloved One, who has come from the Father to transfigure all things in Divine love. *Amen.*

Peter's response was misguided, as it is impossible to capture an experience of the glory of the Divine by erecting a physical memorial. In addition, building three similar dwellings would incorrectly imply that Moses and Elijah were equal to Jesus.

At this point, the disciples were terrified as they became overshadowed by a cloud. Their fear came from a realization that they were in the presence of the Divine.

Then a voice from the cloud proclaimed, "This is my Son, my Chosen; listen to him!" (v. 35). Just as these words affirmed Jesus' identity as he began his ministry at his Baptism (3:22), they once again provide God's endorsement.

Luke tells us that the Apostles "kept silent and in those days told no one any of the things they had seen" (v. 36). It was not until the Resurrection that they could begin to understand what they had just witnessed.

This foretaste of the coming glory of Jesus was for the benefit of the disciples who were witnesses, and was further confirmation that Jesus was God's Messiah. Later on, Peter would recall the Transfiguration as he anticipated his own death and defended the legacy of his teaching on the future coming of Christ.

Peter's opponents maintain that the Apostle's teaching on the second coming of Jesus as judge is a "cleverly devised myth" (2 Pet. 1:16). However, Peter replies that he can proclaim with confidence the "prophetic message" (v. 19) that he brings, because he was present on the holy mountain when Jesus "received honor and glory from God the Father" (v. 17). Peter himself heard the voice of God affirm Jesus as the Beloved Son. Thus he calls his readers to be attentive to the prophecy of Scripture, which shines as a lamp in the darkness until the "morning star rises in your hearts" (v. 19).

ON REFLECTION

W. H. Auden (1907—1973) in "A Christmas Oratorio" came as close as anyone to describing the dynamic involved in the Transfiguration, with his call to follow Jesus, the Way, through the "Land of Unlikeness"—to see rare sights and have unique adventures. Then, in stanza 2, Auden calls us to follow Jesus as the Truth, even as we pilgrimage through the land of Anxiety—until we come to that home that has expected our return all along. Stanza 3 celebrates Jesus as the Life, even here within our "world of the Flesh"—the preliminary celebration of all that in the end shall "dance for joy."

And so these three disciples that would later lead the nascent Jerusalem Church—Peter, James, and John—follow Jesus up this unnamed mountain into "the Land of Unlikeness." Meister Eckhart once said: "God does not work in all hearts alike, but according to the preparation and sensitivity he finds in each." Maybe that is also why they were chosen to climb the mount that day. However spiritually sensitive they were, nothing could have prepared them for what they were about to behold: the incandescence of Jesus, the Lord of Life.

Ever since, we have had a way of "transfiguring Jesus" into our image and likeness—according to our culture and conventional wisdom. Here we can keep Jesus under our control, "on the reservation," so to speak. Like Moses' encounter with the burning bush, the Transfiguration serves as yet another reminder that "God will be who God will be." And Jesus, the Incarnate One, will do the same.

—H. King Oehmig

Jesus, as he comes again in glory, is this "morning star" (cf Num. 24:17; Rev. 22:16). Peter affirms that interpretation of Scripture is not just an individual matter, for prophecy comes through men and women who were moved by God's Holy Spirit (v. 21).

The Transfiguration of Jesus also recalls the experience of Moses on Mt. Sinai. After Moses came down from the mountain bearing the tablets of the Law, the people were afraid because "the skin of his face shone" (Ex. 34:29). When he spoke directly with God, the reflection of God's glory, or Shekinah, remained on his face.

It was generally believed that to encounter the Divine face to face meant death, for who could bear to see the awesome majesty of God? Thus the people were afraid to come near Moses.

Therefore, Moses gave assurance of safety to the Israelites so that they would come near to hear the words that God had given to him.

Once he realized the source of their fear, Moses covered his face with a veil. He removed the veil when he spoke with God and when he communicated the Word of God to the people.

POINTS TO PONDER

1. As you read the Gospel passage, imagine that you are one of the disciples who accompanied Jesus up the mountain. How would you describe what happened? What are some of your thoughts and feelings at this time?

2. In the Gospel of Luke, Jesus often goes off to pray. Why do you think he took Peter, James, and John with him this time? How would you characterize their response to what happened?

3. Why is the appearance of Moses and Elijah significant? What do you imagine they might have talked about with Jesus?

4. In Luke 9:31, we read that Moses, Elijah, and Jesus "appeared in glory." How does this experience empower Jesus, as well as the disciples, for the events that are to come in Jerusalem?

5. Read the Epistle for today in 2 Peter 1:13-21, in which Peter recalls this experience. What is his understanding of the event as he reflects back on it? What is the meaning of the Transfiguration for us today?

THE SEA WALKER

Genesis 37:1-4, 12-28; Psalm 105:1-6, 16-22, 45b; Romans 10:5-15; Matthew 14:22-33

The story of the family of Jacob concludes with the Joseph saga that begins in chapter 37 of Genesis and continues through the end of the book. Joseph's story provides a bridge to the Exodus story that follows.

Although many of the same themes of sibling rivalry, parental favoritism, and deceit are found here, there is a pronounced difference in style. The Joseph story reads like a novella with a well-crafted plot. Most strikingly, God does not appear directly in the narrative; but nonetheless, God's purposes for Israel are carried out.

Jacob had returned to Canaan with his family, and once again sibling rivalry causes conflict. Jacob loved his youngest child Joseph, son of his beloved Rachel, more that his other children. Thus Jacob gave Joseph a special long robe with sleeves (v. 3) that incurred the jealousy of his brothers to the point that "they hated him, and could not speak peaceably to him" (v. 4).

The brothers' animosity toward Joseph was further inflamed by Joseph's unfavorable reports about them to Jacob, and by Joseph's dreams in which his brothers, and even his father, paid homage to him (vv. 5-11).

When Jacob sent Joseph out to check on his brothers who were tending the family flocks, the brothers saw an opportunity to get rid of Joseph by killing him and telling their father he had been attacked by a wild animal. But Reuben intervened and suggested that they throw Joseph into a pit instead.

Thus the brothers seized Joseph, stripped him of his coat, and threw him into a dry pit to die.

When a caravan of Ishmaelites appeared, Judah suggested that they sell Joseph to them instead of killing him—after all, Joseph was their own flesh and blood. Thus the brothers sold Joseph for twenty pieces of silver, and he was taken as a slave to Egypt. There the story will continue to unfold.

Joseph's life had been spared, and this event would ultimately set the stage for saving the lives of his entire family, thus preserving the Lord's promises to Abraham (Gen. 17:1-8).

Psalm 105 gives praise for God's faithfulness and "wonderful works" in the history of Israel. The verses for today tell of the plight of Joseph as he was put in fetters and sold into slavery. This was to test Joseph, who was eventually set free and granted a high place of honor in the house of the king of Egypt. Thus Israel is to sing praises to God and seek the strength of the Lord.

Today's Gospel account of Jesus walking on the water and calming the storm is a further example of God's saving actions, and provides the context for the disciples to witness to the divinity of Jesus.

PRAYER FOR THE DAY

Gracious God, Source of all life, Author of all that is true and good: give us the wind of your Holy Spirit that we may venture beyond the safe confines of an easy faith, and step out bravely from false security to carry the Gospel of Jesus Christ to a perishing world. All this we ask in the unity of the Godhead and in the power of your Holy Name. *Amen.*

After the feeding of the multitude (Mt. 14: 13-21), Jesus dismisses the crowd and continues to search for a deserted place to be alone (his original intention when the throng overtook him). But now he separates from his disciples as well, sending them ahead in the boat while he goes alone up the mountain to pray (14:22-23).

As night falls, a gale blows down the Jordan Valley, creating a strong wind with battering waves that impede the disciples in their journey. Early in the morning, the disciples are terrified when they see Jesus walking toward them across the water, thinking that they are seeing a ghost.

But the presence of Jesus is real, and he immediately reassures them: "Take heart, it is I; do not be afraid" (v. 27).

Peter seeks to imitate the behavior of Jesus. "Lord, if it is you, command me to come to you on the water" (v. 28). In line with the thought that the Lord gives his followers power to do what he does (Jn. 14: 12-14), Jesus calls Peter to come to him.

As long as Peter's attention is focused on Jesus, he is able to walk across the waves.

But as soon as he focuses on the storm, Peter becomes frightened and begins to sink, calling out, "Lord, save me!" Jesus reaches out his hand and pulls him above the water. By saving Peter from drowning, Jesus manifests a further action attributed to God alone (Ps. 144:7).

As Jesus pulls Peter to safety he proclaims, "You of little faith, why did you doubt?" (v. 31). The phrase "you of little faith" occurs elsewhere in Matthew (6:30; 8:26; 16:8; 17:20); and the word for doubt is used in Matthew 28:17 to describe the response of some disciples to the Risen Jesus. However, Jesus never deserts those who doubt.

The storm ceases as Peter and Jesus enter the boat, and the disciples fall down and worship him, confessing, "Truly you are the Son of God" (v. 33). Despite their "little faith," they understand and acknowledge who Jesus is. Their confession anticipates that of Peter in 16:16.

ON REFLECTION

Authors Ron Delbene and Herb Montgomery in their book *Alone With God* (Upper Room, 1992) make an important point regarding the "walking on water" episode from today's Gospel. They point out the role of the wind—especially the direction of the wind. The boat the disciples occupy is heading *into* the wind. Jesus, walking toward the boat, also is heading *into* the wind. But Peter, when he steps out of the boat to go toward Jesus, finds *the wind is at his back.*

We all know what it is to fight a "headwind"—at work, at home, or with an illness. It is hard work. Still, in fighting a headwind, there is a modicum of maneuverability. The opposite is true with a stiff *tailwind.* It can be even more disconcerting. To be caught from behind and thrust forward makes us feel doubly out of control. Matthew says of Peter that "when he noticed the strong wind," he was afraid and began to sink (v. 30).

Have you ever felt the tailwind of God was pushing you out of your own boat? Maybe this "shove" came before you were "ready"—or thought you were. When the tailwind of the Spirit blows stronger than we anticipated—startling us out of the secure and the known—it is there that we may discover the depth of our faith. When we allow ourselves to be blown by the gale of God into holy insecurity, I suspect it is then that we find ourselves closest to God, and God closest to us—even if we get pulled back into the boat, dripping wet from head to toe.

—H. King Oehmig

The Gospel of Mark also tells the story of Jesus walking on the water (6:45-52), but does not mention Peter. And whereas Matthew favorably depicts the disciples as acknowledging the divinity of Jesus, Mark writes that "their hearts were hardened" (6:52).

The Apostle Paul also speaks of the saving power of the Lord: "For, 'everyone who calls on the name of the Lord shall be saved'" (Rom. 10:13.)

In the verses for today he begins by dispelling the notion that we can earn salvation and put God under our obligation. When there is an established set of rules, a person may expect credit for obeying them. As indicated in verse 5, Moses himself proposed that righteousness comes from the law.

But no one can climb to heaven to bring the climax of revelation down to us. Nor is the Anointed One to be sought in the depths. Instead, Paul cites Deuteronomy 30:14 that God's Word is "near you, on your lips and in your heart" (v. 8).

This is the word of faith that *proclaims Jesus as Lord* with total trust that God has raised him from the dead. It is this faith and not our accomplishments that secure salvation. Verse 12 adds that salvation by God's grace, embodied in the Risen Lord, applies to Jew and Gentile alike. To call upon the name of the Lord is to be assured of salvation, and no one who believes in God's Messiah will be put to shame.

However, in order to call upon the Lord, one must have heard the proclamation. Faith comes from what is heard, and what is heard comes through the preaching of Christ. Thus Paul quotes Isaiah 52:7 as a reminder of the importance of those who are called to spread the Gospel: "How beautiful are the feet of those who bring good news!" (v. 15b).

POINTS TO PONDER

1. Read the Gospel passage from the viewpoint of Peter and try to imagine how he might have felt as he started walking out across the stormy waters. Why did he suddenly start to sink?

2. Compare this sense of lostness with what Joseph in the Old Testament experienced in being taken, and then sold by his own brothers. How is God with us when we are in the "pit"?

3. What insights do we find in these readings concerning the relationship between faith and doubt? What risks are involved in the life of faith?

4. As you read the Epistle in Romans 10 for today, how does the fact that we believe that *Jesus Christ is Lord* give us courage in our daily lives?

5. What challenges to your faith do you find in your own life, and how does God rescue you in the midst of them?

GOD'S LIMITLESS LOVE

Genesis 45:1-15; Psalm 133; Romans 11:1-2a, 29-32; Matthew 15:(10-20), 21-28

This final reading from Genesis tells the story of the emotional reunion between Joseph and his brothers, who had earlier conspired to have him sold into slavery (Gen. 37:12-28).

Joseph was brought to Egypt, where he eventually became a powerful leader second only to Pharaoh. When a famine that Joseph had predicted in a dream (Gen. 41: 1-7) became a reality throughout the region, Joseph's father, Jacob, sent his sons to Egypt to purchase food.

In Egypt, Joseph recognized his brothers, but they did not know who he was. When he revealed his identity and asked if his father still lived, the brothers were speechless and dismayed, fearing retaliation.

As Joseph speaks to his brothers in Genesis 45:5-8, he reassures them that all of this was part of the Lord's plan to insure the survival of the family of Jacob: "God sent me before you to preserve life" (v. 5). This story illustrates the theme of Divine providence, and how God uses human actions to create a new reality and a bountiful future (cf Gen. 50:20). Joseph himself models tolerance and reconciliation rather than revenge and anger in his dealings with his brothers.

Since five more years of the famine remained, Joseph made arrangements for his brothers, his father, and all their households to come to Egypt and settle in the land of Goshen, where they would continue to prosper.

The words of the Psalmist eloquently capture the joy of the reunion of Joseph and his brothers: "How very good and pleasant it is when kindred live together in unity!" (133:1).

This unity is compared to the anointing of Aaron to the priesthood with precious oil, and to the refreshing dew on the mountains of Zion, where the Lord's blessings are to be found forevermore.

The Gospel reading tells the story of the healing of the Canaanite woman's daughter (cf Mk. 7:24-30).

As Jesus and his disciples continue their travels, they have altercations with the Pharisees concerning purity issues. These have led to Jesus' teachings on the distinction between ritual practices and moral behavior (15:10-20).

As they come to the Gentile region of Tyre and Sidon in southern Phoenicia, they are approached by a woman. The fact that she is identified as a "Canaanite" emphasizes that, to the Jews, she represents an ancient and godless foe.

The woman shouts at Jesus to have mercy on her and her daughter, as the girl is "tormented by a demon" (15:22). The woman addresses Jesus as "Lord, Son of David."

Lord, as a form of address, is used in Matthew only by true believers. *Son of David* would seem to have little meaning for a Gentile; yet, ironically, it seems to suggest her recognition of Jesus as Messiah.

PRAYER FOR THE DAY

Eternal and immortal God, dwelling in light inaccessible, from before time and forever: place in our hearts the desire to know and serve Jesus Christ, that we may experience the peace that supersedes all understanding, and then share that peace with all whom the Holy Spirit brings to us. This we ask in the power of your blessed Name. *Amen.*

In verse 23, the negative response of Jesus and the disciples to the woman's initial plea seems very out of character. Jesus ignores her, and the disciples encourage him to send her away.

In verse 24, Jesus explains that he cannot help her because he was sent "only to the lost sheep of the house of Israel." This statement echoes Jesus' instructions to the Twelve in 10:5-6, when he tells them not to go to the Gentiles but rather to the "lost sheep of the house of Israel." Here Jesus states clearly that he understands his mission to be limited to the Jews.

But the woman will not be put off so easily. She kneels before Jesus, addresses him again as Lord, and once more asks for his help. Jesus' reply to her in verse 26 is even more definitive and harsh than before. He uses a racial slur, referring to the Gentiles as dogs who are not worthy to receive the same food—i. e., the benefits of his ministry—as the children who are the Jews.

But the woman still will not be deterred. She does not take offense at what Jesus has said. Still addressing him as *Lord,* she redirects his comment by pointing out that "even the dogs eat the crumbs that fall from their masters' table" (v. 27).

This part of the dialog is an example of the sharp verbal exchange much admired in Hebrew culture, in which wits are matched word for word.

The woman does not deny that Jesus' ministry to his own people may have priority, but asserts that the abundance of God's blessings still leaves much for the Gentiles.

The tension has been building steadily throughout this exchange, and reaches its climax in verse 28, as Jesus acknowledges her faith and grants her request. "Woman, great is your faith! Let it be done for you as you wish."

ON REFLECTION

One wonders if the story of Jesus with the Canaanite woman did not give rise to teaching: "From the days of John the Baptist until now the kingdom of heaven has suffered violence, and the violent take it by force" (Mt. 11:12). Here we have a perfect example of taking the kingdom "by force."

Women of that day—let alone *foreign* women—had no business talking with men, especially in broad daylight. Yet she did. Women did not argue with men who dismissed them summarily out of hand. Yet she did. Jesus never told anyone who came to him in need to "get lost; it isn't fair to take children's food and give it to dogs." Yet she took the rebuke.

Did she go away sorrowful, tearful? Not this firebrand! She gives it right back to Jesus, sounding like Hilary Swank in *Million Dollar Baby.* "Even the dogs eat the crumbs that fall from the master's table." A knock-out blow had just been landed on the Son of Man, and he loved it.

Read, mark, and learn: *No one* who came to Jesus in the Gospels with this thing called "faith" ever left disappointed. Nobody. And neither does this woman brimming with the force of importunity. "Woman, great is your faith! Let it be done for you as you wish." When the Canaanite woman returned home to find her daughter healed, how could she have known that millions of people through the millennia following would look upon her courage and thereby find their way into the Kingdom of Jesus—even if by force.

—H. King Oehmig

The woman's faith is the decisive factor, recalling a previous incident with a centurion (Mt. 8:5-13), in which another Gentile's faith results in healing at a distance. These two healings are the only ones in Matthew that explicitly involve Gentiles.

The woman's faith transcends her gender, her race, and salvation history itself. She will not be dissuaded; and Jesus' final words to her are approving.

What finally makes Jesus decide to grant the woman's petition is not only a reassessment of his mission but her great faith (v. 28). This woman is the only person in Matthew's Gospel to earn such high praise from Jesus.

Through her faithful persistence, Gentiles are seen to have a place at the master's table. Although Jesus does not take a full-scale mission to the Gentiles following this incident, the door to this mission has been opened.

The faith of this woman is in sharp contrast to the unbelief of the Jews as the Great Commission of Matthew 28:19 is foreshadowed.

Later Paul, the Apostle to the Gentiles, would address the question of those of Jewish ancestry who rejected Jesus as Messiah. In the passage for today Paul identifies himself as an Israelite and member of the tribe of Benjamin, as he emphatically proclaims that *God does not reject the heirs of Abraham* (Rom. 11:2).

Israel will be saved, and their temporary refusal to accept the completion of the Divine plan in Christ will be overcome. God uses human disobedience—i. e., disbelief in Jesus as the Messiah—as a means for manifesting God's mercy.

POINTS TO PONDER

1. As you read the account of the reunion of Joseph and his brothers, how do you imagine all of them might have felt at this time? What do we learn here about forgiveness and reconciliation?

2. How would you characterize the Canaanite woman and her actions in the Gospel passage? What is the example she sets for us today?

3. How was Jesus, as well as his ministry, challenged and changed by his encounter with this unnamed woman? What do we learn about Jesus himself here?

4. The Canaanite woman represents those who were outside the mainstream of Jewish society. Who are the marginalized in our own world, and how are we called to respond to them?

5. In his letter to the Romans, Paul also speaks of God's acceptance and mercy for all. Thus, in light of all of today's readings, what are we as individuals and as the Church called to do?

"WHO DO YOU SAY THAT I AM?"

Exodus 1:8—2:10; Psalm 124; Romans 12:1-8; Matthew 16:13-20

For the next several weeks, the Old Testament readings focus on the Exodus story, beginning with the account of Moses' rescue in today's passage and continuing to the entry into the promised land. The remembrance of these events forms the core of Israel's liturgical and worship life.

But for these events to unfold, there needed to be an individual who would speak for God to the Hebrew people. Previously, during a time of famine in Canaan, Jacob and seventy in his family (1:1-5) had migrated to Egypt under the protection of his son Joseph, who had become a powerful man in Pharaoh's court (Gen. 45:17-20). The Hebrews prospered there and grew in numbers.

However, as time passed, a new king arose in Egypt who "did not know Joseph" (1:8), and who felt threatened by having so many Hebrews in the land. And even though the Hebrews were forced into oppressive slavery, they grew more numerous than ever.

In an effort to reduce their population, Pharaoh commanded the midwives, Shiphrah and Puah, to kill the male children born to Hebrews. But because "the midwives feared God" (1:17), they refused the king's orders.

Then Pharaoh commanded that all these male children be drowned in the Nile River. When a man from the house of Levi (2:1) and his wife had a son, the mother put the child in a papyrus basket (2:3) and set it afloat in the river, with his older sister watching over him. The word used here for *basket* is the same as that used for Noah's lifesaving ark.

When Pharaoh's daughter came to the river to bathe, she saw the child, took pity on him, and adopted him as her own.

She named the child *Moses* because she "drew him out of the water" (2:10). The sister of the infant then made arrangements for his own mother to be a wet nurse for him.

Once again God's promises to the patriarchs of land and descendants seemed to be imperiled. Although they were now great in numbers, they had no hope of land as long as they were slaves in Egypt. But through the courage and compassion of the women in this story: the midwives, Moses' mother and sister, and the daughter of Pharaoh, the life of the one who would later lead them to the land of promise had been saved.

Psalm 124 expresses thanksgiving for the Lord's deliverance of the people of Israel from their enemies. The rescue of Moses was certainly an example of God's care, thus the Psalmist can proclaim: "Our help is in the name of the Lord, who made heaven and earth" (124:8).

Today's Gospel reading records the pivotal event of Peter's confession that *Jesus is indeed the Messiah.* Mark 8:27-33 and Luke 9:18-22 also record this event, but Matthew's version contains a number of differences. John 6:66-69 also includes a confession of Jesus, but in a different context.

PRAYER FOR THE DAY

Grant us, gracious God, the gift of recognition, that we may come to see your hand at work in the world about us: may we, through the indwelling of the Holy Spirit, come to exalt Jesus as Lord and serve the Gospel of your love with imagination, boldness, and gladness of heart, to your glory. *Amen.*

After the miracle of Jesus walking on the water, the disciples worshiped Jesus proclaiming, "Truly you are the son of God" (Mt. 14:33). But today's passage emphasizes Peter's preeminence among the disciples and his coming to the ultimate truth of Jesus' Messiahship—which could be revealed only through the Father.

Jesus begins by asking the disciples, "Who do people say that the Son of Man is?" (16: 13). Their response includes John the Baptist, Elijah, Jeremiah, or one of the other prophets.

Jesus continues to press the issue by asking, "But who do *you* say that I am?" (v. 15). At this point, Peter steps forward and declares that Jesus is the "Messiah, the Son of the living God" (v. 16). This is the first time that one of the disciples has used the title *Messiah* for Jesus, although it has been used before in Matthew's Gospel (1:1, 16-18; 11:2).

In comparison to the other accounts, only Matthew adds the phrase "Son of the living God," which serves to place the role of the Messiah within the reign of God and apart from any political or military agenda.

Verses 17-19 are also unique to Matthew and make a connection between Peter's confession and the Church. Jesus pronounces a blessing on Peter (v. 17), as this knowledge could have come only from God the Father and not from any human— *i. e.,* "flesh and blood"—source. Peter is the only disciple to receive a specific blessing from Jesus.

The preeminence of Peter is further verified as Jesus goes on to say that "you are Peter, and on this rock I will build my church ..." (v. 18). Although Jesus has already given to Simon the name of Peter (Mt. 10:2), there is a play on words here that is possible in Aramaic as well as Greek. The name "Petros" is similar to the Greek *petra,* which means *boulder* or *rock.* This community of faith is so grounded in Christ and his teachings that even the "gates of Hades will not prevail against it" (v. 18).

Jesus was liberated from this dwelling place of the dead and thus holds its keys (Acts 2:24,

ON REFLECTION

Every teacher has to do it—even if it isn't much fun. It's called "test time." The class gets out its #2 pencils. Question #1: "Who do the people say that I am?" Answer: "Some say John the Baptist, but others Elijah, and still others Jeremiah or one of the prophets." OK. Question #2: "But who do *you* say that I am?"

All those months, trudging the dusty roads of Palestine together. All those nights around the campfire discussing the nature of the Kingdom of heaven. Seeing with their own eyes a withered hand restored, a leper cleansed, the dead being raised. Hearing a teaching that had holy authority. What had all these things taught the students of Jesus? What did it all mean— what had they learned?

Theologian Paul Tillich maintained that Christianity did not begin in Bethlehem's manger; rather it began at Caesarea Philippi. There, a fisherman turned religious pilgrim uttered the words: "You are the Messiah, the Son of the living God." With that statement, everything changed. No longer was Jesus known as a sage, a spirit-person, a prophet; he was *the Christ.* In saying so, Peter became the "rock" on which the Church would be built, was given the keys to the Kingdom, and carried the power to "bind and loose." According to Origen (c. 185—c. 254), "at last, Peter came to Rome and was crucified head-downwards." Sometimes it can be a very dangerous thing to be first in one's class—when the teacher is Jesus.

—H. King Oehmig

27, 31; Rev. 1:18). In conferring authority upon Peter, Jesus assures him and the Church that death's power will not prevail. The authority of Christ has no equal, and Christ's work on earth will triumph.

Peter and the Church as a whole are given a further charge. "I will give you the keys of the kingdom of heaven, and whatever you bind on earth will be bound in heaven, and whatever you loose on earth will be loosed in heaven" (v. 19). The word "key" designates that which allows the opening or securing of a door. As given to Peter, it is another sign of his authority to carry on the work of Jesus.

"To bind" and "to loose" can be understood in the light of a Jewish synagogue custom in which cases were judged through "loosing" or "binding" someone to a vow. In the rabbis' use of this term, which was familiar to Matthew, to bind was to declare something obligatory; whereas to loose one from it was to leave it to individual judgment. In 18:18 this power is given to the community.

The passage ends with Jesus sternly warning the disciples "not to tell anyone that he was the Messiah" (v. 20). They must learn what the Messiahship of Jesus is truly about before they can tell others (Mt. 16:21-28).

In the letter to the Romans, Paul appeals to his brothers and sisters to offer themselves to God as a living sacrifice. They are no longer to follow the ways of the world but to be transformed so that they may discern the will of God for them.

All have been given differing gifts through God's grace (12:6-8), which are to be used for the welfare of the entire community, the Body of Christ. No one can claim that his or her gifts are more important than those of others. Thus we are a body that presents itself to God—a body in which all are needed for wholeness and holiness.

POINTS TO PONDER

1. As you read the Gospel passage, what do you think it meant for Peter when he declared that Jesus was the Messiah? What do you think his expectations of Jesus were at this time?

2. What responsibilities did Jesus bestow upon Peter? What is the vision of the Church that emerges here? How are we called to carry out these tasks in the world today?

3. How do you answer the question of Jesus in Matthew 16:15 for yourself: "But who do you say that I am?"

4. In the story of the infant Moses in the reading from Exodus, imagine what it might have been like to be one of the midwives, Shiphrah, or Puah. What risks did these women take, and what example do they set for us today?

5. According to today's reading from Paul's letter to the Romans, how are members of the faith community to live together?

_____

_____

_____

_____

_____

_____

TAKING UP OUR CROSS

Exodus 3:1-15; Psalm 105:1-6, 23-26, 45c; Romans 12:9-21; Matthew 16:21-28

The Book of Exodus tells us that when the ever-increasing numbers of Israelites residing in Egypt became a threat, the Egyptians made slaves of the descendants of Jacob. In their distress, the Israelites cried out to God for deliverance. Thus God remembered the Divine covenant with the patriarchs and "took notice of them" (2:25).

In today's passage, Moses is called to be God's agent in the liberation of Israel. After being rescued as an infant from the Nile River by Pharaoh's daughter (2:5-10), Moses grew up in the royal household. However, after killing an Egyptian who was mistreating a Hebrew slave (Ex. 2:11-15), Moses fled from Egypt to the desert of Midian, where he married and started a new life.

One day as Moses was tending his father-in-law's sheep in the wilderness near Mt. Horeb (Sinai), his attention was caught by a bush that burned yet was not consumed. As Moses approached the bush, the Lord commanded him to remove his sandals before the Divine presence, as he was on holy ground.

Here the flaming bush serves a twofold purpose: first, to get the attention of Moses; and second as a manifestation of presence of the Divine (Ex. 19:18, Deut. 4:24; Ps. 104: 4; Ezek. 1:27).

The identity of the Lord is then revealed as the One who is the "God of your father, the God of Abraham, the God of Isaac, and the God of Jacob" (v. 6a). Here the Lord immediately makes a connection with Moses' own family while recalling God's historic relationship to these ancestors.

Moses is so filled with awe that he hides his face; to look upon the face of God was too much for a mere mortal to withstand (Gen. 32:30).

The Lord goes on to tell Moses that God has seen the misery of the Israelites, knows their suffering, and will deliver them from their oppression. Furthermore, Moses is to be the one to go to Pharaoh and lead God's people out of bondage in Egypt to a new and prosperous land.

Moses immediately protests that he is not the one for such a vocation. But God assures him that "I will be with you" (v. 12). Moses continues to object, saying that no one will believe that he acts for God—he does not even know God's name.

God then reveals to Moses, "I AM WHO I AM" (v. 14). This was to be God's name forever, "my title for all generations" (v. 15b). God is a dynamic presence who is absolute and unchanging. Unlike the gods of other nations, their God is not named by others.

Psalm 105 gives praise for God's "wonderful works" in the history of Israel. The verses for today recall the sojourn of the family of Jacob in Egypt and the call of Moses and Aaron. "He sent his servant Moses, and Aaron whom he had chosen. ... Praise the Lord!" (vv. 26, 45b).

PRAYER FOR THE DAY

Gracious Lord of all, in whose will there is contentment even in suffering: empower us, through the might of your Holy Spirit, to be the living expression of Jesus Christ and to carry our own crosses wherever you lead, and always to your glory and the well-being of all people. *Amen.*

The Gospel reading also looks at what it means to be called by God. Peter's confession that Jesus was the Messiah, "the Son of the living God" (Mt. 16:16), marks a major turning point in the ministry of Jesus. From "that time on" (v. 21, cf. 4:17), Jesus sets his face toward Jerusalem and begins to teach his disciples what Messiahship, and discipleship, truly mean.

In this first prediction of his Passion, Jesus presents the Apostles with the stunning revelation of the suffering and death he will endure, and of his rising again on the third day (cf Mk. 8:31-33; Lk. 9:18-22).

The followers of Jesus certainly did not associate suffering and death with the Messiah, but rather victory and glory. Even if there was a place in Jewish thought for the suffering servant (Is. 53:3-4), the disciples had no such expectations with regard to Jesus himself.

Thus Peter, speaking for the other disciples, rebukes Jesus saying, "God forbid it, Lord! This must never happen to you" (v. 22).

Jesus' new teaching shatters all of Peter's preconceptions about Messiahship, and his vehement outcry reveals the strength of his reaction.

Jesus responds with the harshest response ever directed toward one of his disciples: "Get behind me, Satan!" (v. 23; cf Mt. 4:10). Just moments before, Jesus had blessed Peter and designated him as the "rock" on which he would build his Church (16:17-19). Now Peter is chastised as a "stumbling block" for setting his mind on human rather than Divine things.

In verses 24-27, Jesus goes on to describe what true discipleship is all about. First of all, the most constant duty of a disciple is to follow (cf 4:19). Therefore, those who would follow Jesus must "deny themselves and take up their cross and follow me" (v. 24). If Jesus himself must suffer in a world where redemption comes through *sacrificial love nailed to a cross,* whoever attempts to follow Jesus must be ready to do likewise.

ON REFLECTION

The first and only association with the Messiah—for the disciples in particular and the people of Israel in general—was "victory and glory," not "suffering and death." The Messiah was to be the promised deliverer of the nation—not a refuted prophet who suffered and died in the most humiliating way possible. For that reason, the Cross was the decisive argument against the Messiahship of Jesus. As Scripture stated: "Anyone hung on a tree is under God's curse" (Deut. 21:23)—the law imposed on idolaters and blasphemers.

It is little wonder then that Peter, who has just confessed him as "Christ," takes Jesus aside and begins to rebuke him, saying, "God forbid it, Lord! This must never happen to you." Of course, Jesus wasn't sick. He wasn't looking forward to dying. Of all the temptations he faced, this one must have been the most intense and tempting of all—to listen to Peter, his "rock," and find another way of salvation. For that reason, I suspect, Jesus gave Peter, on whom he had just bestowed the "keys to the Kingdom," the harshest rebuke he ever gave anyone in the Gospels: "Get behind me, Satan!"

In the Cross, we therefore have the answer to all suffering. There is nothing in this life so terrible, so painful, and so death-dealing that, by God's grace, cannot be healed and turned somehow into good. That the empty Cross has come to be the most traditional—and powerful—symbol in Christianity is not by accident.

—H. King Oehmig

The true pattern of every servant of God must include self-denial—dying to self. To hold on to life in this world is to lose life eternal. To renounce life in this world is to gain what is everlasting.

In an ultimate judgment, the Son of Man would reward everyone to the extent that each agrees to *die to self* in accord with the pattern of the crucified Savior. Indeed, the coming of God's Kingdom is near.

The Apostle Paul gives further instructions to the community of faith on what is required to be a follower of Jesus. Paul was aware of the actuality of evil in the world and the need for Christians to fight against it; therefore he begins by urging the community to "love one another with mutual affection" (Rom. 12:10).

The practice of love was essential, since love was not only the greatest gift (cf 1 Cor. 12:31—13:13), but also the very core of Christian ethics.

He urged patience in suffering, perseverance in prayer, and contributing to the needs of the community (vv. 10-13). Christians should also bless their persecutors while sharing in the joys and griefs of others. They are to claim no special privileges for themselves, and certainly never repay evil for evil.

Finally, they are genuinely to seek to "live peaceably with all" (v. 18), and to refrain from seeking retribution for wrongs done them by others; vengeance is the Lord's concern. By acting in this way, they will see evil overcome by good, and will be true to their call as disciples of Jesus Christ.

POINTS TO PONDER

1. As you read the Gospel passage, why do you think Jesus pulled Peter aside and rebuked him? What misconceptions did Peter and the other disciples have about the Messiahship of Jesus? What difficulties do we continue to have today in understanding the meaning of the life and ministry of Christ?

2. In Matthew 16:23, Jesus accuses Peter of focusing on human rather than Divine things. How would you describe the difference, particularly in reference to experiences in your own life?

3. According to the Gospel passage, what is required of those who would follow Jesus? What does it mean to lose your life in order to find it?

4. What else do we learn about discipleship from the words of Paul in the Epistle reading from Romans?

5. What do today's passages tell us about following God's call? What changes do you need to make in your own life in order to follow God's call for you?

ON COMMUNITY LIFE

Exodus 12:1-14; Psalm 149; Romans 13:8-14; Matthew 18:15-20

After responding to God's call (Ex. 3:1-15), Moses returned to Egypt to confront Pharaoh and bring about the liberation of God's people. After a series of plagues, Pharaoh finally consented to allow the Hebrew slaves to leave Egypt, after God vowed to strike down (in a final plague) all the firstborn of the Egyptians. However, the offspring of the Hebrews would be spared.

In the passage for today, Moses gives detailed instructions to the people on the eve of their departure. This was to be the first act of their existence as the people of God—one they were commanded to celebrate throughout future generations as a "perpetual ordinance" (12:14b). Moreover, the saving power of the original action would continue to be experienced in future keeping of it.

From now on the month of the Exodus would be the beginning of the year. Thus, on this night and in the years to come, each family was to slaughter an unblemished year-old male lamb, roast it whole over a fire, and consume it along with unleavened bread and bitter herbs.

On this night of the Passover, they were to mark the doorposts and lintel of their houses with some of the lamb's blood. This blood was not only a symbol of the Lord's protection but also a reminder of God's promise to liberate Israel.

They were to eat in haste and be prepared to travel because, on that night, the angel of the Lord would carry out the final plague by striking down the firstborn of the Egyptians. This was to be the "passover of the Lord" (v. 11b): the Lord would "pass over" the homes marked with blood—and "no plague shall destroy you when I strike the land of Egypt" (v. 13b).

As a celebration of liberation, the Passover was the defining event in the life of Israel in which God's saving acts on behalf of Israel were fully manifested. As a historical event, it would bring hope to them during later times of oppression. As a ritual, Passover would become the most important of the Jewish festivals and serve to unite the Jewish people for more than three thousand years.

Chapter 18 of Matthew's Gospel comprises the fourth discourse of Jesus in which he focuses on life in the community of believers. It begins with Jesus' response to the disciples' question of who was the greatest in the Kingdom of heaven (18:1), and goes on to give a glimpse of how the early Church handled disputes between members.

Three steps are to be followed when one member of the community sins against another. First, the offended party should go in private to the person who caused the offense and explain the hurt that has been received. Similar instructions are found in Leviticus 19:17 in which individuals are to reason with their neighbor. If both parties desire to end the quarrel, the brother or sister has been won back: "You have regained that one" (Mt. 18:15b).

PRAYER FOR THE DAY

Grant us the grace, Holy Lord, to see one other—from every race, nation, and condition—as your children and worthy of our unconditional love. Set us free in the unity of the Holy Spirit to show forth your sacrificial love for the world, made manifest in the priceless gift of Jesus Christ, the Savior and Lord of all. *Amen.*

But sometimes such a conversation simply does not work. The offender may be more concerned with self-justification than with seeking reconciliation, and any overtures for peace are thus rejected. Then the offended must take action to protect the entire community, since any sin against one member risks the whole fellowship. When the offender continues in the behavior, it soon becomes more than a private grievance and must be brought before the whole community.

Thus, the second step is to call one or two members to witness that the offended one has sought concord (v. 16). Perhaps such public exposure will move the offending party toward agreement, and all will be well once again. This procedure is derived from Deuteronomy 19:15, which states that only on the evidence of two or three witnesses should a charge be sustained.

If the offender still refuses to yield to the overarching good of the community, then the third step is to take the matter before the whole assembly (v. 17b). If the offender still refuses to listen, then the final step may be exclusion from the community and treating such a person as an outsider (v. 17c).

Jesus then goes on to bestow upon the disciples the authority that had previously been given to Peter (16:19). "Whatever you bind on earth will be bound in heaven, and whatever you loose on earth will be loosed in heaven" (18:18). Those things that the disciples declare to be a matter of obligation on earth are to be bound in heaven as well.

In conclusion, Jesus offers assurance of his presence. "For where two or three are gathered in my name, I am there among them" (v. 20).

Today's Psalm 149 exhorts us to praise God's name in dance and song with all the instruments of music that we possess. *The Lord rejoices in the people and gives help to the humble.*

ON REFLECTION

Church fights might be the meanest of all. The fact that Christians are somehow supposed to be "nicer" than earth people—let alone "righter"—just seems to add to the fury. A heavyweight championship prizefight in Las Vegas would be a lot cleaner—and certainly less damaging in the long run. The "walking wounded" from church fights are legion. What a tragedy.

In many ways this teaching for today follows an institutional pattern having little to do with Jesus. The Lord had said to forgive even when forgiveness was refused (Lk. 23:34). Nowhere in the Gospels does he ever refuse fellowship with "Gentiles and tax-collectors"; to the contrary, Jesus always is welcoming notorious sinners to him—without any previous confession or promise of amendment of life. Since there were no "Christian congregations" during the life of Jesus, it makes this kind of teaching sound more like "Matthew's Jesus" dealing with congregational problems.

In his book *The Road Less Traveled* (Touchstone, 1998), M. Scott Peck, M. D., says that the greatest risk of love is to "exercise power with humility." As applied to confrontation, when we tell another "we are right; you are wrong," we can do it in two ways. We can do it with self-righteous arrogance, or we can do it through "care-frontation." The latter consists of rigorous self-scrutiny, combined with a deep empathy for the person being confronted. It is always approached with the words of Jesus in mind: "Do not judge, so that you may not be judged. For with the judgment you make you will be judged, and the measure you give will be the measure you get" (Mt. 7:1-2).

—H. King Oehmig

The Apostle Paul gives further instructions in his letter to the Romans on how those in the community of faith are to relate to one another. First and foremost, such relations are to be based on love for one another, "for the one who loves another has fulfilled the law" (13:8).

Love fulfills the commandments against adultery, murder, theft, and covetousness and leads to the understanding in verse 9 to "love your neighbor as yourself" (cf Lev. 19:18). Only those who are capable of loving themselves can truly love others as well; and in God's intention for humanity, all are neighbors.

Verses 11-14 have an eschatological urgency about them, since Paul believes that salvation is near. Thus it is imperative that Christians live honorably by laying aside the works of darkness and putting on the armor of light (v. 12b). Just as daylight follows the night, so does the new age follow the old age of darkness.

Finally, they are to cast aside irresponsible behavior. There is to be no quarreling and jealousy among them, so they can truly "put on the Lord Jesus Christ" (v. 14).

POINTS TO PONDER

1. As you read Matthew 18:15-17, discuss the three-step procedure for settling disputes within the community. What are the basic principles at work here and how might they be applied in current situations?

2. Under what circumstances do you think expulsion from the Christian community is warranted? At what point do the welfare and harmony of the community take precedence over maintaining relationship with a particular individual?

3. In verses 18-20, Jesus speaks of the spiritual power of the gathered community. What responsibility do we assume when we come together in the name of Jesus?

4. The reading from Exodus includes specific instructions for celebrating the Passover as a "perpetual ordinance" throughout the generations. What is the benefit of maintaining specific rituals, not only in church, but also in our personal and family life?

5. In the Epistle passage, Paul gives directions to the community in Rome on how they are to live together. He sums up the commandments with the familiar injunction to "love your neighbor as yourself." What do we need to do in our relationships with others to make this commandment become a reality?

_____

_____

_____

_____

_____

_____

UNRESTRICTED, ENDLESS FORGIVENESS

Exodus 14:19-31; Psalm 114; Romans 14:1-12; Matthew 18:21-35

When Pharaoh finally allowed the Hebrews to leave Egypt, the Lord guided them as a pillar of cloud by day and a pillar of fire by night (Ex. 13:17-22). However, Pharaoh soon regretted his decision to free the Israelites, and pursued them with horses and chariots, overtaking them as they were camped by the sea.

When the people saw the approaching army, they were afraid and denounced Moses for taking them away to die in the wilderness (Ex. 14:11a). But the angel of God that had been preceding the Israelites in the cloud now moved behind them in protection.

At God's command, Moses stretched out his hand over the sea, and God drove back the waters through a strong east wind that lasted all night and created a dry path for the Israelites to walk through to the other side. When the Egyptians attempted to follow them, God once again commanded Moses to stretch out his hand over the sea. As the Israelites looked on, the Egyptian chariots became mired in the mud, and when the waters closed in again, all the Egyptians and their chariots were destroyed.

The crossing of the sea marked a turning point for Israel, as they witnessed what the Lord did against the Egyptians, and believed in the Lord and in Moses (v. 31).

The Lord acted to save Israel from oppression purely out of love and mercy (Deut. 7:8). Moses was God's chosen agent in this act, as God's promise to be with him at the burning bush was realized (Ex. 3:12).

This saving act was to be recited again and again in Israel's history, beginning with the Song of Moses (Ex. 15:1-18) and the Song of Miriam: "Sing to the Lord, for he has triumphed gloriously; horse and rider he has thrown into the sea" (15:21).

Today's Psalm, 114, appropriately exults in God's power. *Hallelujah!* Israel was brought out of Egypt. The sea fled before God's people, and Jordan was driven back. Mountains trembled, and indeed, they were moved. The whole earth must tremble at the presence of the Lord, who brought forth water from hard rocks and refreshed the people with a flowing spring.

The Gospel passage for today concludes Matthew's fourth discourse, and further illustrates Jesus' instructions on forgiveness in 18:15-20.

The reading begins with Peter, as spokesman for the disciples, asking how often one should forgive, "As many as seven times?" (18:21). Peter thought he was generous in suggesting that one ought to forgive seven times; but Jesus replies that one ought to forgive seventy-seven times.

However, the exact number is not the point here. Jesus is saying that there is to be no limit on forgiveness. The spirit of forgiveness should so pervade our lives that we simply lose count of how many times we are required to forgive.

Elsewhere in the Gospel we find that the appeal for God's mercy can be made only by those who show mercy to others (Mt. 6:12). Thus, we are always to look to our own repentance before God.

PRAYER FOR THE DAY

O God of unrestricted love and limitless grace, by the gift of your Holy Spirit may we daily be willing to set aside unforgiveness of any sort: may we aspire to that Kingdom love that empowered our Lord Jesus Christ to forgive his executioners even as he was perishing on the Cross, and this we ask in the power of your Name. *Amen.*

This understanding of limitless forgiveness is further illustrated in the parable of the unforgiving servant (vv. 23-34), in which a king settles accounts with his servants, one of whom owes him ten thousand talents. This is a highly exorbitant amount, exceeding King Herod's treasury for ten years. It illustrates God's extravagant and limitless forgiveness.

When the servant could not pay back such a debt, the king ordered him and his family to be sold into slavery along with all his possessions. When the servant begged for patience and mercy, the king had pity upon him and forgave the debt.

After being absolved from his tremendous obligation, the servant encountered a fellow servant who likewise owed him a substantial amount—about three months' pay. It would seem that such radical forgiveness and thankfulness for the king's generosity would prompt him to show the same kindness to another.

But instead of reciprocating the forgiveness he had just received, the servant grabbed the other by the throat and demanded payment. When the fellow servant begged for patience and mercy, the first servant refused and had him thrown into prison. Unlike the case of his own vast debt, there was a reasonable chance of repayment in this situation; but he refused to take pity.

When the original servant's actions were reported to the king, he revoked the pardon and ordered punishment. Although torture was not allowed under Jewish law, the reality of the consequences of sin is underscored here.

The actions of the king represent those of God, who forgives freely and without limit. Therefore, we too are called to forgive our brothers and sisters from our heart (v. 35). No one can earn forgiveness from God; forgiveness is a free gift extended to every person. Thus we are to repent and, in mercy and compassion, extend such forgiveness also to others.

ON REFLECTION

C. S. Lewis commented: "Everyone says forgiveness is a lovely idea—until they have something to forgive." How true. In the Greek, the verb "to forgive" is *aphiemi,* meaning "to let go, to set free." Perhaps there is no greater "litmus test" of faith than this Gospel capacity to let go of injury and set free the injurer. Even if it is ourselves.

Simon Tugwell in his book *Living With God* (Templegate, 1975) tells a story of two monks in Japan. They were traveling down a muddy road—with rain still pouring down. Coming around a bend, they met a lovely geisha, dressed in a fine silk kimono and sash, unable to cross an intersection. "Come on," said Tanzan, one of the monks, "I will carry you across." He lifted the girl in his arms and carried her over the mud and rushing water. Ekido, the other monk, did not speak again to Tanzan until they reached the monastery that night. No longer able to restrain himself, Ekido blurted out: "We monks don't go near females—especially young and lovely ones. It is dangerous. Why did you do that?" "I left the girl there," Tanzan said. "Are you still carrying her?"

The Parable of the Two Debtors makes clear the Gospel message that forgiveness is *unlimited* and *forever*—or "seventy times seven." This does not mean that we Christians are bulletproof, or that we don't get hurt or angry. It just means that we *intend* not to nurture unforgiveness, allowing God to heal us of it. In heaven, there are only forgiven sinners. In hell, there are only forgiven sinners too.

—H. King Oehmig

The Apostle Paul likewise offered counsel concerning certain practices within the community in Rome. The passage for today arises from differences concerning abstaining or eating various foods as individuals saw fit (14:1-4).

Paul stressed the importance of motivation rather than specific practice. Whatever is done should be "in honor of the Lord" (v. 6); therefore, they were not to pass judgment on one another. There was to be mutual tolerance that honored each person's conscientious decision as a form of personal response and obedience to God.

There was no room for despising or resenting one another over differences. "Why do you pass judgment on your brother or sister?" (v. 10).

Ultimately, we live and die, not to ourselves, but to the Lord. For this Christ died and rose again.

Thus, every person must stand for his or her own deeds at the day of judgment. All are accountable to the Lord, and therefore everyone shall bow to God Almighty and praise God's name (cf Is. 45:23). Paul calls for mutual respect, tolerance, and the reconciliation that comes when we acknowledge that we are the Lord's.

To God alone belongs judgment, and to God alone are we ultimately accountable. This approach leaves no room for pettiness about variations in practices, but rather encourages charity in all aspects of living.

POINTS TO PONDER

1. As you read over the Parable of the Unforgiving Servant, put yourself in the place of the man who was released from his debt. How do you think he might have felt when he discovered that his debt had been forgiven? How do you explain his later actions toward his fellow servant who owed him money?

2. Here Jesus calls us to practice unlimited forgiveness in our personal relationships. Think of a time when you forgave another person, as well as a time when you yourself were forgiven. As you compare the two experiences, discuss what it is like to forgive as well as to be forgiven.

3. How would you define forgiveness? What does it mean to forgive "from your heart" (v. 35)?

4. What are the attributes of tolerance that Paul proclaims to the Christian community in the reading from Romans? How can we apply these principles?

5. The reading from Exodus tells the story of the escape of the Israelites from the Egyptian army. Through this miraculous event, the people "believed in the Lord and in his servant Moses" (Ex. 14:31b). What are the events in your own life that have strengthened your faith?

THE LABORERS IN THE VINEYARD

Exodus 16:2-15; Psalm 105:1-6, 37-45; Philippians 1:21-30; Matthew 20:1-16

After God had delivered the Israelites from bondage in Egypt, they began their trek through the wilderness to the promised land. However, the hardships in the Sinai Desert soon caused the people to complain bitterly against Moses and Aaron. They seemed to have forgotten their harsh Egyptian slave masters, as they longed for the fleshpots and bread of Egypt, and accused Moses and Aaron of bringing them into the desert to die of hunger.

Previously, when the people had complained about the lack of water, God had provided for their needs (15:22-27). Now God called Moses and Aaron and gave them instructions for the people.

Every morning God would "rain bread from heaven" (Ex. 16:4), which they were to gather for their daily needs. However, on the sixth day they were to gather twice as much, as there would be no bread on the seventh day, the Sabbath. In the evening, quails would settle in the camp so that the Israelites could catch them for food as well.

In the morning when the dew lifted, there was a "fine flaky substance, as fine as frost on the ground" (v. 14). This "bread" or manna is a naturally occurring substance in the Sinai Desert derived from the secretions of scale insects that feed on the sap of tamarisk bushes. It is sweet and full of carbohydrates, but does not keep well, thus the need to gather it daily.

Although the complaints of the Hebrew people led to a supplying of their needs, this crisis was also a test of faith (v. 4). The daily provision of food was another reminder of the saving power of God on behalf of the people (v. 6).

The Psalm for today, 105, is a hymn of praise that recalls God's care and protection of the Israelites during their sojourn in the desert following their escape from Egypt. The Lord provided food and water in abundance and remembered the "holy promise" to Abraham of a new land for Israel, so that they might keep the Lord's statutes and observe the Lord's laws.

The Gospel reading of the parable of the workers in the vineyard is unique to Matthew and provides another illustration of God's generosity and compassion.

After Jesus' conversation with a rich young man who was unable to give up his possessions and follow him (Mt. 19:16-26), the Apostle Peter pointed out that he and the other disciples *had* in fact left everything behind and should thus receive a greater reward (v. 27).

Jesus replied that indeed they "will receive a hundred-fold, and will inherit eternal life" (19:29). But then he goes on to tell a story that illustrates the radical nature of God's grace and mercy.

PRAYER FOR THE DAY

O God, whose property is always to have mercy and to give regardless of merit, may we forever realize that we are saved by grace through faith in our Lord Jesus Christ; therefore, by the overflowing power of the Holy Spirit, may we go forth to serve our neighbors and the world with joy and singleness of heart. *Amen.*

As the parable begins, a landowner goes out at dawn to hire workers for his vineyard (20:1). The laborers agree to the payment of a denarius, the standard daily wage, and set about their work. As the day goes on, the owner continues to hire more workers at 9:00 a. m., noon, and 3:00 p. m. His agreement with these workers is to pay them "whatever is right" (v. 4), and no definite amount is established. At 5:00 p. m., he recruits still others to join the work. At 6:00 p. m. the landowner calls his manager to pay the workers their wages, as was the custom (Lev. 19:13; Deut. 24:14-15).

Up to this point typical labor practices in the ancient world are described. However, the story takes a curious twist in verse 8, when the landowner instructs the manager to pay all the laborers one denarius, beginning with those who had worked only an hour and going on to those who had worked the full twelve hours.

Seeing this, the other workers expect to be paid more, according to the number of hours they worked. However, to their astonishment and anger, they too receive just a denarius.

The disgruntled workers confront the landowner, pointing out that they have worked twelve hours and "borne the burden of the day and the scorching heat" (v. 12). It was unfair that they should receive the same pay as those who had worked only one hour. The owner reminds them that he has paid them exactly what they agreed upon earlier in the day; so they should take their pay and go. "Friend, I am doing you no wrong; did you not agree with me for the usual daily wage?" (v. 13).

The landowner goes on to say that he has the right to give as he chooses. "Am I not allowed to do what I choose with what belongs to me? Or are you envious because I am generous?" (v. 15).

ON REFLECTION

Robert Farrar Capon writes in his book *The Parables of Grace* (Eerdmans, 1990): "To judge from the responses Jesus provoked from the religious experts of the day, it is plain that what he said and did didn't look much like religion to them. Respectable religionists can spot an absence of conventional piety a mile away, and the scribes and Pharisees did just that."

It is hard to blame these by-the-book guys. Not many of us would act differently. When the Johnny-come-lately workers get as much as the early birds, howls of protest go up. The phones ring off the hook at the AFLCIO—or the Better Business Bureau. E-mails to Congress go out. Spouses and family members hear about it over dinner—for weeks. The bishop's office is inundated with complaints. A "special committee" is formed to study what happened and to make recommendations on how to handle it differently next time.

The point of the Parable of the Laborers in the Vineyard, of course, concerns not the workers, but the *vineyard owner.* God will not be placed under any kind of obligation whatsoever. *"I will be who I will be,"* as the Voice from the burning bush said to Moses, and that means "I will be gracious as I will be gracious"—according to *agape* in the New Testament. This love does not *recognize* worth—it *confers* it. It creates and gives acceptance, independent of merit. As unmotivated as it is unwarranted: this is Jesus-love. What a shame it is that there are so many Christians who have yet to hear the Gospel.

—H. King Oehmig

Jesus is telling us that God's Kingdom presents a reversal of what is normally expected, in terms of rewards (cf the Beatitudes in Mt. 5:1-11). There will be equality among the people of God who are obligated to see that the needs of everyone in the community are met regardless of rank, privilege, or length of service. God is extravagantly generous and gives more than we deserve.

Jesus' words that *the last will be first, and the first will be last* (19:30; 20:16) mean that it doesn't matter whether we are lifelong disciples or if we find Christ at the end of our journey; God gives all the gift of eternal life.

The Epistle is the first of four readings from Paul's letter to the church at Philippi in Macedonia—the first church on European soil established by Paul. Paul writes from prison and expresses his appreciation for the Philippians' gifts.

His words reflect how he was torn between wanting to die in order to be fully united with Christ—yet also desired to live to continue his ministry. "For to me, living is Christ and dying is gain. If I am to live in the flesh, that means fruitful labor for me; and I do not know which I prefer" (1:21-22). Given this tension, Paul is confident that either way he will be allowed to accomplish God's will.

Paul believed that his missionary work was not yet complete and that his continued ministry would be of substantial value to his converts. Thus he anticipated a time of extended work among them (v. 25).

He relied on the prayers of the community and the help of the Holy Spirit to continue the work he was given to do. He expressed faith that the people would be able to stand firm against their opponents and prevail through any suffering they might encounter for the *privilege* of believing in Christ (v. 29).

POINTS TO PONDER

1. Reflect on the parable in the Gospel passage first from the perspective of the landowner; then of the early laborers; and finally from the viewpoint of the last workers hired. Discuss the issues and insights that arise from these different points of view.

2. What human assumptions about fairness and merit are challenged in the parable? What comforts as well as disturbs you here?

3. The parable ends with the phrase "so the last will be first, and the first will be last" (Mt. 20:16). In light of the parable, what do these words mean for you? What is the most important learning for you from this parable?

4. As you read the words of Paul in his letter to the Philippians, what do you think it meant for Paul to live a life that is "worthy of the gospel of Christ" (1:27)? What does it mean for you to live in such a manner?

5. All of the readings for today show the abundance of God's care and mercy. How have you experienced this generosity in your own life?

_____

_____

_____

_____

_____

THE AUTHORITY OF JESUS

Exodus 17:1-7; Psalm 78:1-4, 12-16; Philippians 2:1-13; Matthew 21:23-32

As the Israelites continued across the Sinai wilderness after leaving Egypt, they camped at Rephidim, but found no water there. Slavery had provided them with a measure of security in that they had adequate food and water; but now, in their discomfort and need, they quarreled with Moses and demanded water for themselves and their livestock. Moses responded, "Why do you test the Lord?" (Ex. 17:2).

As they persisted in their complaints, Moses turned to the Lord for help to avoid a revolt endangering his own life (v. 4). God answered Moses by instructing him to go, along with elders, ahead of the people. He was to use the staff he used to strike the Nile (Ex. 14:16) to *strike a rock* at Horeb that would yield drinking water.

Moses did as the Lord commanded, and called the place Massah (to put to the test) and Meribah (to quarrel or contend), because the Israelites had tested the Lord, saying "Is the Lord among us or not?" (v. 7).

Again and again, the Lord provided for the safety and sustenance of Israel, despite their doubt and unfaithfulness.

The Psalmist called attention to this provision of water in the desert as well as "the glorious deeds of the Lord" and all the wonders God had done (78:4). God's people were to tell these stories to their children so that they would never forget the compassion and power of the Lord on behalf of Israel.

As Jesus continued on his journey to Jerusalem, he continued to encounter opposition from the religious establishment. In the verses preceding today's Gospel passage (Mt. 21:23-27), the authority of Jesus to teach was questioned by the chief priests and elders: "By what authority are you doing these things, and who gave you this authority?" (v. 23). In posing this question, Jesus' opponents hoped to discredit and trap him into declaring that his authority came from God, which would make him vulnerable to a charge of blasphemy.

In true rabbinic style, Jesus replied with another question: "Did the baptism of John come from heaven, or was it of human origin?" (v. 25). The priests and elders argued the question among themselves. If they answered that John's baptism was from God, then they would need to explain why they did not acknowledge and affirm John. However, if they replied that John's baptism was "of human origin" (v. 26), they were afraid of the response of the crowds, who revered John as a prophet.

Jesus' query had put the priests and elders in a quandary, forcing them to admit, "We do not know" (v. 27a). Jesus had the last word as he dismissed the authority of the religious leaders to question him. "Neither will I tell you by what authority I am doing these things" (v. 27b).

PRAYER FOR THE DAY

Lord Jesus, who taught with freedom and authority, and called us to follow you in the way that leads to abundant life: give us the grace of your Holy Spirit, that we may with sure confidence and a steadfast faith express your will to draw all people to know the Holy God in the intimate way you have shown. *Amen.*

To illustrate his point, Jesus then went on to tell a series of parables, beginning with the story of a man and his two sons. The man asked his first son to go and work in the vineyard, but the son refused. However, he later changed his mind and went to work after all. The father went to his second son and requested the same thing. This son answered, "I go, sir" (v. 30); but in fact he did nothing. Jesus asked, "Which of the two did the will of his father?" (v. 31).

The priests and elders replied that the first son obeyed the will of his father, and in doing so, they exposed their own hypocrisy. For the first son could be compared to the tax collectors and prostitutes who represented corruption and immorality, but who eventually heard and believed in John's message of repentance. Thus these so-called sinners would enter the Kingdom of heaven first.

On the other hand, the religious authorities were like the second son, who professed to be righteous, but rejected John and all that he taught. Even after they saw the changed lives of the tax collectors and prostitutes, they still refused to believe. They continued to play the part of the second son who would say "yes" but never follow through.

The message here is that what matters is *what we actually do* in response to God's call. The religious respectability of affirming the right thing, but not acting upon it, stands in the way of authentic response to God.

It is the "poor in spirit" (5:3) who understand that they must look to a source of provision beyond themselves. Such people find the Kingdom; while those who regard themselves as self-sufficient do not receive the highest gift.

ON REFLECTION

We human beings don't like being justified by anything outside our control. Our self-worth is made up of what we do—according to the way we look, the amount of money we make, and the number of trophies we win. Either we "measure up"—or we don't. Marcus Borg called them the "three As" of life: Affluence, Attractiveness, and Achievement.

Of course, Gospel "worthiness" has nothing to do with any of these things; in fact, the more successful we are in achieving them, the harder it is to come to Jesus. Just read the story of the man who had many possessions and went away from Jesus sorrowful (Mk. 10:17-22)—or the Parable of the Great Banquet (Lk. 14:16-24).

As Frederick Buechner writes in *Wishful Thinking:* "The Beautiful People all send in their excuses—their real estate, their livestock, their sex lives—so the host sends his social secretary out into the streets to bring in the poor, the maimed, the blind, and the lame. The string ensemble strikes up the overture to *The Bartered Bride,* the champagne glasses are filled, the cold pheasant is passed around, and there they all sit by candlelight with their white canes and their empty sleeves, their orthopedic shoes, and aluminum walkers. A woman with a hair-lip proposes a toast. An old man, with the face of Lear on the heath, rises to his feet. A deaf-mute thinks people are starting to go home and pushes back from the table. Rose petals float in the finger bowls. The strings shift into the *Liebestod.* With parables and jokes both, if you have to have them explained, don't bother."

—H. King Oehmig

The passage for today from Paul's letter to the Philippians includes an eloquent Christ hymn (2:6-11). Paul begins by encouraging the believers to be of one mind and spirit by having the same love and thus making his own joy complete (vv. 1-2).

Such unity can occur only if the disciples renounce selfish ambition as Christ has done. In humility they must treat the needs of others as more important than their own. Thus they are to "Let the same mind be in you that was in Christ Jesus" (v. 5).

This mind of Christ is expressed in Christ's incarnation and mission. This self-expenditure on God's part to become fully human in the person of Jesus Christ is the essence of the Gospel message. He who in eternity is God did not see his likeness or equality with God as a prize to be grasped (v. 6). Christ's godliness was self-emptying; he became human and was subject to a painful and shameful death on the cross (vv. 7-8).

Therefore, the Father exalted that humility, and "gave him the name that is above every name, so that at the name of Jesus every knee should bend" (vv. 9-10). And so also should every tongue acknowledge that Jesus Christ is Lord, to the glory of God the Father.

When Paul goes on to exhort the Philippians to "work out your own salvation" (v. 12), this is not to contradict justification by grace. Rather, they are to take responsibility for that salvation, and with fear and trembling to remember that, while they are responsible to God, the Lord is also at work in their lives, enabling them to persevere for God's good pleasure.

POINTS TO PONDER

1. Consider the actions of the two sons as you read the Gospel parable. Which one of the sons do you think ultimately obeyed the will of his father, and why do you think this?

2. Reflect on the responses of the two sons in terms of your own relationship with God. How are you sometimes like one or the other? According to this parable, what will be required to enter the Kingdom of heaven?

3. The parables of Jesus are meant to turn our human assumptions about life upside down. What comfortable attitudes are challenged by the parable of the two sons?

4. In the Epistle, Paul encourages the Philippians to live in humility and obedience as Christ himself did. How would you define these two qualities, and how can you make them a part of your own daily living?

5. As you look at all of the passages for today, what do they suggest about personal responsibility in our relationship with God and others?

THE WICKED TENANTS

Exodus 20:1-4, 7-9, 12-20; Psalm 19; Philippians 3:4b-14; Matthew 21:33-46

The giving of the Ten Commandments in today's Old Testament passage is the culmination of the covenantal relationship between God and Israel that began with Abraham. Israel has been chosen and redeemed by God, who now gives them the gift of *Torah*—i. e., instruction, or teaching—which will not only shape every aspect of their lives, but also provide a means of response to God's redemptive love (cf Deut. 5:6-21).

More accurately translated as "ten words" or "ten statements," the commandments are arranged with the first four pertaining to relationship with God, and the remaining six relating to others.

The opening words, "I am the Lord your God" (v. 2), serve as an introduction, and establish the authority and identity of God as the one who liberated Israel from slavery. Because of God's actions on behalf of Israel, "you shall have no other gods before me" (v. 3).

This relationship with God also prohibited the worship of idols (v. 4) and making "wrongful use of the name of the Lord" (v. 7). God's name is not to be used to support false statements.

The fourth commandment requires that the seventh day be given to the Lord through abstaining from normal labor (v. 8). This day is holy, since the Lord rested on the seventh day of creation (Gen. 2:3) and thereby sanctified it.

Relationships with others in the next six commandments are to be characterized first of all by giving honor and respect, especially to the care of elderly parents in order to insure that future generations will have the right to inherit (v. 12).

The next three commandments deal with civil issues, beginning with "You shall not murder" (v. 13). This is sometimes translated as *you shall not kill,* which implies a much broader prohibition. In fact, there are cases in the Torah for which the punishment is death (Ex. 21:12-17). However, the commandment is concerned with protecting human life, which belongs to God.

The prohibition against adultery (v. 14) points to respect for marriage and the importance of family stability. Not only is adultery a violation of the marital relationship, it is a sin against God (Gen. 39:9).

Stealing (v. 15) is prohibited, as is bearing false witness against one's neighbor (v. 16). This goes beyond legal perjury and includes slander or injurious, deceptive ruining of another's reputation.

The final commandment warns against coveting or lusting after anything belonging to one's neighbor. True obedience to God involves not only the avoidance of certain specific acts, but also intentions of the heart. Trespass against a neighbor is also sin against God.

PRAYER FOR THE DAY

Gracious and ever-faithful God, friend of sinners and sanctifier of the faithful: suffuse us in the wonder and power of the Holy Spirit, that we may know the Gospel of Jesus Christ as a banquet of liberation, a celebration of the magnificence of your love. And may we witness, in word and deed, to this eternal truth unto the ends of the earth. *Amen.*

The initial reaction of the Israelites was fear. But Moses urged them not to be afraid, as what they witnessed was another sign of God's power on behalf of Israel.

Psalm 19 reminds us that the heavens themselves are telling the glory of God. The Creator God who made all has also given us laws to live by—perfect decrees that rejoice the heart when kept in faith. In this understanding is victory and ultimate peace.

In the Gospel passage, Jesus uses the imagery of Isaiah's Song of the Vineyard in the parable of the wicked tenants (cf Mk. 12: 1-12; Lk. 20:9-19), as the religious leaders continue to question his authority (Mt. 21:23). Jesus begins by describing a common practice in first-century Palestine in which an absentee landowner planted a vineyard and then leased it out to tenants for a share of the final crop in payment.

At harvest time, the landowner sent his slaves to collect his share. However, the tenants beat the slaves and killed one of them. When the landowner sent even more slaves a second time, they too were beaten and driven away. Thus the landowner decided to send his son in the belief that "They will respect my son" (v. 37). However, the tenants plotted together and killed the son in order to seize his inheritance.

Jesus then asks the scribes and Pharisees what the landowner should do to the tenants when he learns that his son has been killed. They reply that the tenants deserve a "miserable death" (v. 41), and that the landowner should lease the vineyard to other tenants.

In this allegory, the vineyard represents Israel, and the landowner stands for God. The slaves who are sent to bring the owner the produce from the vineyard are the historic prophets who endured insult, imprisonment, beating, and even death to bring God's message to the people.

ON REFLECTION

Webster defines "karma" in Eastern religions this way: "The totality of a person's actions in one of the successive states of existence is thought of as determining the person's fate in the next." Call it the law of "cause and effect." And there is a certain truth to it in the Bible. "Do not judge, so that you may not be judged," Jesus taught (Mt. 7:1). "You reap whatever you sow" (Gal. 6:7). Even the Ten Commandments suggest a kind of karma: "the iniquity of parents" is visited upon the third and fourth generations (Ex. 20:4-6).

Christianity throws the concept of "karma" upside down: "While we were still weak ... Christ died for the ungodly." God's love for us is proven in that "while we still were sinners Christ died for us" (Rom. 5:6-8). Jesus dies, in other words, not for the well behaved or the deserving, but for those who have erred and strayed like lost sheep.

In the Parable of the Wicked Tenants—clearly an allegory on the mistreatment of the prophets and the murder of Jesus—the "karma" that the chief priests and elders invoke on the wicked tenants is what most of us would imagine: "He will put those wretches to a miserable death" (Mt. 21:41). Justice demands no less. And yet—what happens on Easter morning is not a holocaust unleashed by a vengeful Father-God, but the miracle of *Resurrection.* God's Gospel love remains constant—giving us the best even when we have done our worst. The only "karma," Christianly speaking, is grace.

—H. King Oehmig

The final messenger is God's son—the Messiah and heir.

The wicked tenants are not Israel as a nation, but the people who have ruled Israel, including those who held authority in the time of Jesus. As the leaders of Israel, they should be faithful stewards, but they have not borne good fruit (Mt. 3:8, 10; 7:16-20; 12:33; 13:8). Thus their authority should be taken away and given into the care of those who would render to God what the Lord demands (v. 43).

Jesus goes on to predict his own suffering and death at the hands of the religious authorities as he cites Psalm 118:22-23 in verse 42 (cf Acts 4: 11; 1 Pet. 2:7). Furthermore, those who oppose him will not only lose their authority, they will also be crushed by that very same stone (v. 44)—the cornerstone that is Jesus.

As the religious authorities realized that they were in fact the wicked tenants of whom Jesus spoke, they sought to apprehend him, but were afraid to do so because the people regarded Jesus as a prophet.

True devotion to God demands a way of life that results in the fruits of God's Kingdom. When those who manage the vineyard become obstacles to giving worthy fruit back to God, God will find new workers.

In his letter to the Philippians, Paul writes that there is nothing in life that can compare to the surpassing value of knowing Christ—not even his own impeccable heritage. For Jesus' sake he was willing to consider all else as "rubbish" (3:8b).

The only righteousness of value comes from God, through faith in Jesus Christ. Paul hoped to know for himself the power of Christ's Resurrection through sharing in Christ's sufferings (v. 10). Paul does not claim that he has reached that status; but he presses toward "the prize of the heavenly call of God in Christ Jesus" (v. 14).

POINTS TO PONDER

1. The story of the wicked tenants describes an economic arrangement that would have been familiar to Jesus' listeners. What does the relationship between the landowner and his tenants suggest about our relationship with God? What is God like in this story?

2. What do you think should happen to the tenants who killed the landowner's slaves and his son?

3. In Mathew 21:42, Jesus is described as the "cornerstone." What does this image suggest to you about Jesus? How is Jesus the cornerstone for your own life?

4. In the final verse, Jesus calls us to produce the "fruits of the kingdom." What are these fruits? What can happen if we fail to be good stewards of God's gifts?

5. Read the other Lessons for today as well. How do the commandments given by Moses relate to our work in God's vineyard? What changes are we called to make in our lives through these insights?

THE WEDDING BANQUET

Exodus 32:1-14; Psalm 106:1-6, 19-23; Philippians 4:1-9; Matthew 22:1-14

After their release from bondage in Egypt, the Israelites had received the Commandments and pledged themselves to a covenant relationship with God. But while they were encamped in the desert awaiting Moses' return from Mt. Sinai, they grew impatient and begged Aaron for a visible representation for devotion—after they had just pledged not to make idols (Ex. 20:4).

So Aaron ordered the people to bring him their gold, and had it melted down and fashioned into a calf. Aaron constructed an altar and proclaimed a festival day with burnt offerings and sacrifices. "These are your gods, O Israel, who brought you up out of the land of Egypt!" (Ex. 32:4).

The Lord was very angry at the sight of the people reveling before the golden calf, and ordered Moses to "Go down at once!" (v. 7). In the face of such disobedience, God vowed to "consume" the people (v. 10). The promise to make Israel a great nation would now pass to Moses: "... of you I will make a great nation" (v. 10; cf Gen. 12:2).

Moses answered God's wrath by interceding for Israel. He first asked why the Lord was so angry with the people after so mightily bringing them out of Egypt. By destroying them now, he suggests, God would damage the Divine reputation among the other nations (v. 12).

"Turn from your fierce wrath; change your mind and do not bring disaster on your people" (v. 12b). Moses went on to remind the Lord of the promises of land and descendants made to the ancestors of Israel.

The passage ends with a simple statement of the Lord's "change of heart" (v. 14). Moses acted as a mediator with God, who listened and turned away from anger—reminding us once again that God's justice is always tempered with mercy.

"Who can utter the mighty doings of the Lord, or declare all his praise?" Psalm 106: 2 asks. It recounts how, when the Israelites forgot God, Moses served as a buffer to keep God from destroying them.

In the Gospel reading Jesus tells the third in a series of parables directed to those who refuse to accept the message of God's Messiah.

The occasion here is a royal marriage banquet. Such marriage feasts could last for several days, and so, as is the custom, the king sent his slaves to remind the invited guests that it was time to come. When they did not arrive, the king sent more slaves to compel them to come to the banquet.

However, the guests still refused to come; they "made light" (Mt. 22:5) of the invitation. Some went about their usual occupations of tending to their farms and businesses, but others killed the king's slaves.

PRAYER FOR THE DAY

Holy God, author and giver of peace, source of all well-being: instill in our hearts through the working of your Holy Spirit a true sense of gratitude, that we may show forth the boundless riches of knowing Jesus Christ as Lord, living in the power of your creative abundance, and this we pray in your holy Name. *Amen.*

In his anger, the king sent his army to destroy the murderers and the city in which they lived. The destruction of the city can be taken as a reference to the fall of Jerusalem in A. D. 70.

The host commands his slaves to go out into the streets and bring in everyone they find to partake of the feast. The slaves do as they are instructed and gather all the people they can find, "both good and bad; so the wedding hall was filled with guests" (v. 10). This points out the mixed nature of those who are called by Jesus to God's Kingdom.

Those who might be expected to respond to the Divine call show only contempt for it; while those who seem disqualified accept the invitation and are welcomed. Those God uses are often the most unlikely candidates for service. And if we do not heed the call, God's work will be carried out by others. Furthermore, those who, like the religious leaders here, assume they are the heirs to God's Kingdom, will finally be rejected if they put other concerns first.

The rest of the parable is unique to Matthew and may have once been a separate story. Although the guests brought in from the streets must have been told the nature of the occasion, one of them had not bothered to wear the necessary wedding garment. Like the refusals of the first invitees, this omission was taken as an insult by the king. When the man can offer no explanation for his negligence, he is bound and thrown "into the outer darkness, where there will be weeping and gnashing of teeth" (v. 13; cf Mt. 8:12; 13:42, 50; 24:51; 25:30).

Failure to wear an appropriate garment to the wedding symbolizes neglecting to behave in a manner befitting God's standards. This points to the necessity of being prepared to answer God's call—to model true discipleship and reflect life in God's Kingdom.

In the final verse, Jesus proclaims that "many are called, but few are chosen" (v. 14).

ON REFLECTION

Bennett J. Sims, the late Episcopal Bishop of Atlanta and founder of the Institute of Servant Leadership, wrote an article entitled: "Must the Church Be So Boring?" After existing over the course of eighty generations, the Church has had to fight "fossilization"—that is, becoming more of a museum or a repository of relics than a "banquet hall" of newness of life.

Old hymns, stiff pew arrangements, repetitive liturgies, dry sermons, and antiquated stained glass all can make for a boring experience at church—let alone an anachronistic one. Clergy are not exempt from the malaise either. Sims tells the story of a minister who presided over a village church for fifty years. At 95 years of age, he was gently told by his bishop that he must retire. The cleric looked at the bishop with a rheumy stare and huffed: "Your Grace, when I accepted this call I was not told that my appointment would be temporary!"

Tertullian, the African Church Father (160—225), once said, "We only live by remaining in the waters." Of course, he was talking about baptismal "waters," but the same truth could apply regarding the image of the "marriage feast" in today's parable. We only live by "remaining at the party." We only live by dancing and partying in the newness of the Gospel celebration—not by remaining in fossilized forms that are not the banquet themselves. If your church is more of a fossil than a feast, something needs to change. The Gospel of Jesus might be disturbing, or confounding, or astonishing—it should never be *boring*.

—H. King Oehmig

All are called to the unity and fellowship of God's banquet, but not all will pass God's judgment. Being invited to the celebration does not guarantee being allowed to stay. Final inclusion in the Kingdom involves being prepared to share fully in God's life.

In writing to the Philippians, who had been Paul's most loyal congregation—"my joy and my crown" (4:1)—the Apostle also sounds a note of rejoicing: "Rejoice in the Lord always; again I will say, Rejoice" (v. 4).

He counsels them to "stand firm in the Lord" (v. 1), and let nothing undermine their faith, including dissention among themselves. He alludes to a disagreement between two women in the community, and urges them to come to a common mind in the Lord.

The rest of the community is to assist these women in their struggle for the Gospel that they have shared with Paul.

With the assurance of God's presence ("the Lord is near," v. 5b), they are not to worry about anything (cf Mt. 6:25-33). Reliance on God will dispel anxiety for those who know that God is with them. In their life of faith, consistent prayer, and thanksgiving, they will know the "peace of God, which surpasses all understanding" (v. 7). Thus they can give their minds unreservedly to truth, justice, purity, and all that Paul has taught them.

POINTS TO PONDER

1. In today's Gospel parable, the invited guests were so absorbed in their own pursuits that they did not heed the invitation to the wedding banquet. What are some of the distractions in your own life that interfere with your call from God? What do you need to do to eliminate them?

2. As you read Matthew 22:11-14, how do you think the guest who was thrown out for not wearing the proper attire might have felt? What do you think the reaction of the other guests might have been? What does this suggest to us about our own preparation for God's Kingdom?

3. When the slaves went out and gathered the guests (v. 10), both "good and bad" came. And in verse 14, Jesus says that "many are called, but few are chosen." What is the difference between being called and being chosen? How have you been both called and chosen?

4. Jesus says that the Kingdom of heaven is like a wedding banquet (v. 1). What do you think Jesus wanted his listeners to understand about God and the Kingdom from this parable?

5. In today's Epistle in Philippians 4:1-9, Paul calls upon his readers to "Rejoice in the Lord always." What does Paul mention as cause for rejoicing? What do you have to celebrate in your own life?

_____

_____

_____

_____

_____

_____

GOD OR CAESAR?

Exodus 33:12-23; Psalm 99; 1 Thessalonians 1:1-10; Matthew 22:15-22

After the people of Israel had broken God's commandment against idols by worshiping a golden calf (Ex. 32:1-14), the Lord sent a plague among them (v. 35). God then commanded the Israelites to continue on their journey to the land promised them, "but I [the Lord] will not go up among you, or I would consume you on the way, for you are a stiff-necked people" (Ex. 33:3).

Now the Lord "used to speak to Moses, face to face, as one speaks to a friend" (v. 11); thus, in the text for today, Moses asks for God to stay, and points out that the continuing Divine presence makes Israel stand out among nations (v. 16).

When the Lord consents to Moses' request (v. 17), Moses then asks to see God's glory. However, to look upon the face of God is too much for mere mortals to withstand (v. 20); therefore God seals the promises to Moses with Moses being allowed to see God's "back."

Once again, Moses has acted as a mediator between the Lord and Israel. And once again, God acts with compassion toward the wayward Israelites: "I will be gracious to whom I will be gracious, and will show mercy on whom I will show mercy" (v. 19).

The Psalmist celebrated the Lord's glory as King, exalted above all peoples. He proclaimed the Lord's greatness, and did obeisance to the Holy One (99:5), remembering how God had spoken to the people out of a pillar of cloud. The Psalm calls for the entire nation to worship the Holy One on the Holy Hill.

In today's Gospel text, Jesus' antagonists set yet another trap for him, devising a trick question. But once again, Jesus disarms his opponents and uncovers the truth in an unexpected way.

In this encounter the Pharisees and supporters of Herod in Jerusalem plot together to "entrap" Jesus by posing the following question: "Is it lawful to pay taxes to the emperor, or not?" (Mt. 22:17).

If Jesus declares that Torah forbids paying the taxes that sustain the Roman occupation (including its pagan temples), he can be arrested for sedition by Pilate's security forces. On the other hand, if he claims that Torah allows paying this tax, his teaching will be denounced by those who are rigorous in their interpretation of religious obligation.

However, Jesus does not fall into the leaders' trap, even though they cleverly start out by praising him as a courageous teacher of God's way (v. 16). Jesus immediately recognizes their ploy and asks: "Why are you putting me to the test, you hypocrites?" (v. 18).

The tax in question here was levied by the Roman occupation on every man, woman, child, and slave. The amount of the usual tax was a Roman denarius, the average daily wage for a laborer. Jesus asks for such a coin.

PRAYER FOR THE DAY

Almighty and merciful God, you alone can order our wills and affections: through the wisdom of your Word, Jesus Christ, assist us in distinguishing what is holy and lasting in life from what is transient and not worthy of our allegiance, so that, through the working of the Holy Spirit within and among us, we may know where true joys are to *Amen.*

While local coins that carried no human or animal image were minted for the required offerings at the temple, normal commerce and payment of taxes required the imperial coinage bearing Caesar's likeness.

When Jesus asks whose image is stamped on the coin, the inevitable answer is "the emperor's" (v. 21). Thus he puts himself in the position of *questioner* rather than *respondent;* and his "answer" to their original question becomes a command to "Give therefore to the emperor the things that are the emperor's ..." (v. 21). The coin is already Caesar's, hence it should be given back to him. This reply leaves no opportunity for Jesus' enemies to denounce him to the Romans as a rebel. And neither nationalists nor religious zealots can say that he is disloyal to their faith.

But the full genius of Jesus' answer is revealed in the rest of the sentence. They are to give back to Caesar the things that belong to Caesar, "... and to God the things that are God's" (v. 21). Jesus' audience would know well the biblical teaching that God had created humanity in the Divine image (Gen. 1:26). Each listener was thus stamped with the image of God—a living visual reminder that God had a claim on every aspect of life.

To give back to God what, by right of creation itself, belongs to God, means to return all that we are and all that we have. No one can argue with the point Jesus has made. The Pharisees and Herodians have been caught in their own hypocrisy by trying to force a choice between loyalty to God or Rome. They are ultimately amazed by the response of Jesus and leave him, going on their way.

ON REFLECTION

Jesus was fully aware of "God and mammon"—and the tension between the two. He knew about living in "two worlds," and the constant struggle to keep priorities straight. Call it the "tension between commitments." Maybe that is why Jesus talked about the relationship between a person and her or his possessions more than of any other single subject in the Gospels—more even than prayer or peace or evangelism. He knew that where one's treasure was, one's heart would be also (Mt. 6:21).

It was a perfect setup for entrapment. If Jesus recommends paying tribute to Caesar, he in effect supports the Roman occupation of Palestine—making him a limp Messiah-Liberator. If he teaches against paying the tax, then the Roman IRS will arrest him for sedition. The answer Jesus gave to the religious big-shots was brilliant—and silenced them. Jesus told them to render to Caesar the things that are Caesar's, and to give to God the things that are God's. By putting the answer in that order, Jesus was saying that God and the emperor were not equals. One must render to Caesar only what the state deserves *in light of what God first desires from us.*

In cases when the Church has ceased to be in tension with Caesar, one of two things has happened, said theologian Carlyle Marney. One, either Caesar has been converted; or, two, the Church has so watered down the Gospel of Jesus that it has lost the capacity to speak truth to power. It doesn't take a Ph. D. in the sociology of religion to know which of these two options occurs most often.

—H. King Oehmig

This text has often been used to frame debates over church and state doctrine; however, Matthew's concern here was to illustrate Jesus' skill in evading the trap that his enemies tried to set for him by *turning the issue back on his questioners*. In so doing, Jesus called attention to the fact that what God asks of us—our total devotion and obedience—does not belong to Caesar, and therefore cannot be given back to him.

Thessalonica was the capital of the Roman province of Macedonia. Paul began his ministry there by preaching in the synagogue. Although he gained a number of converts, he also incurred the enmity of the synagogue leaders, who incited a riot as a pretext for the city authorities to arrest Paul. Thus Paul's converts sent him away to Berea, and later to Athens for his own safety (Acts 17:1-15).

Paul's first letter to the Thessalonians is generally considered to be the oldest piece of literature in the New Testament. It begins with the usual greetings of grace and peace to the recipients. Silvanus and Timothy were co-workers with Paul in his ministry there.

Paul gives thanks for the Thessalonians and assures them of his prayers. He commends their faith, love, and "steadfastness of hope in our Lord Jesus Christ" (1:3). They have responded to the Gospel message brought by Paul and have become "imitators of us and of the Lord" (v. 6), even in the face of persecution. "... in every place your faith in God has become known" (v. 8). Such devotion Paul saw as a glorious work of God, as the Thessalonians waited for the coming of God's "Son from heaven" (v. 10) who would rescue them from judgment.

POINTS TO PONDER

1. What is the nature of the trap that the Pharisees try to set for Jesus? How does Jesus extricate himself from this potentially dangerous situation?

2. As Jesus responds to his critics, what do we learn here about Jesus and his ministry? What is the point that Jesus makes here?

3. Just as the coin that Jesus held up had the image of the emperor engraved on it, we have been imprinted with the image of God. What implication does the fact that we are made in God's image have on our lives?

4. Why do you think the Pharisees were amazed at Jesus and went away (Mt. 22: 22)? How do you continue to be amazed by Jesus in your own life?

5. What other insights do the Lessons for today contribute to your understanding of the challenge of living the Christian life?

THE SUMMARY OF THE LAW

Deuteronomy 34:1-12; Psalm 90:1-6, 13-17; 1 Thessalonians 2:1-8; Matthew 22:34-46

The reading from Deuteronomy marks not only the final chapter of the Pentateuch, but also the death of Moses and empowerment of his successor, Joshua (cf Num. 27). Moses had faithfully led Israel from bondage in Egypt through the trials of the journey in the wilderness.

However, now that they were finally poised to enter the land of promise, Moses would not be going with them as a consequence of the incident at Meribah, where Moses disobeyed the Lord by striking the rock instead of speaking to it (Num. 20:1-13).

Instead, the Lord commanded Moses to go up Mount Nebo, where he could see a panoramic view of the whole land that God had promised to the patriarchs and their descendants (Deut. 34:4b). There, in solitude, Moses died. He was 120 years old; but because he died "at the Lord's command" (v. 5), he did not die of old age or infirmity (v. 7).

The exact place of his burial remains unknown, adding a further sense of mystery to the story of the prophet. The Israelites mourned Moses for thirty days in honor befitting a parent.

When the period of mourning for Moses had ended, Joshua became the leader of Israel. Joshua is described as "full of the spirit of wisdom, because Moses had laid his hands on him" (v. 9); and thus the people obeyed him. With this transfer of power, Israel is ready to leave their past and follow Joshua into the future.

Verses 10-12 provide a fitting climax to the legacy of Moses: "Never since has their arisen a prophet in Israel like Moses, whom the Lord knew face to face" (v. 10).

Moses was the greatest of the prophets, having a relationship with God like no other. He was a charismatic leader who spoke for and with God to perform mighty "signs and wonders" (v. 11) on behalf of Israel.

Psalm 90 begins with the statement that *the Lord has been our dwelling place.* The Psalmist also describes the eternal transcendence of the Lord. In God's sight, a thousand years are like yesterday. But humans fade away like the grass. So we ask for God's favor and for God to prosper our works.

The Gospel reading for today includes two incidents, one dealing with the commandments (Mt. 22:34-40) and the other concerning the nature of messiahship (vv. 41-46). Both situations reflect the continuing tension between Jesus and the religious leaders, as they try to find cause to denounce Jesus following his triumphal entry into Jerusalem (21:1-11).

Previously, Jesus had effectively silenced the Sadducees in an exchange concerning resurrection (22:23-33). Now the Pharisees approach Jesus and ask, "Teacher, which commandment in the law is the greatest?" (v. 36).

PRAYER FOR THE DAY

Eternal God, in you we find genuine peace and the strength to love: draw us ever closer to you through the mediation of the Holy Spirit, that you may love others through us. May we live no longer for ourselves alone, but for the Gospel of Jesus Christ in the supreme virtues of faith, hope, and love. *Amen.*

According to Jewish tradition, there were a total of 613 distinct commandments. Was there a primary commandment in light of which all the rest could be understood?

Jesus responds in verse 37 by quoting Deuteronomy 6:5: "You shall love the Lord your God with all your heart, and with all your soul, and with all your mind." This is the first and greatest of the commandments—love of God has priority over everything else.

A second—and an equally important commandment—to "love your neighbor as yourself" (v. 39), is derived from Leviticus 19:18. Taken together, love of God and love of neighbor summarize "all the law and the prophets" (v. 40).

Jesus' words here represent an orthodox understanding of Jewish law and draw attention to the covenant relationship with God. Just as the Lord shows loving kindness to us, we are to respond with complete devotion to God.

How we treat our neighbor is integral to our faith, since God's love is worked out through our dealings with others.

Then Jesus asked: "What do you think of the Messiah? Whose son is he?" (v. 42a). The Pharisees replied by stating the general belief that the Messiah would be a descendant of David (v. 42b).

However, Jesus responds that it is not such a simple matter: Why did David call the Messiah "Lord" instead of Son? He goes on to quote Psalm 110:1 as proof: "The Lord said to my Lord ..." (v. 44).

These words from Psalm 110 were often used at coronations, and it was traditionally assumed that King David was the Psalm's author. Jesus points out that the Messiah is designated as David's Lord, and one does not address one's heirs in this fashion. Therefore, instead of accepting that the Messiah would restore the past glories of David, Jesus calls for a deeper understanding.

ON REFLECTION

The rabbis counted 613 commands in the Law. Of these, 248 were positive commands—the same number as parts of the body. That left 365 negative commands, a number that represented the number of days in a year. The question of which of these commandments were the greatest tempted theological joisting; but reverence for all the commandments kept the debate to a minimum. What *human being* could decide which of *God's* edicts outweighed the others? What person had the "right" to prioritize Divine law?

Rather than giving an answer that chose a single commandment, Jesus offered the lawyers a combination of two, yoking Deuteronomy 6:5 with Leviticus 19:18. The former was the command to love God with the totality of one's being, the latter the command to love one's neighbor as oneself. In putting them together, Jesus made them *equal* in importance, and also inseparable. If you love one, in effect, you love both.

In 1 John it says, "We love because God first loved us" (4:19)—meaning that any capacity we have for love is derived from God, not human nature on its own. Let's face it, we have a devil of a time loving those closest to us, let alone our "neighbor." Just because we "ought" to do something does not mean that we "can." When the Gospel happens in relationships—when we truly love God and neighbor—it is the Holy Spirit at work in us, the power of *agape*, which alone has survival value in this world (1 Cor. 13:8).

—H. King Oehmig

The glories of David's reign represented one stage of God's revelation in history. Unity under David had enabled Israel to overcome enemies and achieve military strength; but this was not the ultimate goal of God's revelation. The reign of the Messiah will not be a mere military victory, but *triumph over sin and death.*

In this final debate with the Pharisees before his arrest, Jesus once again silences his adversaries and proves himself to be the authoritative interpreter of Scripture: "...nor from that day did anyone dare to ask him any more questions" (v. 46).

In the Epistle, Paul continues to describe his ministry in Thessalonica. He addresses the members of the community as his brothers and sisters on whose behalf his work and suffering were not in vain. He refers to his own imprisonment and suffering at Philippi. He and his companions, Silvanus and Timothy (1:1), have been entrusted by God with the message of the Gospel, which they courageously declare despite opposition.

As stewards of the Gospel, the Thessalonians are to be examples of sincerity and integrity. Just as Paul and his associates do not speak to please mortals, but rather to serve God (2: 4)—the Thessalonians are never to resort to impure motives or trickery, and to let all their dealings emanate from *the heart of love where Christ dwells.*

They are not to seek gain from their work, whether as profit or as power. Flattery and greed are to be avoided as well. In this way, converts may recognize Christ not only in their words, but in their lives, for *their fidelity is to the cause of the Lord.*

Paul ends with a statement of his own affection for the community at Thessalonica. He has shared not only the message of the Gospel with them, but himself as well.

POINTS TO PONDER

1. As you read Matthew 22:37-39, notice that the word "love" is used here as a verb requiring action. How do we express our love for God with all our heart, soul, and mind?

2. How do we demonstrate our love for our neighbor? How do the actions of Jesus himself serve as an example of the way we are to love God and neighbor?

3. What do you think Jesus means in verse 40 when he says that "all the law and the prophets" hang on these two commandments?

4. In verse 42, Jesus asks, "What do you think of the Messiah?" What do you think the people of Jesus' own time expected the Messiah to be? What are our own perceptions of the Messiah today? How does Jesus describe the Messiah here?

5. How does the Apostle Paul's example in our Epistle for today add to your comprehension of how to be true stewards of the Gospel?

ALL SAINTS' SUNDAY

Revelation 7:9-17; Psalm 34:1-10, 22; 1 John 3:1-3; Matthew 5:1-12

The early festivals of the Church included commemorations of the martyrs who had died for their faith. However, All Saints' Day is not only a celebration of the great host of witnesses who have gone before, but also a time to remember *all God's faithful people* in every place and time.

The Book of Revelation provided hope to the persecuted church near the end of the first century. In the vision of chapter 7, the faithful who have been marked with a seal on their foreheads (v. 3) will be protected during the coming tribulation.

The text for today depicts a scene of countless multitudes in heaven, people from every nation, tribe, and language before the throne of God. Robed in white, they carry palm branches as symbols of victory. They join the angels in worship, proclaiming blessing, glory, wisdom, thanksgiving, honor, power, and might to God forever.

They are the ones who have come out of the "great ordeal" (v. 14)—the persecution that caused the death of many and suffering for others. Their robes have been made white in the blood of the Lamb sacrificed for their salvation. Now they can worship eternally in the presence of God. They will no longer suffer or experience hunger and thirst, for the Lamb "will guide them to springs of the water of life, and God will wipe away every tear from their eyes" (v. 17).

Later on, the author of Revelation would provide further assurance of God's love and care, not only in the future, but in the here and now.

God's love is shown by the fact that we are "called children of God" (1 Jn. 3:1). Genesis tells us that men and women were made in God's image (1:27); thus we are called to reflect God's intentions for us by living up to our Divine calling. The world does not recognize these believers because the world did not know Jesus either (cf Jn. 15:18-19; 16:3; 17:25).

The writer goes on to say that we have not been shown our future, but we do know that we will be transformed into the likeness of Christ and see the glory of God the Father (cf 2 Cor. 3:18). Thus we are called to live a godly and virtuous life that is worthy of this calling—to be pure as Jesus is pure.

The way of life called for by the author of 1 John reflects the approach expected of the followers of Jesus. The admonitions of Matthew 5:1-12 especially relate to the proclamation of Jesus that "the kingdom of heaven has come near" (Mt. 4:17).

A "beatitude" is a blessing or announcement of God's favor in the present as well as the future. As a part of Matthew's First Discourse or Sermon on the Mount (5:1—7:29), the Beatitudes are addressed directly to Jesus' chosen disciples.

PRAYER FOR THE DAY

Gracious Lord, who sent your Son Jesus Christ to deliver us from the power of evil and make us your children by adoption and grace: may your anointing with the Holy Spirit guide us into becoming "little Christs" to all whom you give us, that we may be transparent to your unfailing Presence in the world as your saints. *Amen.*

The Gospel of Luke also includes Beatitudes (6:20-26) that feature four blessings contrasted with four woes. Matthew's version consists not so much of promises to the needy as *a challenge to believers to take on "Kingdom" attitudes.*

The first four Beatitudes (vv. 3-6) focus on those who suffer now, but who will receive justice in the coming reign of God. The remaining verses (vv. 6-11) promise blessings upon those who strive to alleviate the conditions described in the first four Beatitudes.

First Jesus calls for blessings on the "poor in spirit" (v. 3). While Luke refers simply to the "poor," Matthew is not as concerned with economic need as with a *deeper acknowledgment of our spiritual dependence before God.* The poor in spirit are those who have no reason to hope in this world, but will receive solace in the Kingdom of heaven.

The next blessing is for those who mourn and have no joy in their lives (v. 4). Their mourning is genuine sorrow over the wrongs and suffering in the world. They will be comforted when God's rule is established.

The third blessing is for the meek who "will inherit the earth" (v. 5). This Beatitude reflects the sentiment of Psalm 37:11 in promising future prosperity. The meek represent the dispossessed of the world who will not be denied forever.

Next Jesus speaks of those who hunger and thirst for righteousness (v. 6). This suggests a desire to see vindication for those who suffer unjustly. Their blessing is that *such hunger for justice will be satisfied in God's reign.* In these first four Beatitudes, Jesus promises reversals of present conditions in the coming Kingdom.

The fifth blessing is for the merciful who in their turn *shall receive mercy* (v. 7). God's mercy is freely extended to all and is used here in the sense of forgiveness.

ON REFLECTION

Joan of Arc, in George Bernard Shaw's *St. Joan,* is trying desperately to get Charles—the weak, insipid dauphin—to show some initiative. Frustrated, she raises her voice at him and tells Charles that there is one thing he has never learned. Curious, he asks her what it is. "Charlie, you have never learned that we are put here on this earth not to do our own business, but to do God's!"

Today we honor and celebrate the "saints" of the faith who, one way or another, realized that they were put here on earth for more than the business of personal gratification and fulfillment. They were sent to express God's will: *human well-being,* whether they were conscious of it or not. Far from being sin-free, or oozing virtue—such as breaking into Alleluias when they stubbed their toe on the way to the bathroom at midnight—these "saints" were everyday, earthy people that allowed themselves to be used by God: to be transparent to the reality of Jesus in their lives.

St. Therese (1873—1897), known as "The Little Flower" in England, entered a Carmelite convent in Lisieux, France, at the age of 15, died of tuberculosis at 24, and in 1947 was named, with Joan of Arc, as patroness of France. Although a figure of great piety and spiritual distinction, Therese may have best summed up what it takes to be a "saint." She said, "If you are willing to serenely bear the trial of being displeasing to yourself, you will be for Jesus a pleasant place of shelter." How true.

—H. King Oehmig

Those who are recipients of this mercy and forgiveness are called to do likewise. Only those who practice mercy will have the understanding to receive it themselves.

Next comes blessing for the "pure in heart" (v. 8) who have risen above temptation to *seek God in all aspects of their lives.* Thus they will see God now as well as in the age to come.

A seventh blessing is pronounced for the peacemakers (v. 9) who seek to bring about reconciliation. They are named as "children of God," for their acts reflect the reconciling nature of God.

The final blessings declare God's favor upon those who suffer persecution for their loyalty to God (vv. 10-11). To be so committed to God, even in the midst of suffering, signals entrance into God's realm. They can be compared to the persecuted prophets and can "rejoice and be glad" (v. 12a)—for there is eternal reward for them in heaven!

The Beatitudes point to a life of holiness, and illustrate a reversal of the expectations of the world: in God's Kingdom, the first will be last, and the last will be first (Mt. 19:30; 20: 16). Here the call to discipleship overshadows worldly recognition and achievement, as Jesus portrays a *new realm* in which God's will and purpose for creation are fully realized.

In the same spirit, Psalm 34 celebrates the Lord's care for the faithful. It tells of deliverance from perils, provision for needs, consolation in distress, and security of life. The Psalmist calls upon the people to praise the Lord at all times, and declares that those who trust in God are blessed.

POINTS TO PONDER

1. As you begin your discussion of the Gospel reading, reflect on the word "blessed." How would you explain this word from your own understanding, as well as the way it is used in the Gospel context?

2. Jesus describes eight blessings. As you consider each blessing and its accompanying promise, how do these qualities relate to your own life? For example, when have you mourned, been a peacemaker, or hungered for righteousness? How have you felt blessed at these times?

3. Which of the Beatitudes best describes your own idea of what it means to be blessed?

4. Who are some individuals that exemplify the virtues of the Beatitudes for you? According to these words, what must we do to become true disciples? How can we make the vision of the Beatitudes a reality in our world?

5. Read the other Lessons appointed for today. What do we learn here about God and our relationship with God and others?

THE HUMBLE WILL BE EXALTED

Joshua 3:7-17; Psalm 107:1-7, 33-37; 1 Thessalonians 2:9-13; Matthew 23:1-12

Moses had led the Israelites from bondage in Egypt and guided them through the years of wandering in the wilderness. But Moses died just as the people were ready to cross the Jordan River and take possession of the promised land (Deut. 34:1-12).

In the passage for today, the Israelites finally enter the land under Joshua. Moses, before he died, had laid hands on Joshua and empowered him to take his place. Thus, the events that are about to occur are to endorse Joshua's leadership (Josh. 3:7).

Joshua called the people together and selected one man from each of the twelve tribes. The priests then came forward carrying the Ark of the Covenant and stepped into the Jordan River. The Ark was the sacred representation of *the presence of God* which had gone before them and would now lead them into the land.

As the priests stepped into the river, the "waters flowing from above stood still, rising up in a single heap" (v. 16) so that the Israelites could cross to Jericho on dry ground. The priests remained in the riverbed holding the Ark until all the people had crossed over. The narrative points out that the river was unusually high, as it was spring, and the waters held back were substantial indeed.

The story of the crossing of the Jordan River is similar in many respects to the earlier crossing of the Red Sea when the Israelites left Egypt (Ex. 14). The emphasis is once again on the saving work of the Lord on behalf of Israel, with Joshua as the new Moses.

This event marks a transition point in the history of Israel as the nation embarks upon its future in a new land with a new leader.

"Give thanks to the Lord," *for God is good,* begins Psalm 107. This Psalm was probably sung by a group of pilgrims traveling to Jerusalem for one of the festivals. The Lord turns rivers into deserts, and sometimes deserts into pools of water, ordering the lives of all people. But *God's mercy endures forever,* and when we cry to the Lord, we will find deliverance.

In the Gospel, Jesus had been engaged in a series of disputes with the religious authorities (ch. 21-22). Now as he speaks to the crowd before the temple, he points out the hypocrisy of these leaders, and warns his disciples against following their example.

The scribes and Pharisees had oversight of the daily governance of the Jewish community, and thus would sit on "Moses' seat" of authority. In telling his disciples to follow their teaching, Jesus upholds the importance of the Law and the prophets, but also warns: "Do not do as they do, for they do not practice what they teach" (23:3).

PRAYER FOR THE DAY

Grant us, gracious Lord God, the blessing of humility through the gift of your Holy Spirit: anoint us that we may understand ourselves as sons and daughters of the Most High. Let us forever seek to express the holy will of Jesus Christ, who humbled himself and died on the Cross, liberating the world from the power of sin and death. *Amen.*

The scribes and Pharisees made the application of the Law impossibly difficult to follow. The heavy burdens they imposed on the people were minute, multiple rules and regulations so detailed that the people could never totally observe them. Thus religion had become an unbearable burden; yet the scribes and Pharisees refused to lighten the load by simplifying the system. In contrast to the heavy burden of the Pharisees, the burden that Jesus brings is *light* (Mt. 11:30).

All their actions are for public show of piety and not true devotion, as witnessed by their exaggerated use of phylacteries and fringes. Phylacteries were small leather boxes containing pieces of parchment with Scripture passages, and were worn on the forehead and arm during morning prayers (Ex. 13:16; Deut. 6:4-9). Jews wore tassels on the corners of their robes as a mark of devotion (Num. 15:38-39; Deut. 22:12); but the Pharisees also carried this practice to extremes.

In a culture where religion played such a central role in establishing ethnic identity, the respect for religious leaders was strong; but the scribes and Pharisees exploited this by insisting on public seats of honor. They expected deference from others, including being addressed as Rabbi.

But Jesus says that his followers are not to claim the title of Rabbi, as all disciples are equal under a single teacher—the Messiah. In like manner, they have one Father who is in heaven.

In calling attention to the behavior of the scribes and Pharisees, Jesus was admonishing his followers not to act as they did. The one who is greatest among them is the one who serves others most. The passage ends with the familiar pattern of reversal: whoever claims exalted status will be humbled, while whoever is consistently humble will be raised (v. 12).

ON REFLECTION

Alan Jones, the Dean of Grace Cathedral in San Francisco, said that clergy suffer from the collision of two dynamics: *low self-esteem* and *high idealism*. It's most likely a problem with the un-ordained as well, but to a lesser degree. To be called "reverend," to dress in distinctive clothing, to have people be forced to listen to what you say week after week (as you look down on them) can be an elixir for people who, though doing the Lord's work, still think they are "nobodies."

New Testament scholar J. D. M. Derrett, in his work *Jesus' Audience* (Seabury Press, 1973), made an observation that helps us more nearly understand the Gospel teaching for today: "In the oriental world, prestige is more important than any other factor, and people will commit suicide rather than forfeit it." For Jesus to discount the prestige that comes from religious prominence—from wearing elaborate vestments, claiming places of honor at banquets, and bearing the title of "teacher"—was indeed radical. Then, to proclaim the truth that *the greatest of all is the servant of all* really turned things upside down.

Jesus was not against excellence in itself, nor opposed to being successful in life. He did caution, however, against these human-made criteria that were used to define *who you were as a person.* The only self-definition Jesus cared about was being named as *a child of the Most High*—all else was commentary. To a world driven by hunger for notoriety—yet laboring and travailing under its effects (such as eating disorders, sleep difficulties, and personality disorders)—maybe this teaching of Jesus is just the good news we need to hear.

—H. King Oehmig

Because the Pharisees claimed to come in the name of Moses and the prophets, but failed to live up to their high calling, they put themselves and others at great peril rather than ushering in the Kingdom (v. 15).

Paul also set forth the proper way in which true followers of Jesus were to behave in his correspondence with the Thessalonians. Paul had a fond relationship with the community there and spoke in terms of mutual support and integrity in upholding the Gospel.

Paul declined to accept any support from the congregation while he served them and supported himself by his trade as a tentmaker (Acts 18:3). He speaks of the blameless conduct that he and his colleagues demonstrated among them.

Paul compares his relationship with his converts to that of a loving father to his children. In his teaching, he encourages them to remember that as disciples they are called to lead exemplary lives worthy of the glory of God's Kingdom.

He expresses his gratitude for the manner in which the Thessalonians received God's Word and allowed it to work in their lives. Although they received the Gospel from Paul, he reminds them that as an Apostle he acts merely as an agent of the Gospel by proclaiming *the work of God in Jesus Christ.*

POINTS TO PONDER

1. What are the specific issues for which Jesus condemns the scribes and Pharisees in the Gospel passage? It is very easy to think that these criticisms are applicable only to the situation in Jesus' own time. How are we as individuals and as the Church today also guilty of the same shortcomings?

2. What expectations do we have of our own religious and secular leaders and institutions today? How realistic are these expectations? What is our response when these expectations are not met?

3. In Matthew 23:8-9, Jesus indicates that we are all sisters and brothers under one teacher, one Father, and one Messiah. What implications does this pronouncement have for our relationships with others?

4. What kind of model does the Apostle Paul offer in our Epistle today for a life of serving God through Christ?

5. What do we learn about discipleship from today's passages? What challenges do we face as we strive to live into this ideal of Christian living?

KEEP AWAKE

Joshua 24:1-3a, 14-25; Psalm 78:1-7; 1 Thessalonians 4:13-18; Matthew 25:1-13

The idea of a Covenant with God recurs often in the Hebrew Bible. After the Deluge, God made a Covenant with Noah. Later there was a promise to Abraham, and a pledge delivered from Sinai. In the final chapter of the Book of Joshua, when the Hebrews have gained possession of the land, it is time to ratify what formerly was agreed.

Before the Lord called Abraham, his ancestors had worshiped the gods of the land beyond the Euphrates. In Egypt, Abraham's descendants had come to know of a different group of gods. Now that they were in Canaan, the gods that had been worshiped there might be thought to have claims in the land.

Therefore choose! they are admonished (24: 15). Shall it be the One God who led them out of Egypt, or the many who might be thought to have great powers?

For Joshua there was no hesitation. "I and my house will serve the Lord." Flushed with their victories, the people gladly echoed Joshua's commitment. Joshua then warned them that the Lord would make an exclusive claim. If they were to revere alien gods, the Lord would turn from the Divine graciousness they had experienced—and destroy them.

Again the people promised, "We will serve the Lord." Joshua then called on them to be witnesses that they had made their choice, and to prove it by getting rid of all symbols and tokens of other gods that they still possessed. On that basis, the people could be in Covenant with their God.

Psalm 78 is a summary of God's saving acts for the chosen people, and of the nation's repeated failures to fulfill its Covenant obligations.

The Psalm tells how the Lord provided quail as well as manna to sustain the people in their journey from Egypt to the promised land. God's mighty acts have been told by parents to children, and they must be repeated to coming generations.

In the Gospel, Jesus told a story based on the wedding customs of the time. In those days the bridegroom went to take his bride from her family home to her new dwelling. When they arrived there would be a gala celebration. The arrival might be delayed—and in this story, it was.

Ten designated bridesmaids were to be vigilant while awaiting the bridegroom's arrival. Five (the "wise") had come prepared with extra oil for their lamps. The other five (the "foolish") had none.

The maidens in the story represent two classes found among those who are called to be God's people. Some respond to the call with prudence, while others expect God to satisfy every need, thinking it enough just to be invited.

Indeed, this latter group holds that it is more or less God's duty to take care of those needs resulting from their own neglect. Both types are recognizable in the story and in our present generation as well.

PRAYER FOR THE DAY

O God of grace and glory, in whose service we find perfect freedom and true purpose, by the invisible working of your Holy Spirit, keep us forever awake to the needs of the world and alert to respond in the Name of Jesus Christ our Lord, until the end of the age. *Amen.*

As the time of arrival was more and more delayed, all of the bridesmaids became drowsy and slept. But the call to arise came at midnight. The wise were able to trim their lamps; but they did not have enough oil to save the foolish. The unprepared bridesmaids found themselves excluded from the celebration. Therefore *everyone must be watchful,* for no one can know the day or the hour when God's climactic act will take place.

The bridegroom, of course, is the Messiah, the Agent through whom God's work is to be completed. And Matthew believes that the bridegroom is the *Risen Christ,* whose return in glory he soon expects.

In the story as Jesus tells it, however, the Messiah could be a figure other than himself. During his earthly ministry, Jesus never publicly claimed to be the Messiah; and many scholars hold that he never made such a claim even among the inner circle of disciples.

The arrival of the bridegroom at midnight, rather than at sundown, could suggest the delay in Christ's return that was being experienced at the time that Matthew wrote.

In the story, the bridegroom's arrival is greeted with a shout to awaken those who are to attend the celebration. In just this way will the Messiah be expected to arrive unheralded, with everyone taken by surprise. Five of the young women—the wise ones—are prepared with oil in their lamps; but the other five are not. Jesus would have called for those who had oil to share with those who had none; but the Last Judgment offers no such option.

Therefore *Keep awake!* since we do not know the day or the hour of the Lord's coming. This is not to be a *paranoid* preparedness. It is rather the call to live each day as though it were one's last—not in mortal fear of the worst, but in animated hope for the best: the new heaven and the new earth.

ON REFLECTION

Psychologists say it is one of our worst nightmares: to be caught *unprepared.* We have a huge power point presentation to make before the boss and potential new clients—and it comes up blank. A preacher finds himself in the pulpit on Easter Day—minus a manuscript or notes. A student goes in to take a final exam—only to find she has studied the wrong material.

The Parable of the Wise and Foolish Virgins deals with the same kind of psychological torment. The "unprepared" run out of oil just at the time it is most needed—at the moment when the bridegroom is about to arrive. Home Depot isn't open. Neither is Lowe's, nor the local 711. It is just tough luck. None of the other "prepared" virgins seems eager to share oil supplies, either.

Walker Percy, the noted Southern novelist, would manifest a common theme in his books—that is, the "fulfillment, yet unfulfillment" of the "successful." Often his protagonist is a male professional who has clawed his way to the top. Or a suburban mom with a car full of well-coiffed kids, driving an expensive car to a soccer game. They have fulfilled the "American dream." And yet, Percy asks the reader, why do they look out a window and feel a terrible sadness? *What are they looking for?* There is only one reality worth looking for. Jesus taught that it was *the Kingdom of the Father;* and whether it comes tomorrow—or at the End of the Age—those who find it have everything (Mt. 6:33).

—H. King Oehmig

The Apostle Paul's picture of the Day of the Lord combined an expected general resurrection with a return of Christ in glory—to pass God's judgment on those who would be raised as well as those who were alive at the time. He did not pretend to know the day or the hour, but he expected it to be very soon—indeed, within his own lifetime (1 Thess. 4:17). The shout of the archangel and God's trumpet were the only warning anyone would have. When those raised from death were given the reward due to them, then the disciples who had not experienced death would be caught up to be forever with the Lord.

To live each day as if judgment might happen was good for Paul's Thessalonian converts, and it is equally good for us. So be forever ready! Who can say that it might not be *tomorrow*—and if it isn't, we shall be better people if we live as though it could be.

POINTS TO PONDER

1. As you read the Gospel parable, consider the following questions: Imagine that you are one of the "wise" maidens. Why do you act as you do? In particular, why do you refuse to share your oil with the "foolish" maidens?

2. Put yourself in the role of one of the maidens who was not prepared. What are the motivations for your behavior in this situation? What is your reaction when the bridegroom refuses to admit the unprepared maidens, saying that he does not know them?

3. According to this parable, who will be admitted to the Kingdom of heaven, and why? How would you characterize your response to this parable? What do you find disturbing here? What is comforting?

4. What do you think Jesus wanted to convey with this story?

5. Refer to all of the Lessons appointed for today. What do we learn about the coming of the Lord, judgment, and salvation from these passages?

ON THE STEWARDSHIP OF TALENTS

Judges 4:1-7; Psalm 123; 1 Thessalonians 5:1-11; Matthew 25:14-30

After their liberation from Egypt and years of wandering in the wilderness, the Israelites entered Canaan under the leadership of Joshua and began to take possession of the land. After Joshua died, the Israelites continued their conquest over the next 400 years under a succession of leaders.

The Book of Judges tells the stories of twelve of these leaders who lived at various times from Joshua's death until the beginning of the era of the monarchy, as recorded in 1 Samuel.

The judges were actually local tribal leaders. They were military leaders, warriors, prophets, and priests. Among the judges was a woman, the prophet Deborah, who did function as a judge to settle disputes (Jdg. 4:5).

The Israelites had again done "what was evil in the sight of the Lord" (v. 1), and thus had been oppressed by the army of Sisera under King Jabin. When Israel cried out for help, the Lord had called Deborah to be the instrument of liberation.

Deborah summoned a military commander named Barak and ordered him to assemble his troops to meet Sisera in battle. Although Deborah assured Barak of victory as promised by the Lord, he refused to leave unless Deborah accompanied the army.

Deborah complied with Barak's request, and Sisera's army was destroyed by the Israelites (v. 16b). However, Sisera himself escaped, only to be killed later by a woman named Jael (vv. 17-22). Finally, King Jabin himself was destroyed as well (v. 24). This victory over Israel's enemy is celebrated in the Song of Deborah (Jdg. 5:1-31).

This story illustrates the usual pattern in the Book of Judges of sin, punishment, and rescue. The emphasis here is on God's power to destroy Israel's enemies, as well as the Lord's mercy in saving a sinful Israel.

Psalm 123 is a plea for mercy that compensates for scorn and contempt from the proud. We look to God for deliverance, as a servant looks to his or her master.

As we near the end of the Church Year, the lectionary focuses as well on themes of final judgment. The Parable of the Talents is the third in a series of parables (Mt. 24:45-51; 25:1-13) that treat *what must be done to prepare for the coming of the Son of Man.*

As a man left on a journey, he entrusted his property to his slaves: to one he gave five talents, to another two talents, and to a third, one talent: "to each according to his ability" (25:15). The first two slaves doubled the amount given to them through trade and investment; while the third dug a hole and hid his single talent.

When the master returned to settle his accounts, he praised the first two slaves:

PRAYER FOR THE DAY

Almighty God, we ask for the coming of your Kingdom and glory in all its fullness; and, we pray, anoint us with the Holy Spirit that we may live out the giftedness with which we have been blessed: that Jesus Christ may be proclaimed in thought, word, and deed until his coming again in glory. *Amen.*

"Well done, good and trustworthy slave; you have been trustworthy in a few things, I will put you in charge of many things; enter into the joy of your master" (vv. 21, 23). These slaves had taken a risk and skillfully managed their resources; therefore, they would be entrusted with even more responsibility and would experience the joy of their master's presence.

However, when the third slave returned his single talent, the master took the talent from him and gave it to the slave who had secured the greatest return. Although the third slave was not dishonest and did not lose his master's money, he was accused of being wicked and lazy (v. 26).

He replied that he had acted out of fear since the master was a "harsh man" (v. 24). The master did not deny this assessment, but asserted that, for that very reason, the slave should have invested the talent to obtain interest on it.

The harsh summation concludes that more will be given to those who have much, while "from those who have nothing, even what they have will be taken away" (v. 29). The spiritual truth here is that one must act responsibly and be willing to take a risk in the face of *the coming of the Son of Man.*

The prudence and caution of the third slave was self-protective and ultimately self-serving. He was further punished by being thrown into the "outer darkness, where there will be weeping and gnashing of teeth" (v. 30). The darkness symbolizes the condemnation of the last judgment and is in direct opposition to entering the joy of the master.

God's call demands that we take the risks that must accompany growth. Rather than just living safely, we are called to act in ways that reflect the creativity and commitment of our Creator in sending the Son.

ON REFLECTION

The Parable of the Talents is told in Matthew's twenty-fifth chapter on the "coming kingdom," and it deals with what believers are to do—in light of the "delayed" return of the master. As the parable and Madeleine L'Engle put it, we are *to serve our gifts.* We are to "serve them" by expressing them in a bent world. And we are to "serve them" by working on them, enhancing them, expanding them.

Elizabeth O'Connor gives even greater emphasis to expressing giftedness in her book *The Eighth Day of Creation* (Word Books, 1971): "Because our gifts carry us out into the world and make us participants in life, the uncovering of them is one of the most important tasks confronting any one of us. When we talk about being true to ourselves—being the persons we are intended to be—we are talking about our gifts.

"When we talk about vocation, whether we are artists or engineers, we are talking about our gifts. We perceive the will of God in our lives when we discern our gifts ... our obedience and surrender to God are, in large part, our obedience and surrender to our gifts. This is the message wrapped up in the parable of the talents."

O'Connor would also say that the purpose of the Church was to help members of the Body of Christ to discover their gifts, and then to hold us accountable for using them—in the face of our wanting to "bury them." To enter into the joy of creating, we must create. It is as simple and as complicated as that.

—H. King Oehmig

We are to be good stewards by proclaiming the Good News and not by hiding it away. The reward is the everlasting joy of our Lord.

The Apostle Paul also spoke of the coming day of the Lord to the community in Thessalonica. He warned that it would come unexpectedly to an unprepared world "like a thief in the night" (1 Thess. 5:2). Any attempt to predict the exact day or time was futile. Like the ancient prophets, he saw this as sudden destruction for those who sought peace and safety in human efforts.

However, Paul was primarily speaking words of comfort for his converts, "children of light and children of the day" (v. 5). As God's chosen, they were to act in accord with that privilege by taking up their calling. They were to stay awake and be sober in their habits. To those who had not committed themselves to the fellowship of disciples, the day of the Lord might indeed come as a thief to rob them of their expected well-being.

In their alertness the disciples were destined by God for salvation and not for wrath. Thus they were to prepare themselves by putting on the armor of God—the breastplate of faith and love and the helmet of hope and salvation.

As they experience salvation through Jesus Christ, the believers recognize fellowship with the Lord that cannot be broken. Because Jesus gave his life for all believers, whether they are alive or have entered into the sleep that the world calls death, *they have life eternal.* Therefore they are to continue to encourage one another as they have been doing.

POINTS TO PONDER

1. As you read the Gospel passage in Matthew 25, put yourself in the place of each of the three slaves in the story. How do you think each of them felt as they received their money as the master was leaving?

2. What do you think might have been the motivating factors for each of them as they decided what to do with the money? How do you think each slave might have felt as he anticipated the return of the master?

3. With which slave do you identify most easily? What did the master expect of his slaves? What is your reaction to his treatment of each of the three slaves?

4. This parable challenges us to take risks as a part of our call from God. What risks have you taken in relation to your faith? What other messages does this story have for you?

5. Today's passages offer us examples of the Divine mercy and a vision of the coming day of the Lord. Contrast the various images and discuss your own understanding of how we are to prepare ourselves for the Lord's coming.

JESUS SHALL REIGN

Ezekiel 34:11-16, 20-24; Psalm 100; Ephesians 1:15-23; Matthew 25:31-46

Following three parables about the preparations necessary for the coming of the Son of Man (Mt. 24:45-51; 25:1-13, 14-30), the Gospel for this Christ the King Sunday presents a vision of final judgment unique to Matthew's Gospel.

Universal judgment was an established belief in which the wicked would be punished and cast out, while the righteous were invited to share the joy of God's Kingdom. As Matthew presents this scene, all nations gather before the Son of Man (cf Dan. 7:13-14), who will come in glory with his angels.

The Son of Man is understood to be Jesus, who is further referred to as king (Mt. 25:34), a title identified with Jesus in Matthew's infancy (2:2) and Passion narratives (27:11, 29, 37, 42).

The king will divide the people in the same way that a shepherd separates the sheep from the goats. Mixed flocks of sheep and goats were common, but it was necessary to separate them when night came. The goats needed shelter from the cold, while the sheep preferred to remain outdoors. Sheep were more valuable and thus received preferential treatment.

The king puts the sheep at his right hand and the goats at his left. The "sheep" are blessed by God and will "inherit the kingdom prepared for you from the foundation of the world..." (v. 34). In contrast, the goats are "accursed" and cast out into the "eternal fire prepared for the devil and his angels" (v. 41).

The king identifies with those who have endured suffering. Thus to give food and water to the hungry, to offer shelter to the stranger, to provide clothing to the naked, and to visit those who are sick or in prison is to show the same kindness to the Lord himself.

Those on his right have followed this example of the Lord by caring for the afflicted and unfortunate. Because they have done these deeds without any expectation of return, they respond with astonishment that they have done such acts (vv. 37-39). Jesus responds, "Truly I tell you, just as you did it to one of the least of these who are members of my family, you did it to me" (v. 40). Thus they will receive the promise of eternal life.

In contrast, those at his left hand who have ignored the needs of the less fortunate are astounded that they are to be cursed and condemned to eternal punishment. They bore no malice toward the hungry, the homeless, the sick, or prisoners; they simply did not recognize them as their responsibility.

However, more than altruistic deeds are demanded here. When the character of Christ is formed in any disciple, there is no ulterior motive behind deeds of compassion. When Christ lives within us, it truly *will be* Christ's deeds and not our own that will come forth; this is the essence of discipleship.

PRAYER FOR THE DAY

Almighty and ever merciful God, whose purpose is to bring to consummation all things in Jesus Christ our Lord: give to all peoples of the earth, in spite of ongoing rebellion and division, the grace to come together under the rule of the King of kings and Lord of lords, through the unity of the Holy Spirit, who lives and reigns with you, one God, forever and ever. *Amen.*

Here we see Jesus as the exalted Son of Man, as king, as judge and as "one of the least of these" (v. 40). But it is in his identification with the needy and outcast that Jesus' kingship is most fully manifested.

The Prophet Ezekiel also speaks of God's care for the outcast and afflicted. The image of the shepherd was often used as a symbol for the king or leader of a nation in the ancient Near East. In the passage for today, the Lord is depicted as the shepherd-king who cares for the flock, in contrast to the corrupt shepherds—i. e., leaders of Israel who have abused their power and exploited the people (34:1-10).

During the time of Ezekiel, God's people were scattered in the Exile, a situation that the prophet believed related to the failed leadership of Israel's kings. But God would search for the lost sheep, gather them together, and bring them back to their own land.

In contrast to the predatory leaders of Israel, God's role was to protect the flock, bind up the injured, search for the strayed, and provide sustenance.

The Lord would also provide justice by holding accountable those who had gained prosperity at the expense of others. They would pay for the ills they had allowed to occur (v. 16b). In like manner, the Lord gives warning of judgment to the flock itself. In vowing to "judge between sheep and sheep, between rams and goats" (v. 17), the Lord declares that the people are responsible for their own behavior.

Finally, God will establish a shepherd-king to rule over all to ensure the well-being of the flock. This Davidic king will carry out gracious and compassionate deeds in the name of the Lord. "And I, the Lord, will be their God, and my servant David shall be prince among them" (v. 24).

ON REFLECTION

It won't be because of how well you knew the Bible. It won't be because of how religious or prayerful you were—or how successful you were at appearing "stainless" before the world. It will hinge on one thing when the Cosmic King comes at the End. It will have to do with your *faith-in-action.*

Jesus had taught: "Not everyone who says to me, 'Lord, Lord,' will enter the kingdom of heaven, but only the one who does the will of my Father in heaven" (Mt. 7:21). And the parable on The Last Judgment fleshes out the teaching. The Cosmic King will confront us about *to what degree our faith was a verb rather than a noun.* Yet this "verb-centered faith" has nothing to do with "success." It is not about moving mountains, or building crystal cathedrals. Nor is it about feeding the hungry *perfectly.* It is about *showing up.* It is along the lines of what Wordsworth described as "the best portion of a good man's life, his little nameless, unremembered acts of kindness and love."

Finally, it is worth noting that the "sheep" herded into eternal life had no clue that they were to be "saved." They were not performing these kindnesses to "the least of these" to obtain a reward—to get to heaven. They did what they did because there were simple needs to be met, and they met them. To their surprise, they found they were doing these things *to Jesus himself*—incognito among the poor and the oppressed—where he still lives today.

—H. King Oehmig

In the context of Ezekiel's time, this is a yearning for the restoration of the Davidic monarchy following the return from Exile. These words set the scene for the Incarnation of Jesus and the further promise of his Second Coming.

Jesus came into his kingly power through his Resurrection, and the letter to the Ephesians gives us a further understanding of the exalted Christ. As the passage for today begins, the genuine faith of the community and their love for one another is acknowledged with an assurance of continuing prayer for their *further spiritual wisdom and revelation* through "the God of our Lord Jesus Christ, the Father of glory" (1:17).

Such enlightenment will give understanding of the hope to which God calls them, as well as to the rich and glorious inheritance God provides. They must understand the boundless power that God exercises on behalf of believers, as demonstrated when God raised Jesus and set him in the heavenly places (v. 20).

They are to acknowledge his establishment in heaven above all powers, temporal and eternal, whether of the present age or of the coming age of fulfillment. Here the sovereignty of Jesus as *Lord over all* is fully proclaimed.

This exalted Christ has been made head over all existence for the sake of the Church that is his Body. It is through his presence that all things are brought to completion.

Psalm 100 gives us words to praise God for having made us and keeping us as well-loved sheep. We enter God's gates with thanksgiving in our worship and praise, blessing the Divine Name. "For the Lord is good," and God's steadfast love endures to all generations. *Amen!*

POINTS TO PONDER

1. Describe the scene that Matthew presents in the Gospel passage. What is your initial response to these words?

2. Why do you think the sheep are astonished when they learn that they will inherit the Kingdom (Mt. 25:34-40)? On the other hand, why are the goats surprised that they have been condemned (vv. 41-46)?

3. What are we called here to do, as individuals and as the Church?

4. What do we learn in the Gospel passage about final judgment?

5. Also read the Old Testament Lesson for today in Ezekiel 34:11-16, 20-24 and compare the imagery of sheep and judgment as described by Ezekiel with that of Jesus in the Gospel reading.

_____

_____

_____

_____

_____

_____

_____

UNDERSTANDING THE SUNDAY SCRIPTURES
A Companion to
The Revised Common Lectionary
Year A

is published by:

READMARKPRESS

P.O. Box 11428
Chattanooga, TN 37401

Telephone: 800.722.4124
Fax: 423.242.4266

www.readmarkpress.com
info@readmarkpress.com

Watch for UNDERSTANDING THE SUNDAY SCRIPTURES,
Year B and *Year C,* coming soon!

If you think your study group or organization might benefit from the use of this book in a group setting, please contact us. Group discounts are available.

Retail price $21.95
ISBN Number 978-0-9795581-0-8

Cover design and typesetting by Deena Fisher, Drollerie.com. Title font is *Augustea Open Letter.* Chapter title font is *Apple Garamond.* Content font is *Times New Roman. On Reflection* and *Points to Ponder* title font is *Trajanus Bricks.* Initial paragraph dropped capitals font is *Trajanus Bricks Extra* by Manfried Klein.

Printed in the United States
97097LV00005B/40/A